The Voltairine de Cleyre Reader

Edited by A. J. Brigati

The Voltairine de Cleyre Reader
ISBN 1-902593-87-1

© 2004, A.J. Brigati

AK Press
674A 23rd St, Oakland, California 94612-1163
www.akpress.org

PO Box 12766, Edinburgh, Scotland EH89YE
www.akuk.com

Library of Congress Cataloguing in-Publication data

A catalog record for this book is available from the Library of Congress
Library of Congress Control Number: 2003097106

Editorial Assistants:
Ben Prickett
Patrick R. Sessions

Research Assistants:
Joy Dement
Kelley McKee

Special Thanks to Barry Pateman

Book Design: Fourteen Little Men, Inc. / www.fourteenlittlemen.com

Cover art: *Night* by Virginia Allison
printed from the original charcoal on canvas

Printed in Canada

About the Editor

A.J. Brigati professes Eighteenth and Nineteenth Century British Literature, Marxist and Anarchist Theory and Sports Literature at the University of Montevallo, Montevallo, Alabama.

Contents

Preface

n his obituary of his friend and comrade, Voltairine de Cleyre, published in the August 1912 London *Freedom*, Harry Kelly wrote that, "to her the Anarchist ideal was something more than a dream of the future; it was a guide for everyday life, and not to be compromised with. Most of us can find excuses for ourselves when we deviate from the straight line; but Voltairine kept herself to it unflinchingly." As we can imagine, such vigorous and firm commitment to her ideal led to tensions between her and other anarchist and radical contemporaries. She was not sparing in criticism both of herself and others. Difficult, complex, and driven by an unflinching integrity grounded in everyday experience, Voltairine de Cleyre wrote some of the most prescient and perceptive essays on anarchism that we could hope to read. Essays that refuse to lie dormant as comfortable artifacts, but still challenge us today.

In many of her essays, de Cleyre consciously set out to create a specifically anarchist history. Work on the Paris Commune, her series of talks and writings on Haymarket, her attempt to articulate and evidence an innate and organic American anarchism, all form part of a larger work that analyzes, memorializes and informs present practice. Her historical pieces reflect her wide reading, her literary passionate nature and a respect and admiration for those militants who died for their beliefs. Indeed, the dead Haymarket men were a constant presence in her life providing strength and inspiration.

Like her companion Dyer D. Lum, de Cleyre favored the idea of anarchism without adjectives. Initially an individualist anarchist and supporter of the ideas reflected in Benjamin Tucker's paper, *Liberty,* she stayed constant to the paper's initial Proudhonist mutualism while gradually recognizing class as more and more of an important aspect of her anarchism. Although she never adopted anarchist communism, de Cleyre was influenced in the idea of a unifying anarchism by Lum as well as the Spanish anarchists, Ricardo Mella and Fernando Tarrida del Marmol, whom she met in London in 1897. As she wrote to Emma Goldman in 1907, "I am an Anarchist Simply without economic labels attached." Such a position would later be adapted in some form by Malatesta, Max Nettlau, Voline and Sebastien Faure. This view of anarchism considerably affected de Cleyre's writing on anarchism. Her essays reflect a struggle with language, a tension if you will, centered on finding the right word for the right feeling, the right action. Very rarely does she use hyperbolic rhetoric. Her essays are precise explorations meant to clarify, guide or interrogate.

Her belief and work reflected a commitment both to education and action. At various times in her life her work consisted of teaching young Jewish immigrants English. (Jewish anarchists were for de Cleyre, "the most liberal minded and active comrades in the movement as well as the most transcendental dreamers.") She was a regular contributor to anarchist newspapers such as *Lucifer, Free Society, The Rebel* and *Mother Earth,* as well as to a whole series of freethought and radical journals and papers, where her uncompromising atheism and feminism, bedrocks of her anarchism, were regularly on show.

In 1892 she helped form the Philadelphia Ladies Liberal League. Belying its rather genteel name it encouraged discussion on sex, anarchism and all kinds of revolutionary and radical material ("we have done this" she wrote in *The Rebel* of October 20, 1895, "because we love liberty and hate authority"). The Ladies Liberal League later merged with the Radical Library, another organization created by de Cleyre and her comrades, whose aim was to provide radical material that workingmen and women could read at their leisure.

Just who should be the focus of this education was startlingly obvious to de Cleyre. On undertaking a speaking tour in 1910, she was dismayed by the nature of some of her venues and audiences, arguing, "comrades, we have gone upon a wrong road. Let us get back to the point that our work should be chiefly among the poor, the ignorant, the brutal, the disinterested, the men and women who do the hard and brutalizing work of the world." (*Mother Earth,* December 1910) Her comments precipitated a sharp response from Emma Goldman in the same issue of the magazine, who argued in a rejoinder, "the men and women who first take up the banner of new liberating ideas generally emanate from the so called respectable classes" and "Anarchism builds not on classes, but on men and women."

We would be wrong however if we saw de Cleyre as a woman lost in books, learning and propaganda. She had a fierce and intuitive support of those anarchists taking individual or group action against oppression. Her story, *The Heart of Angiolillo,* her poem *Santa Agueda* (in praise of the assassination of the Spanish Prime Minister Canovas by Angiolillo), her poetic celebration of the executions of the anarchist militants, Valliant, Henry and Caserio, *In the Face of Vultures,* all reflect her unwavering support of those who have used violence, and her desire to memorialize and celebrate their courage. In her essay *McKinley's Assassination from the Anarchist Standpoint* she argued that "the hells of capitalism create the desperate; the desperate act desperately." She believed this statement. It had an ironic darkness in her own life. In 1902 de Cleyre was shot by a former pupil, Herman Helcher (initially her wounds were pronounced fatal). She refused to appear as a witness against her assailant and wrote a letter to the anarchist newspaper, *Free Society,* asking comrades to forgive him.

De Cleyre would regularly quote her mentor Dyer D. Lum that "Events are the true schoolmasters." Her ideas were never conceived in an intellectual vacuum, but from an attempt to work out practical ideas and experiences that we could learn from on the road towards anarchism. Such a relationship between experience and practice makes this publication a most welcome and pertinent one. Not since the collection of de Cleyre's work by Alexander Berkman in 1914 has such a selection of her ideas been made available. Despite Paul Avrich's excellent and thoughtful *An American Anarchist: The Life of Voltairine de Cleyre* (Princeton: Princeton University Press, 1978) and numerous editions of some of her individual essays, Voltairine de Cleyre's name is still known to too few people—and the richness of a large selection of her work to a mere handful. She is a clear, thoughtful and sophisticated writer who, at her best, out of her long days of loneliness, writes with a clarifying brilliance and, just as importantly, an impressive level of common sense. This volume will provide a fine introduction to a woman whose "life was a protest against all show, a challenge to all hypocrisy, and an inspiration for social rebellion." (Hippolyte Havel in *The Road to Freedom,* June–July 1928, 5)

—*Barry Pateman*

Short Chronology of Significant Dates

November 17, 1866   Voltairine de Cleyre born in Leslie, Michigan.

1885   After convent education becomes a freethinker.

1886   Edits *The Progressive Age* a small free thought journal.

1887   Begins to give public lectures on free thought, often on behalf of the American Secular Union.

November 11, 1887   Execution of Haymarket anarchists.

December   Hears Clarence Darrow talk on socialism at the Thomas Paine Memorial Convention at Linesville, PA. Impressed by his ideas she becomes a socialist.

1888   Becomes an anarchist.

1889   Writes *The Drama of the Nineteenth Century*. Meets Dyer D. Lum, "her teacher, her confidant, her comrade."

1890   Has child (Harry) with James B. Elliot, freethinker who later became secretary of the Thomas Paine Historical Association of America.

1891   Begins English lessons for Jewish anarchist immigrants. Learns Yiddish.

1892   Helps found the Philadelphia Ladies Liberal League.

April 6, 1893   Dyer D. Lum commits suicide.

August   Meets Emma Goldman in Philadelphia. Towards the end of the year visits Goldman in Blackwell's Island Prison, New York. Begins correspondence with Alexander Berkman, serving 22 years for the attempted murder of Henry Clay Frick, chairman of the Carnegie Steel Company.

1894   Publishes *In Defense of Emma Goldman* (Lecture originally given on December 16, 1893).
Meets Charles Mowbray, an English anarchist who is on a speaking tour in America.

May   Meets Johann Most in New York.

1895   Publishes *The Past and Future of the Ladies Liberal League.*

1896   Meets John Turner, English anarchist who is on a speaking tour in America.

June 13, 1897   Travels to Britain. Meets Peter Kropotkin, Louise Michel, Jean Grave, Fernando Tarrida del Marmol, Max Nettlau, and other militants including John Turner and William Wess. Also meets Spanish anarchists released after being tortured in Barcelona's Montjuich Prison. Publishes *The Gods and the People*.

Writes the poem, "Germinal" celebrating Michelle Angiolillo's assassination of the Spanish Prime Minister in revenge for the tortures. Lectures in Scotland.

1899   Translates Jean Grave's *Moribund Society and Anarchy* from the French.

1900   Publishes book of poetry, *The Worm Turns*.

1901   Helps form Philadelphia Social Science Club. With others, de Cleyre organizes series of open-air meetings. After the assassination of President McKinley on September 6, meetings were broken up by the police.

March 1902   Senator JR Hawley offers $1000 to have a shot at an anarchist. De Cleyre offers herself as a target—and states she will give the $1000 "to the propaganda of the ideal of a free society."

December 19   Shot by Herman Helcher.

June 24, 1903   Travels to Norway, Scotland and England. Publishes *Crime and Punishment*.

1904   Ill for much of the year.

October   *Lucifer* prints a premature obituary of her.

1905   Attempts suicide through an overdose of morphine.

1906   Her health slowly recovers. Meets Alexander Berkman after his release from prison. Encourages him to write.

March 18   Takes part in a celebration of the Paris Commune.

Begins regular schedule of public speaking toward the end of the year.

1907   Publishes *McKinley's Assassination from the Anarchist Standpoint*.

February 20, 1908   Jewish and Italian anarchists call a mass meeting on unemployment. De Cleyre is one of the speakers. A demonstration follows. De Cleyre and others are arrested. Eventually found "not guilty." Four Italian anarchists, though, sentenced to five years at hard labor.

June 30, 1909   Mass meeting organized by national Free Speech Campaign at Cooper Union, New York. De Cleyre speaks. Other speakers include Clarence Darrow and Jack London.

Publishes *Anarchism and American Traditions*.

October 1910   Begins a speaking tour. Speaks on topics such as "Ferrer" and "Modern Educational Reform." Moves to Chicago.

        Lectures to adults for two months at Chicago Modern School.

        Publishes *The Dominant Idea*.

February 1911   Turns down invitation from Alexander Berkman and Leonard Abbott to become Business Manager of the Ferrer Modern School in New York City.

        Becomes energized by the events in Mexico and enlists support for the PLM (Partido Liberal Mexicano), the exiled Mexican anarchist group. Campaigns for the group's paper, *Regeneración,* and for bail money when its leading militants are arrested.

        Publishes *The Mexican Revolt*.

March 18, 1912   Addresses Memorial meeting for Paris Commune.

June 20   Dies.

June 23   Buried in Waldheim Cemetery near the Haymarket Martyrs.

1914   Emma Goldman's publishing house, Mother Earth Publishing Association, publishes *The Selected Works of Voltairine de Cleyre,* edited by Alexander Berkman, with an introduction by Hippolyte Havel.

Introduction

Anyone who wishes to consider the life and works of Voltairine de Cleyre is ultimately indebted to the scholarship of Paul Avrich[1], her principal biographer, as well as the many archives and public domains which have preserved many of her most widely read works. Although some archives have maintained several of de Cleyre's works, she still remains little known to most of academia. In fact, until the time of commencing this undertaking, much of her original manuscripts were relatively dormant within various collections. As such, this publication is able to serve as a much-needed annotated scholarly edition of de Cleyre's works, the first modern collection of its kind to date.

Voltairine de Cleyre may be considered one of the most influential free thinkers of the late nineteenth and early twentieth century. Her roles as both a political activist and women's rights advocate will become evident to the reader in her discussions of anarchism, labor rights, the need for women to have private space and access to education and sport. Of further interest in light of twenty-first century women's studies, within these texts, scholars may note de Cleyre's admiration for Mary Wollstonecraft and the influences the works of the latter had upon her own. Also, one will take note of her personal and professional relations with a more well-known women's rights activist and anarchist, Emma Goldman. Nevertheless, in considering her treatment of gender issues, the contemporary reader will likely leave with the sentiment that de Cleyre represents a voice of reason with thoughts for equality much advanced for her time.

The intention of releasing this annotated edition of selected works undoubtedly suggests the need for the work of such a significant, yet often neglected, figure to be considered more widely in the arena of academic discourse. May it also serve as an invitation for further study in considering de Cleyre's contributions to literature, politics and cultural studies in light of current academic concerns.

The woman who Emma Goldman would call "the most gifted and brilliant anarchist woman America ever produced"[2] was born on November 17, 1866 in Leslie, Michigan. Voltairine de Cleyre was born into poverty; however, her family was rooted in intellectual free thought. Such a lineage of free thought advocacy may be noted in that her name was given to her by her father in celebration of Voltaire and his free thought philosophy.

Given the unfavorable economic conditions of the de Cleyre family, de Cleyre's father thought it best to send her away to a convent school, the Convent of Our Lady of Port Huron in Ontario, regardless of the polarity between religious doctrine and the idea of free thought. In essence, he wished his daughter anything but the impoverished home he could provide.

Although de Cleyre despised the convent, she took from the experience several key features which would mold her later life. She was educated in music, which she loved, and would later teach to earn a modest living. Also, the convent provided her a basis for an adequate education, allowing her to develop basic skills as a writer and speaker. Furthermore, her experience with the rearing by the nuns gave her a sense of asceticism and moral consciousness that she would carry with her in later life. Moreover, though, having been punished at the convent for often expressing her opinions, the experience helped her to realize her need to become active as a freethinker and a champion of such philosophy.

Once she took leave of the convent, she began a career offering private lessons in English, music, French and penmanship. However, in 1886 when the Haymarket Affair took place, her life became more complex. Having heard that an explosion brought about the arrests of anarchist suspects, de Cleyre's initial response was that they should be hanged. Later, she would live to regret her hasty response and mourn her indiscretion upon each anniversary of the Haymarketers' executions. Subsequent to the events of the Haymarket Affair, de Cleyre began to promote anarchism, labor rights and the free thought movement. Given her realization of her role as an anarchist, the year 1888 marks de Cleyre's earliest anarchist essays[3].

Although de Cleyre preferred not to label her expressions of anarchism, her writings reveal her tendencies as an individualist anarchist. Her essay *Anarchism and American Traditions* serves to outline her openness to experiment with economy, faith and social structure while revealing the individualist anarchist's disdain for any centralized organization, including the state. Just as de Cleyre placed anarchism open to various belief structures and even religious experimentation, she emphasized the need to bring about change through education and labor organizing, while at the same time demonstrating understanding, compassion, and support for those who resort to violence.

On December 19, 1902 an act of violence touched her own life and placed her philosophy to trial. A former student of hers named Herman Helcher shot de Cleyre three times at point blank range. After surviving the malicious attack, de Cleyre later would appeal on the boy's behalf. In a letter to the journal *Free Society*, de Cleyre writes, "What this poor half-crazed boy needs is not the silence and cruelty of a prison, but the kindness, care and sympathy which heal." Aside from her own suffering, de Cleyre suggests that Helcher suffers from mental illness and places a necessity upon prioritizing mental health treatment rather than punishment. Further evidence of this sentiment is revealed in a letter published by a Philadelphia daily in which de Cleyre writes:

> *The boy who, they say, shot me is crazy. Lack of proper food and healthy labor made him so. He ought to be put in an asylum. It would be an outrage against civilization if he were sent to jail for an act which was the product of a diseased brain.*

De Cleyre empathizes with Helcher as she too was no stranger to poverty and unfavorable circumstances. She suffered frequent illness and terrible bouts with depression throughout her life. On several occasions de Cleyre is thought to have contemplated or attempted suicide as her presumed lover and counterpart Dyer Lum had in 1893.

It is believed that Lum and de Cleyre engaged in an intermittent relationship for five years leading up to his death. While little is known regarding specifics of the relationship, it seemed their dealings inspired de Cleyre's intellectual curiosity and production of individualist anarchist and free thought material. The relationship also seems to have played a major role in de Cleyre's development as what one would now consider a feminist theorist. The relationship seems to have yielded material, in *Sex Slavery, They Who Marry Do Ill* and *Mary Wollstonecraft*, which begins to explore and question the roles women play in society and the opportunities, or lack thereof, they face.

From consideration of the limits of women's access to sports, as in her critique on the restrictive clothing assigned to women equestrians in *Sex Slavery*, to the need for individual space expressed in *They Who Marry Do Ill*, de Cleyre bridges the gap between the early feminist expressions of Mary Wollstonecraft (1759–1797) and Virginia Woolf (1882–1941) and the later solidified feminist movements as defined by Adrienne Rich (1929–). To this end, Emma Goldman noticed de Cleyre for her views on anarchism but also her feminist stance. The two both shared the desire to advocate for the rights of women and also one another. De Cleyre writes *In Defense of Emma Goldman* in response to Goldman being imprisoned for her activism, while Goldman writes an essay in praise of de Cleyre (*Voltairine de Cleyre*, Oriole Press, 1931). According to Avrich[4], the two corresponded seldom and met infrequently. Aside from the essays in support of one another's efforts not much more interaction between them is known other than a few kind words exchanged when Goldman visited de Cleyre at her sick bed. De Cleyre would often become bedridden for days from discomfort as a result of speaking in public.

Although it caused her great anxiety, by 1888, de Cleyre had well entered the public speaking circuit which found her traveling between Michigan and such cities as Chicago, Philadelphia, New York and occasionally London. During this year, de Cleyre was asked to lecture before the Friendship Liberal League in Philadelphia. There she met James B. Elliot, an organizer in the free thought movement. Around this time, de Cleyre took residence in the city and the two began a short relationship resulting in a son. On June 12, 1890, Harry de Cleyre was born.

Through the year 1910, de Cleyre continued to be one of the most renowned anarchist, women and labor rights activist lecturers in the nation. She helped organize a series of lectures to the Ladies Liberal League as well as to numerous labor and trade organizations and unions. Her lectures were translated into several languages and were read by human rights groups both domestically and abroad.

By 1910, however, de Cleyre began to suffer again from the chronic illness and depression which lingered throughout her life. At this time, she moved back to Chicago and continued to lecture and write. Perhaps feeling her own inevitable demise, or an intolerance for her continued suffering, de Cleyre would regularly suffer from bouts of bleak pessimism. For the last two years of her life, news of revolt in Mexico had her and other anarchists active in advocating the cause of the laboring class and, more specifically, the PLM (Mexican Liberal Party), an avowedly anarchist group whose leadership was in exile in America. De Cleyre became a correspondent in Chicago of a radical pamphlet appealing to labor rights solidarity groups to help raise funds for the revolution. This turn of events also prompted de Cleyre to produce such works as *Direct Action* and *The Mexican Revolt*.

Though active in the cause for labor equity until the time of her death, on June 20, 1912, Voltairine de Cleyre died in Chicago succumbing to the plague of persistent illness. Her funeral was held, and she was buried at Waldheim Cemetery alongside the Haymarket martyrs.

A Note on the Texts

I n an effort to maintain the condition of the original, or at least documentary integrity of these collected works, I have purposefully not edited or tampered with the original manuscript representations in any form or manner other than to insert indications of notations and adapt the typeset to a uniform font style for the purpose of publication and ease of reading. As a result, many textual, style, grammatical and spelling imperfections may be found throughout the texts as they were presumably from the hand of de Cleyre. Upon examining numerous errors in the works, one should consider that some of these works were scripted to be delivered orally and may therefore not have been prepared with the author's intention to seek print publication.

In preparing text for presentation in this edition, where multiple editions and/ or imprints of the same work were considered, the principles of Greg's copy text method for textual analysis was employed with the philosophy of maintaining as adequately as possible the original form of the author's intended copy. Here too, it should be mentioned that although the grammatical errors, or "accidentals," in some instances seem obviously contrary to normal practices in written English language, the dangers of editorial correction has the potential to alter subtle meanings which may be detected upon close readings by curious readers and scholars. With this, I rely on privileging the accidentals while adding notes where clarification is necessary in making the text more accessible to the contemporary reader. Essentially, I leave the reader to use their discretion in determining which elements of mechanics and style are placed intentionally for meaning and effect and which are simply positioned in haste or error.

Further, the specific origin of each text considered and subsequent publication information is noted under the appropriate title headings in the section entitled "Notes."

In Defense of Emma Goldman and the Right of Expropriation

Voltairine de Cleyre
Philadelphia, 1894
(3515 Wallace Street)

"A starving man has a natural right to his neighbor's bread".

Cardinal Manning[1]

"I have no idea of petitioning for rights. Whatever the rights of the people are, they have a right to them, and none have a right to either withold or grant them".

Paine's "Rights of Man"[2]

"Ask for work; if they do not give you work ask for bread; if they do not give you work or bread then take bread".

Emma Goldmann[3]

A Lecture / Delivered in New York, Dec. 16. 1894

1

The light is pleasant, is it not my friends? It is good to look into each other's faces, to see the hands that clasp our own, to read the eyes that search our thoughts, to know what manner of lips give utterance to our pleasant greetings. It is good to be able to wink defiance at the Night, the cold, unseeing Night. How weird, how gruesome, how chilly it would be if I stood here in blackness, a shadow addressing shadows, in a house of blindness! Yet each would know that he was not alone; yet might we stretch hands and touch each other, and feel the warmth of human presence near. Yet might a sympathetic voice ring thro' the darkness, quickening the dragging moments.—The lonely prisoners in the cells of Blackwell's Island have neither light nor sound! The short day hurries across the sky, the short day still more shortened in the gloomy walls. The long chill night creeps up so early, weaving its sombre curtain before the imprisoned eyes. And thro' the curtain comes no sympathizing voice, beyond the curtain lies the prison silence, beyond that the cheerless, uncommunicating land, and still beyond the icy, fretting river, black and menacing, ready to drown. A wall of night, a wall of stone, a wall of water! Thus has the great State of New York answered EMMA GOLDMANN; thus have the classes replied to the masses; thus do the rich respond to the poor; thus does the Institution of Property give its ultimatum to Hunger!

"Give us work" said EMMA GOLDMANN; "if you do not give us work, then give us bread; if you do not give us either work or bread then we shall take bread."—It wasn't a very wise remark to make to the State of New York, that is—Wealth and its watch-dogs, the Police. But I fear me much that the apostles of liberty, the fore-runners of revolt, have never been very wise. There is a record of a seditious person, who once upon a time went about with a few despised followers in Palestine, taking corn out of other people's corn-fields; (on the Sabbath day, too). That same person, when he wished to ride into Jerusalem told his disciples to go forward to where they would find a young colt tied, to unloose it and bring it to him, and if any one interfered or said anything to them, were to say: "My master hath need of it". That same person said: "Give to him that asketh of thee, and from him that taketh away thy goods ask them not back again". That same person once stood before the hungry multitudes of Galilee and taught them, saying: "The Scribes and the Pharisees sit in Moses' seat; therefore whatever they bid you observe, that observe and do. But do not ye after their works, for they say, and do not. For they bind heavy burdens, and grievous to be borne, and lay them on men's shoulders; but they themselves will not move them with one

2

of their fingers. But all their works they do to be seen of men; they make broad their phylacteries, and enlarge the borders of their garments: and love the uppermost rooms at feasts, and the chief seats in the synagogues, and greetings in the markets, and to be called of men, 'Rabbi, Rabbi.'" And turning to the scribes and the pharisees, he continued: "Woe unto you, Scribes and Pharisees, hypocrites! for ye devour widows' houses, and for a presence make long prayers: therefore shall ye receive the greater damnation. Woe unto you, Scribes and Pharisees, hypocrites! for ye pay tithe of mint, and anise, and cummin, and have omitted the weightier matters of the law, judgment, and mercy, and faith: these ought ye to have done and not left the other undone. Ye blind guides, that strain at a gnat and swallow a camel! Woe unto you, Scribes and Pharisees, hypocrites! for ye make clean the outside of the cup end plaster, but within they are full of extortion and excess. Woe unto you, Scribes and Pharisees, hypocrites! For ye are like unto whited sepulchres, which indeed appear beautiful outward, but within are full of dead men's bones and all uncleanness. Even so ye outwardly appear righteous unto men, but within ye are full of hypocrisy and iniquity. Woe unto you, Scribes and Pharisees, hypocrites! Because ye build the tombs of the prophets and garnish the sepulchres of the righteous; and say, 'if we had been in the days of our fathers we would not have been partakers with them in the blood of the prophets'. Wherefore ye be witnesses unto yourselves that ye are the children of them which killed the prophets. Fill ye up then the measure of your fathers! Ye serpents! Ye generations of vipers! How can ye escape the damnation of hell!"

Yes; these are the words of the outlaw who is alleged to form the foundation stone of modern civilization, to the authorities of his day. Hypocrites, extortionists, doers of iniquity, robbers of the poor, blood-partakers, serpents, vipers, fit for hell!

It wasn't a very wise speech, from beginning to end. Perhaps he knew it when he stood before Pilate[4] to receive his sentence, when he bore his heavy crucifix up Calvary, when nailed upon it, stretched in agony, he cried: "My God, my God, why hast thou forsaken me!"

No, it wasn't wise—but it was very grand.

This grand, foolish person, this beggar-tramp, this thief who justified the action of hunger, this man who set the right of Property beneath his foot, this Individual who defied the State, do you know why he was so feared and hated, and punished? Because, as it is said in the record, "the common people heard him gladly"; and the accusation before Pontius Pilate was, "we found this fellow perverting the whole nation. He stirreth up the people, teaching throughout all Jewry".

3

Ah, the dreaded "common people"!

When Cardinal Manning wrote: "Necessity knows no law, and a starving man has a natural right to his neighbor's bread", who thought of arresting Cardinal Manning? His was a carefully written article in the *Fortnightly Review*[5]. Who read it? Not the people who needed bread. Without food in their stomachs, they had not fifty cents to spend for a magazine. It was not the voice of the people themselves asserting rights. No one for one instant imagined that Cardinal Manning put himself at the head of ten thousand hungry men to loot the bakeries of London. It was a piece of ethical hair-splitting to be discussed in after-dinner speeches by the wine-muddled gentlemen who think themselves most competent to consider such subjects when their dress-coats are spoiled by the vomit of gluttony and drunkenness. But when EMMA GOLDMANN stood in Union Square and said, "if they do not give you work or bread then take bread", the common people heard her gladly and as of old the wandering carpenter of Nazareth addressed his own class, teaching throughout all Jewry, stirring up the people against the authorities, so the dressmaker of New York addressing the unemployed working-people of New York, was the menace of the depths of society, crying in its own tongue. The authorities heard and were afraid: therefore the triple wall.

It is the old, old story. When Thomas Paine, one hundred years ago, published the first part of "The Rights of Man", the part in which he discusses principles only, the edition was a high-priced one, reaching comparatively few readers. It created only a literary furore. When the second part appeared, the part in which he treats of the application of principles, in which he declares that "men should not petition rights but take them", it came out in a cheap form, so that one hundred thousand copies were sold in a few weeks. That brought down the prosecution of the government. It had reached the people that might act, and prosecution followed prosecution till Botany Bay[6] was full of the best men of England. Thus were the limitations of speech and press declared, and thus will they ever be declared so long as there are antagonistic interests in human society.

Understand me clearly. I believe that the term "constitutional right of free speech" is a meaningless phrase, for this reason: the constitution of the United States, and the Declaration of Independence, and particularly the latter, were, in their day, progressive expressions of progressive ideals. But they are, throughout, characterized by the metaphysical philosophy which dominated the thought of the last century. They speak of "inherent rights", "inalienable rights", "natural rights", etc: They declare that men are equal because of a supposed, mysterious wetness, existing somehow apart from matter. I do not say this to disparage those grand men who dared to put themselves against the authorities of the monarchy, and to conceive a better ideal of society, one which they certainly thought would secure equal rights to men; because I realize fully that no one can live very far in advance of the time-spirit, and I am positive in my own mind that, unless some cataclysm destroys the human race before the end of the twentieth century the experience of the next hundred years will explode many of our own theories. But the experience of this age has proven that metaphysical quantities do not exist apart from materials, and hence humanity cannot be made equal by declarations on paper. Unless the material conditions for equality exist, it is worse than mockery to pronounce men equal. And unless there is equality (and by equality I mean equal chances for every one to make the most of himself) unless, I say, these equal chances exist, freedom, either of thought, speech, or action, is equally a mockery.

I once read that one million angels could dance at the same time on the point of a needle; possibly one million angels might be able to get a decent night's lodging by virtue of their constitutional rights; one single tramp couldn't. And whenever the tongues of the non-possessing class threaten the possessors, whenever the disinherited menace the privileged, that moment you will find that the constitution isn't made for you. Therefore I think anarchists make a mistake when they contend for their constitutional rights. As a prominent lawyer, Mr. Thomas Earle White of Phila.[7], himself an anarchist, said to me not long since: "What are you going to do about it? Go into the courts, and fight for your legal rights? Anarchists haven't got any." "Well", says the governmentalist, "you can't consistently claim any. You don't believe in constitutions and laws." Exactly so; and if any one will right my constitutional wrongs I will willingly make him a present of my constitutional rights. At the same time I am perfectly sure no one will ever make this exchange; nor will any help ever come to the wronged class from the outside. Salvation on the vicarious plan isn't worth despising. Redress of wrongs will not come by petitioning "the powers that be". "He has rights who dare maintain them." "The Lord helps them who help themselves." (And when one is able to help himself, I don't think he is apt to trouble the Lord much for his assistance.) As long as the working-people fold hands and pray the gods in Washington to give them work, so long they will not get it. So long as they tramp the streets, whose stones they lay, whose filth they clean, whose sewers they dig, yet upon which they must not stand too long lest the policeman bid them "move on"; as long as they go from factory to factory, begging for the opportunity to be a slave, receiving the insults of bosses and foremen, getting the old "no", the old shake of the head, in these factories they built, whose machines they wrought; so long as they consent to herd like cattle,

5

in the cities, driven year after year, more and more, off the mortgaged land, the land they cleared, fertilized, cultivated, rendered of value; so long as they stand shivering, gazing thro' plate glass windows at overcoats, which they made, but cannot buy, starving in the midst of food they produced but cannot have; so long as they continue to do these things vaguely relying upon some power outside themselves, be it god, or priest, or politician, or employer, or charitable society, to remedy matters, so long deliverance will be delayed. When they conceive the possibility of a complete international federation of labor, whose constituent groups shall take possession of land, mines, factories, all the instruments of production, issue their own certificates of exchange, and, in short, conduct their own industry without regulative interference from law-makers or employers, then we may hope for the only help which counts for aught—Self-Help; the only condition which can guarantee free speech, (and no paper guarantee needed).

But meanwhile, while we are waiting, for there is yet much grist of the middle class to be ground between the upper and nether millwheels of economic evolution; while we await the formation of the international labor trust; while we watch for the day when there are enough of people with nothing in their stomachs and desperation in their heads, to go about the work of expropriation; what shall those do who are starving now?

That is the question which EMMA GOLDMANN had to face; and she answered it by saying: "Ask, and if you do not receive, take,—take bread".

I do not give you that advice. Not because I do not think that bread belongs to you; not because I do not think you would be morally right in taking it; not that I am not more shocked and horrified and embittered by the report of one human being starving in the heart of plenty than by all the Pittsburgs, and Chicagoes, and Homesteads, and Tennessees, and Coeur d'Alenes[8], and Buffaloes, and Barcelonas, and Parises; not that I do not think one little bit of sensitive human flesh is worth all the property rights in N. Y. city; not that I think the world will ever be saved by the sheep's virtue of going patiently to the shambles; not that I do not believe the expropriation of the possessing classes inevitable, and that that expropriation will begin by just such acts EMMA GOLDMANN advised, viz: the taking possession of wealth already produced; not that I think you owe any consideration to the conspirators of Wall Street, or those who profit by their operations, as such nor ever will till they are reduced to the level of human beings having equal chances with you to earn their share of social wealth, and no more, not that I would have you forget the consideration they have shown to you; that they have advised lead for strikers, strychnine for tramps, bread and water as good enough for working people; not that I cannot hear yet in my ears the words of one who said to me of the Studebaker Wagon Works' strikers[9], "if I had my way I'd mow them down with gatling guns"; not that I would have you forget the electric wire of Ft. Frick[10], nor the Pinkertons[11], nor the militia, nor the prosecutions for murder and treason; not that I would have you forget the 4th of May, when your constitutional right of free speech was vindicated, nor the 11th of Nov. when it was assassinated; not that I would have you forget the single dinner at Delmonico's[12] which Ward Mc.Allister[13] tells us cost ten thousand dollars! Would I have you forget that the wine in the glasses was your children's blood? It must be a rare drink—children blood! I have read of the wonderful sparkle on costly champagne;—I have never seen it. If I did I think it would look to me like mother tears over the little, white, wasted forms of dead babies;—dead—because—there was no milk in their breasts! Yes, I want you to remember that these rich are blood-drinkers, tearers of human flesh, gnawers of human bones! Yes, if I had the power I would burn your wrongs upon your hearts in characters that should glow like live coals in the night!

I have not a tongue of fire as EMMA GOLDMANN has; I cannot "stir the people"; I must speak in my own cold, calculated way. (Perhaps that is the reason I am let to speak at all.) But if I had the power my will is good enough. You know how Shakespeare's Marc Antony[14] addressed the populace of Rome:

> "I am no orator, as Brutus is,
> But as you know me all, a plain blunt man
> That love my friend. And that they know full well
> That gave me public leave to speak of him.
> For I have neither wit, nor words, nor worth,
> Action, nor utterance, nor the power of speech
> To stir men's blood. I only speak right on.
> I tell you that which you yourselves do know,
> Show you sweet Caesar's wounds, poor, poor dumb mouths,
> And bid them speak for me. But were I Brutus
> And Brutus Antony, there were an Antony
> Would ruffle up your spirits, and put a tongue
> In every wound of Caesar's, that should move
> The stones of Rome to rise and mutiny."

If, therefore, I do not give you the advice which EMMA GOLDMANN gave, let not the authorities suppose it is because I have any more respect for their constitution and their law than she has, or that I regard them as having any rights in the matter.

No. My reasons for not giving that advice are two. First, if I were giving advice at all, I would say: "My friends, that bread belongs to you. It is you who toiled and sweat in the sun to sow and reap the wheat; it is you who stood by the thresher, and breathed the chaff-filled atmosphere in the mills, while it was ground to flour; it is you who went into the eternal night of the mine and risked drowning, fire-damp, explosion, and cave-in, to get the fuel for the fire that baked it; it is you who stood in the hell-like heat, and struck the blows that forged the iron for the ovens wherein it is baked; it is you who stand all night in the terrible cellar shops, and tend the machines that knead the flour into dough; it is you, you, you, farmer, miner, mechanic, who make the bread; but you haven't the power to take it. At every transformation wrought by toil some one who didn't toil has taken part from you; and now he has it all, and you haven't the power to take it back! You are told you have the power because you have the numbers. Never make so silly a blunder as to suppose that power resides in numbers. One good, level-headed policeman with a club, is worth ten excited, unarmed men; one detachment of well-drilled militia has a power equal to that of the greatest mob that could be raised in New York City. Do you know I admire compact, concentrated power. Let me give you an illustration. Out in a little town in Illinois there is a certain capitalist, and if ever a human creature sweat and ground the grist of gold from the muscle of man, it is he. Well, once upon a time, his workmen, (not his slaves, his workmen,) were on strike; and fifteen hundred muscular Polacks armed with stones, brickbats, red hot pokers, and other such crude weapons as a mob generally collects, went up to his house for the purpose of smashing the windows, and so forth; possibly to do as those people in Italy did the other day with the sheriff who attempted to collect the milk tax. He alone, one man, met them on the steps of his porch, and for two mortal hoers, by threats, promised, cajoleries, held those fifteen hundred Poles at bay. And finally they went away, without smashing a pane of glass or harming a hair of his head. Now that was power! And you can't help but admire it, no matter if it was your enemy who displayed it; and you must admit that so long as numbers can be overcome by such relative quantity, power does not reside in numbers. Therefore, if I were giving advice, I would not say, "take bread", but take counsel with yourselves now to get the power to take bread.

There is no doubt but that power is latently in you; there is little doubt it can be developed; there is no doubt the authorities know this, and fear it, and are ready to exert as much force as is necessary to repress any signs of its development. And this is the explanation of EMMA GOLDMANN'S imprisonment. The authorities do not fear you as you are, they only fear what you may become. The dangerous thing was "the voice crying in the wilderness" foretelling the power which was to come after it. You should have seen how they feared it in Phila. They got out a whole platoon of police and detectives, and executed a military maneuver to catch the little woman who had been running around under their noses for three days. And when she walked up to them, why then, they surrounded and captured her, and guarded the city hall where they kept her over night, and put a detective in the next cell to make notes. Why so much fear? Did they shrink from the stab of the dressmakers needle? Or did they dread some stronger weapon?

Ah!—the accusation before the New York Pontius Pilate was: "she stirreth up the people". And Pilate sentenced her to the full limit of the law, because, he said, "you are more than ordinarily intelligent". Why is intelligence dealt thus hardly with? Because it is the beginning of power. Strive, then, for power.

My second reason for not repeating EMMA GOLDMANN'S words is, that I, as an anarchist, have no right to advise another to do anything involving a risk to himself; nor would I give a fillip for an action done by the advice of some one else, unless it is accompanied by a well-argued, well-settled conviction on the part of the person acting, that it really is the best thing to do. Anarchism, to me, means not only the denial of authority, not only a new economy, but a revision of the principles of morality. It means the development of the individual as well as the assertion of the individual. It means self-responsibility, and not leader worship. I say it is your business to decide whether you will starve and freeze in sight of food and clothing, outside of jail, or commit some overt act against the institution of property and take your place beside TIMMERMANN[15] and GOLDMANN. And in saying this I mean to cast no reflection whatever upon Miss Goldmann for doing otherwise. She and I hold many differing views on both Economy and Morals; and that she is honest in hers she has proven better than I have proven mine. Miss Goldmann is a communist; I am an individualist[16]. She wishes to destroy the right of property, I wish to assert it. I make my war upon privilege and authority, whereby the right of property, the true right in that which is proper to the individual, is annihilated. She believes that co-operation would entirely supplant competition; I hold that competition in one form or another will always exist, and that it is highly desirable it should. But whether she or I be right, or both of us be wrong, of one thing I am sure: *the spirit which animates EMMA*

GOLDMANN is the only one which will emancipate the slave from his slavery, the tyrant from his tyranny—the spirit which is willing to dare and suffer.

That which dwells in the frail body in the prison-room to-night is not the New York dressmaker alone. Transport yourselves there in thought a moment; look steadily into those fair, blue eyes, upon the sun-brown hair, the sea-shell face, the restless hands, the woman's figure, look steadily till these fade from sight, as things will fade when gazed long upon, look steadily till in place of the person, the individual of time and place, you see that which transcends time and place, and flits from house to house of Life, mocking at Death. Swinburne[17] in his magnificent "Before a Crucifix" says:

> "With iron for thy linen bands,
> And unclean cloths for winding-sheet,
> They bind the people's nail-pierced hands,
> They hide the people's nail-pierced feet:
> And what man, or what angel known
> Shall roll back the sepulchral stone?"

Perhaps in the presence of this untrammeled spirit we shall feel that something has rolled back the sepulchral stone; and up from the cold wind of the grave is borne the breath that animated ANAXAGORAS[18], SOCRATES, CHRIST, HYPATIA[19], JOHN HUSS[20], BRUNO[21], ROBERT EMMET[22], JOHN BROWN, SOPHIA PEROVSKAYA[23], PARSONS, FISCHER, ENGEL, SPIES, LINGG[24], BERKMANN[25], PALLAS[26]; and all those, known and unknown, who have died by tree, and axe, and fagot, or dragged out forgotten lives in dungeons, derided, hated, tortured by men. Perhaps we shall know ourselves face to face with that which leaps from the throat of the strangled when the rope chokes, which smokes up from the blood of the murdered when the axe falls; that which has been forever hunted, fettered, imprisoned, exiled, executed, and never conquered. Lo, from its many incarnations it comes forth again, the immortal Race-Christ of the Ages! The gloomy walls are glorified thereby, the prisoner is transfigured: And we say, reverently we say:

> "O sacred Head, O desecrate,
> O labor-wounded feet and hands,
> O blood poured forth in pledge to fate
> Of nameless lives in divers lands!
> O slain, and spent, and sacrificed
> People! The gray-grown, speechless Christ."

They Who Marry Do Ill

(A lecture presenting the negative side of the question, whose positive was argued under the heading "They who marry do well," by Dr. Henrietta P. Westbrook[1]; both lectures delivered before the Radical Liberal League, Philadelphia, April 28, 1907.)

L et me make myself understood on two points, now, so that when discussion arises later, words may not be wasted in considering things not in question: First—How shall we measure doing well or doing ill; Second—What I mean by marriage.

So much as I have been able to put together the pieces of the universe in my small head, there is no absolute right or wrong; there is only a relativity, depending on the consciously though very slowly altering condition of a social race in respect to the rest of the world. Right and wrong are social conceptions: mind, I do not say *human* conceptions. The names "right" and "wrong," truly, are of human invention only; but the conception "right" and "wrong," dimly or clearly, has been wrought out with more or less effectiveness by all intelligent social beings. And the definition of Right, as sealed and approved by the successful conduct of social beings, is: That mode of behavior which best serves the growing need of that society.

As to what that need is, certainly it has been in the past, and for the most part indicated by the unconscious response of the structure (social or individual) to the pressure of its environment. Up till a few years since I believed with Huxley[2], Von Hartman[3], and my teacher Lum[4], that it was wholly so determined; that consciousness might discern, and obey or oppose, but had no voice in deciding the course of social development: if it decided to oppose, it did so to its own ruin, not to the modification of the unconsciously determined ideal.

Of late years I have been approaching the conclusion that consciousness has a continuously increasing part in the decision of social problems; that while it is a minor voice, and must be for a long time to come, it is, nevertheless, the dawning power which threatens to overhurl old processes and old laws, and supplant them by other powers and other ideals. I know no more fascinating speculation than this, of the role of consciousness in present and future evolution. However, it is not our present speculation. I speak of it only because in determining what constitutes well-being at present, I shall maintain that the old ideal has been considerably modified by unconscious reaction against the superfluities produced by unconscious striving towards a certain end.

The question now becomes: What is the growing ideal of human society, unconsciously indicated and unconsciously discerned and illuminated?

By all the readings of progress, this indication appears to be the *free individual;* a society whose economic, political, social and sexual organization shall secure and constantly increase the scope of being to its several units; whose solidarity and continuity depend upon the free attraction of its component parts, and in no wise upon compulsory forms.

Unless we are agreed that this is the discernable goal of our present social striving, there is no hope that we shall agree in the rest of the argument. For it would be vastly easy to prove that if the maintenance of the old divisions of society into classes, each with specialized services to perform—the priesthood, the military, the wage earner, the capitalist, the domestic servant, the breeder, etc.—is in accord with the growing force of society, then marriage is the thing, and they who marry do well.

But this is the point at which I stand, and from which I shall measure well and ill-doing; viz.: that the aim of social striving now is the free individual, implying all the conditions necessary to that freedom.

Now the second thing: What shall we understand as marriage?

Some fifteen or eighteen years ago, when I had not been out of the convent long enough to forget its teachings, nor lived and experienced enough to work out my own definitions, I considered that marriage was "a sacrament of the Church" or it was "civil ceremony performed by the State," by which a man and a woman were united for life, or until the divorce court separated them. With all the energy of a neophyte freethinker, I attacked religious marriage as an unwarranted interference on the part of the priest with the affairs of individuals, condemned the "until death do us part" promise as one of the immoralities which made a person a slave through all his future to his present feelings, and urged the miserable vulgarity of both the religious and civil ceremony, by which the intimate personal relations of two individuals are made topic of comment and jest by the public.

By all this I still hold. Nothing is more disgustingly vulgar to me than the so-called sacrament of marriage; outraging of all delicacy in the trumpeting of private matters in the general ear. Need I recall, for example, the unprinted and unprintable floating literature concerning the marriage of Alice Roosevelt, when the so-called "American princess"[5] was targeted by every lewd jester in the country, because, forsooth, the whole world had to be informed of her forthcoming union with Mr. Longworth! But it is neither the religious nor the civil ceremony that I refer to now, when I say that "those who marry do ill." The ceremony is only a form, a ghost, a meatless shell. By marriage I mean the real thing, the permanent relation of a man and a woman, sexual and economical, whereby the present home and family life is maintained. It is of no importance to me whether this is a polygamous, polyandric or monogamous marriage, nor whether it is blessed by a priest, permitted by a magistrate, contracted publicly or privately, or not contracted at all. It is the permanent dependent relationship which, I affirm, is detrimental to the growth of individual character, and to which I am unequivocally opposed. Now my opponents know where to find me.

In the old days to which I have alluded, I contended, warmly and sincerely, for the exclusive union of one man and one woman as long as they were held together by love, and for the dissolution of the arrangement upon the desire of either. We talked in those days most enthusiastically about the bond of love, and it only. Nowadays I would say that I prefer to see a marriage based purely on business considerations, than a marriage based on love. That is not because I am in the least concerned with the success of the marriage, but because I am concerned with the success of love. And I believe that the easiest, surest and most applicable method of killing love is marriage—marriage as I have defined it. I believe that the only way to preserve love in anything like the ecstatic condition which renders it worthy of a distinctive name— otherwise it is either lust or simply friendship—is to maintain the distances. Never allow love to be vulgarized by the indecencies of continuous close communion. Better to be in familiar contempt of your enemy than the one you love.

I presume that some who are unacquainted with my opposition to legal and social forms, are ready to exclaim: "Do you want to do away with the relation of the sexes altogether, and cover the earth with monks and nuns?" By no means. While I am not over and above anxious about the repopulation of the earth, and should not shed any tears if I knew that the last man had already been born, I am not advocating sexual total abstinence. If the advocates of marriage had merely to prove the case against complete sexual abstinence, their task would be easy. The statistics of insanity, and in general all manner of aberrations, would alone constitute a big item in the charge. No: I do not believe that the highest human being is the unsexed one, or the one who extirpates his passions by violence, whether religious or scientific violence. I would have people regard all their normal instincts in a normal way, neither gluttonizing nor starving them, neither exalting them beyond their true service nor denouncing them as the servitors of evil, both of which mankind are wont to do in considering the sexual passion. In short, I would have men and women so arrange their lives that they shall always, at all times, be free beings in this regard as in all others. The limit of abstinence or indulgence can be fixed by the individual alone, what is normal for one being excess for another, and what is excess at one period of life being normal at another. And as to the effects of such normal gratification of such normal appetite upon population, I would have them conscientiously controlled, as they can be, are to some extent now, and will be more and more through the progress of knowledge. The birth rate of France and of native-born Americans gives evidence of such conscious control.

"But," say the advocates of marriage, "what is there in marriage to interfere with the free development of the individual? What does the free development of the individual mean, if not the expression of manhood and womanhood? And what is more essential to either than parentage and the rearing of young? And is not the fact that the latter requires a period of from fifteen to twenty years, the essential need which determines the permanent home?" It is the scientific advocate of marriage that talks this way. The religious man bases his talk on the will of God, or some other such metaphysical matter. I do not concern myself with him; I concern myself only those who contend that as Man is the latest link in evolution, the same racial necessities which determine the social and sexual relations of allied races will be found shaping and determining these relations in Man; and that, as we find among the higher animals that the period of rearing the young to the point of caring for themselves usually determines the period of conjugality, it must be concluded that the greater attainments of Man, which have so greatly lengthened the educational period of youth, must likewise have fixed the permanent family relation as the ideal condition for humanity. This is but the conscious extension of what unconsciousness, or perhaps semi-conscious adaptation, had already determined for the higher animals, and in savage races to an extent. If people are reasonable, sensible, self-controlled (as to other people they will keep themselves anyway, no matter how things are arranged), does not the marriage state secure this great fundamental purpose of the primal social function, which is at the same time an imperative demand of individual development, better than any other arrangement? With all its failures, is it not the best that has been tried, or with our present light has been conceived?

In endeavoring to prove the opposite of this contention, I shall not go to the failures to prove my point. It is not my purpose to show that a vast number of marriages do not succeed; the divorce court records do that. But as one swallow doesn't make a summer, nor a flock of swallows either, so divorces do not in themselves prove that marriage in itself is a bad thing, only that a goodly number of individuals make mistakes. This is, indeed, an unanswerable argument against the indissolubility of marriage, but not against marriage itself. I will go to the successful marriages—the marriages in which whatever the friction, man and wife have spent a great deal of agreeable time together; in which the family has been provided for by honest work decently paid (as the wage-system goes), of the father, and preserved within the home by the saving labor and attention of the mother; the children given a reasonable education and started in life on their own account, and the old folks left to finish up life together, each resting secure in the knowledge that he has a tried friend until death severs the bond. This, I conceive, is the best form that marriage can present, and I opine it is oftener dreamed of than realized. But sometimes it is realized. Yet from the viewpoint that the object of life should be the development of individuality, such have lived less successfully than many who have not lived so happily.

And to the first great point—the point that physical parentage is one of the fundamental necessities of self-expression: here, I think, is where the factor of consciousness is in process of overturning the methods of life. Life, working unconsciously, blindly sought to preserve itself by generation, by manifold generation. The mind is simply staggered by the productivity of a single stalk of wheat, or of a fish, or of a queen bee, or of a man. One is smitten the appalling waste of generative effort; numbed with helpless pity for the little things, the infinitude of little lives, that must come forth and suffer and die of starvation, of exposure, as a prey to other creatures, and all to no end but that out of the multitude a few may survive and continue the type! Man, at war with nature and not yet master of the situation, obeyed the same instinct, and by prolific parentage maintained his war. To the Hebrew patriarch as to the American pioneer, a large family meant strength, the wealth of brawn and sinew to continue the conquest of forest and field. It was the only resource against annihilation. Therefore, the instinct towards physical creation was one of the most imperative determinants of action.

Now the law of all instinct is, that it survives long after the necessity which created it has ceased to exist, and acts mischievously. The usual method of reckoning with such a survival since such and such a thing exists, it is an essential part of the structure, not obliged to account for itself and bound to be gratified. I am perfectly certain, however, that the more conscious consciousness becomes, or in other words, the more we become aware of the conditions of life and our relations therein, their new demands and the best way of fulfilling them, the more speedily will instincts no longer demanded be dissolved from the structure.

How stands the war upon nature now? Why, so that short of a planetary catastrophe, we are certain of the conquest? Consciousness! The alert brain! The dominant will! Invention, discovery, mastery of hidden forces. We are no longer compelled to use the blind method of limitless propagation to equip the race with hunters and trappers and fishers and sheep-keepers and soil-tillers and breeders. Therefore, the original necessity which gave rise to the instinct of prolific parentage is gone; the instinct itself is bound to die, and is dying, but will die faster as men grasp more and more of the whole situation. In proportion as the parenthood of the brain becomes more and more prolific, as ideas spread, multiply, and conquer, the necessity for great physical production declines. This is my first contention. Hence the development of individuality does no longer *necessarily* imply numerous children, nor indeed, *necessarily* any children at all. That is not to say that no one will want children, nor to prophecy race suicide. It is simply to say that there will be fewer born, with better chances of surviving, developing, and achieving. Indeed, with all its clash of tendencies, the consciousness of our present society is having this driven home to it.

Supposing that the majority will still desire, or let me go further and say *do* still desire, this limited parentage, the question now becomes: Is this the overshadowing need in the development of the individual, or are there other needs equally imperative? If there are other needs equally imperative, must not these be taken equally into account in deciding the best manner of conducting one's life? If there are not other needs equally imperative, is it not still an open question whether the married state is the best means of securing it? In answering these questions, I think it will again be safe to separate into a majority and a minority. There will be a minority to whom the rearing of children will be the great dominant necessity of their being, and a majority to whom this will be one of their necessities. Now what are the other necessities? The other physical and mental appetites! The desire for food and raiment and housing after the individual's own taste; the desire for sexual association, not for reproduction;

the artistic desires; the desire to know, with its thousand ramifications, which may carry the soul from the depths of the concrete to the heights of the abstract; the desire to do, that is, to imprint one's will upon the social structure, whether as a mechanical contriver, a force harnesser, a combiner, a dream translator, —whatever may be the particular mode of the personal organization.

The desire for food, shelter, and raiment, it should at all times lie within the individual's power to furnish for himself. But the method of home-keeping is such that after the relation has been maintained for a few years, the interdependence of one on the other has become so great that each is somewhat helpless when circumstance destroys the combination, the man less so, the woman wretchedly so. She has done one thing in a secluded sphere, and while she may have learned to do that thing well (which is not certain, the method of training is not at all satisfactory), it is not a thing which has equipped her with the confidence necessary to go about making an independent living. She is timid above all, incompetent to deal with the conditions of struggle. The world of production has swept past her; she knows nothing of it. On the other hand, what sort of an occupation is it for her to take domestic service under some other woman's rule? The conditions and pay of domestic service are such that every independent spirit would prefer to slave in a factory, where at least the slavery ends with the working hours. As for men, only a few days since a staunch free unionist told me, apparently without shame, that were it not for his wife he would be a tramp and a drunkard, simply because he is unable to keep a home; and in his eyes the chief merit of the arrangement is that his stomach is properly cared for. This is a degree of helplessness which I should have thought he would have shrunk from admitting, but is nevertheless probably true. Now this is one of the greatest objections to the married condition, as it is to any other condition which produces like results. In choosing one's economic position in society, one should always bear in mind that it should be such as should leave the individual uncrippled -an all-round person, with both productive and preservative capacities, a being pivoted within.

Concerning the sexual appetite, irrespective of reproduction, the advocates of marriage claim, and with some reason, that it tends to preserve normal appetite and satisfaction, and is both a physical and moral safeguard against excesses, with their attendant results, disease. That it does not do so entirely, we have ample and painful proof continuously before our eyes. As to what it may accomplish, it is almost impossible to find out the truth; for religious asceticism has so built the feeling of shame into the human mind, on the subject of sex, that the first instinct, when it is brought under discussion, seems to be to lie about it. This is especially the case with women. The majority of women usually wish to create the impression that they are devoid of sexual desires, and think they have paid the highest compliment to themselves when they say, "Personally, I am very cold; I have never experienced such an attraction." Sometimes this is true, but oftener it is a lie—a lie born of centuries of the pernicious teachings of the Church. A roundly developed person will understand that she pays no honor to herself by denying herself fullness of being, whether to herself or of herself; though, without doubt, where such a deficiency really exists, it may give room for an extra growth of some other qualities, perhaps of higher value. In general, however, notwithstanding women's lies, there is no such deficiency. In general, young, healthy beings of both sexes desire such relations. What then? Is marriage the best answer to the need? Suppose they marry, say at twenty years, or thereabouts, which will be admitted as the time when sexual appetite is most active; the consequence is (I am just now leaving children out of account) that the two are thrown too much and too constantly in contact, and speedily exhaust the delight of each other's presence. Then irritations begin. The familiarities of life in common breed contempt. What was once a rare joy becomes a matter of course, and loses all its delicacy. Very often it becomes a physical torture to one (usually the woman), while it still retains some pleasure to the other, for the reason that bodies, like souls, do most seldom, almost never, parallel each other's development. And this lack of parallelism is the greatest argument to be produced against marriage. No matter how perfectly adapted to each other two people may be at any given time, it is not the slightest evidence that they will continue to be so. And no period of life is more deceptive as to what future development may be than the age I have just been speaking of, the age when physical desires and attractions being strongest, they obscure or hold in abeyance the other elements of being.

The terrible tragedies of sexual antipathy, mostly for shame's sake, will never be revealed. But they have filled the Earth with murder. And even in those homes where harmony has been maintained, and all is apparently peaceful, it is mainly so through the resignation and self-suppression of either the man or the woman. One has consented to be largely effaced, for the preservation of the family and social respect.

But awful as these things are, these physical degradations, they are not so terrible as the ruined souls. When the period of physical predominance is past, and soul-tendencies begin more and more strongly to assert themselves, how dreadful is the recognition that one is bound by common parentage to one to remain in the constant company of one from whom one finds oneself going farther and farther away in thought every day. "Not a day," exclaim the advocates of "free unions." I find such exclamation worse folly than the talk of "holy matrimony" believers. The bonds are there, the bonds of life in common, the love of the home built by joint labor, the habit of association and dependence; they are very real chains, binding both, and not to be thrown off lightly. Not in a day or a month, but only after long hesitation, struggle, and grievous, grievous pain, can the wrench of separation come. Oftener it does not come at all.

A chapter from the lives of two men recently deceased will illustrate my meaning. Ernest Crosby[6], wedded, and I assume happily, to a lady of conservative thought and feeling, himself the conservative, came into his soul's own at the age of thirty-eight, while occupying the position of Judge of the International Court at Cairo. From then on, the whole radical world knows Ernest Crosby's work. Yet what a position was his compelled by honor to continue the functions of a social life which he disliked! To quote the words of his friend, Leonard Abbott[7], "a prisoner in his palatial home, waited on by servants and lackeys. Yet to the end he remained enslaved by his possessions." Had Crosby not been bound, had not union and family relations with one who holds very different views of life in faith and honor held him, should we not have had a different life-sum? Like his great teacher, Tolstoy, likewise made absurd, his life contradicted by his works, because of his union with a woman who has not developed along parallel lines.

The second case, Hugh O. Pentecost[8]. From the year 1887 on, whatever were his special tendencies, Pentecost was in the main a sympathizer with the struggle of labor, an opposer of oppression, persecution and prosecution in all forms. Yet through the influence of his family relations, because he felt in honor bound to provide greater material comfort and a better standing in society than the position of a radical speaker could give, he consented at one time to be the puppet of those he had most strenuously condemned, to become a district attorney, a prosecutor. And worse than that, to paint himself as a misled baby for having done the best act of his life, to protest against the execution of the Chicago Anarchists[9]. That this influence was brought to bear upon him, I know from his own lips; a repetition, in a small way, of the treason of Benedict Arnold, who for his Tory wife's sake laid everlasting infamy upon himself. I do not say there was no self-excusing in this, no Eve-did-tempt-me taint, but surely it had its influence. I speak of these two men because these instances are well known; but everyone knows of such instances among more obscure persons, and often where the woman is the one whose higher nature is degraded by the bond between herself and her husband.

And this is one side of the story. What of the other side? What of the conservative one who finds himself bound to one who outrages every principle in his or hers? People will not, and cannot, think and feel the same at the same moments, throughout any considerable period of life; and therefore, their moments of union should be rare and of no binding nature.

I return to the subject of children. Since this also is a normal desire, can it not be gratified without the sacrifice of individual freedom required by marriage? I see no reason why it cannot. I believe that children may be as well brought up in an individual home, or in a communal home, as in a dual home; and that impressions of life will be far pleasanter if received in an atmosphere of freedom and independent strength than in an atmosphere of secret repression and discontent. I have no very satisfactory solutions to offer to the various questions presented by the child-problem; but neither do the advocates of marriage. Certain to me it is, that no one of the demands of life should ever be answered in a manner to preclude future free development. I have seen no great success from the old method of raising children under the indissoluble marriage yoke of the parents. (Our conservative parents probably consider their radical children great failures, though it probably does not occur to them that their system is in any way at fault.) Neither have I observed a gain in the child of the free union. Neither have I observed that the individually raised child is any more likely to be a success or a failure. Up to the present, no one has given a scientific answer to the child problem. Those papers which make a specialty of it, such as *Lucifer*, are full of guesses and theories and suggested experiments; but no infallible principals [sic] for the guidance of intentional or actual parents have as yet been worked out. Therefore, I see no reason why the rest of life should be sacrificed to an uncertainty.

That love and respect may last, I would have unions rare and impermanent. That life may grow, I would have men and women remain separate personalities. Have no common possessions with your lover more than you might freely have with one not your lover. Because I believe that marriage stales love, brings respect into contempt, outrages all the privacies and limits the growth of both parties, I believe that "they who marry do ill."

Anarchism and American Traditions

American traditions, begotten of religious rebellion, small self-sustaining communities, isolated conditions, and hard pioneer life, grew during the colonization period of one hundred and seventy years from the settling of Jamestown to the outburst of the Revolution. This was in fact the great constitution-making epoch, the period of charters guaranteeing more or less of liberty, the general tendency of which is well described by Wm. Penn[1] in speaking of the charter for Pennsylvania: "I want to put it out of my power, or that of my successors, to do mischief."

The revolution is the sudden and unified consciousness of these traditions, their loud assertion, the blow dealt by their indomitable will against the counter force of tyranny, which has never entirely recovered from the blow, but which from then till now has gone on remolding and regrappling the instruments of governmental power, that the Revolution sought to shape and hold as defenses of liberty.

To the average American of today, the Revolution means the series of battles fought by the patriot army with the armies of England. The millions of school children who attend our public schools are taught to draw maps of the siege of Boston and the siege of Yorktown, to know the general plan of the several campaigns, to quote the number of prisoners of war surrendered with Burgoyne[2]; they are required to remember the date when Washington crossed the Delaware on the ice; they are told to "Remember Paoli[3]," to repeat "Molly Stark's a widow[4]," to call General Wayne "Mad Anthony Wayne[5]," and to execrate Benedict Arnold; they know that the Declaration of Independence was signed on the Fourth of July, 1776, and the Treaty of Paris in 1783; and then they think they have learned the Revolution—blessed be George Washington! They have no idea why it should have been called a "revolution" instead of the "English War," or any similar title: it's the name of it, that's all. And name-worship, both in child and man, has acquired such mastery of them, that the name

"American Revolution" is held sacred, though it means to them nothing more than successful force, while the name "Revolution" applied to a further possibility, is a spectre detested and abhorred. In neither case have they any idea of the content of the word, save that of armed force. That has already happened, and long happened, which Jefferson foresaw when he wrote:

> "The spirit of the times may alter, will alter. Our rulers will become corrupt, our people careless. A single zealot may become persecutor, and better men be his victims. It can never be too often repeated that the time for fixing every essential right, on a legal basis, is while our rulers are honest, ourselves united. From the conclusion of this war we shall be going down hill. It will not then be necessary to resort every moment to the people for support. They will be forgotten, therefore, and their rights disregarded. They will forget themselves in the sole faculty of making money, and will never think of uniting to effect a due respect for their rights. The shackles, therefore, which shall not be knocked off at the conclusion of this war, will be heavier and heavier, till our rights shall revive or expire in a convulsion."

To the men of that time, who voiced the spirit of that time, the battles that they fought were the least of the Revolution; they were the incidents of the hour, the things they met and faced as part of the game they were playing; but the stake they had in view, before, during, and after the war, the real Revolution, was a change in political institutions which should make of government not a thing apart, a superior power to stand over the people with a whip, but a serviceable agent, responsible, economical, and trustworthy (but never so much trusted as not to be continually watched), for the transaction of such business as was the common concern and to set the limits of the common concern at the line of where one man's liberty would encroach upon another's.

They thus took their starting point for deriving a minimum of government upon the same sociological ground that the modern Anarchist derives the no-government theory; viz., that equal liberty is the political ideal. The difference lies in the belief, on the one hand, that the closest approximation to equal liberty might be best secured by the rule of the majority in those matters involving united action of any kind (which rule of the majority they thought it possible to secure by a few simple arrangements for election), and, on the other hand, the belief that majority rule is both impossible and undesirable; that any government, no matter what its forms, will be manipulated by a very small minority, as the development of the States and United States governments has strikingly proved; that candidates will loudly profess allegiance to platforms before elections, which as officials in power they will openly disregard, to do as they please; and that even if the majority will could be imposed, it would also be subversive of equal liberty, which may be best secured by leaving to the voluntary association of those interested in the management of matters of common concern, without coercion of the uninterested or the opposed.

Among the fundamental likenesses between the Revolutionary Republicans and the Anarchists is the recognition that the little must precede the great; that the local must be the basis of the general; that there can be a free federation only when there are free communities to federate; that the spirit of the latter is carried into the councils of the former, and a local tyranny may thus become an instrument for general enslavement. Convinced of the supreme importance of ridding the municipalities of the institutions of tyranny, the most strenuous advocates of independence, instead of spending their efforts mainly in the general Congress, devoted themselves to their home localities, endeavoring to work out of the minds of their neighbors and fellow-colonists the institutions of entailed property, of a State-Church, of a class-divided people, even the institution of African slavery itself. Though largely unsuccessful, it is to the measure of success they did achieve that we are indebted for such liberties as we do retain, and not to the general government. They tried to inculcate local initiative and independent action. The author of the Declaration of Independence, who in the fall of '76 declined a re-election to Congress in order to return to Virginia and do his work in his own local assembly, in arranging there for public education which he justly considered a matter of "common concern," said his advocacy of public schools was not with any "view to take its ordinary branches out of the hands of private enterprise, which manages *so much better* the concerns to which it is equal"; and in endeavoring to make clear the restrictions of the Constitution upon the functions of the general government, he likewise said: "Let the general government be reduced to foreign concerns only, and let our affairs be disentangled from those of all other nations, except as to commerce, *which the merchants will manage the better the more they are left free to manage for themselves,* and the general government may be reduced to a very simple organization, and a very inexpensive one; a few plain duties to be performed by a few servants." This then was the American tradition, that private enterprise manages better all that to which it is equal. Anarchism declares that private enterprise, whether individual or cooperative, is equal to all the undertakings of society. And it quotes the particular two instances, Education and Commerce, which the governments of the States and of the United States have undertaken to manage and regulate, as the very two which in operation have done more to destroy American freedom and equality, to warp and distort American tradition, to make of government a mighty engine of tyranny, than any other cause, save the unforeseen developments of Manufacture.

It was the intention of the Revolutionists to establish a system of common education, which should make the teaching of history one of its principal branches; not with the intent of burdening the memories of our youth with the dates of battles or the speeches of generals, nor to make the Boston Tea Party Indians[6] the one sacrosanct mob in all history, to be revered but never on any account to be imitated, but with the intent that every American should know to what conditions the masses of people had been brought by the operation of certain institutions, by what means they had wrung out their liberties, and how those liberties had again and again been filched from them by the use of governmental force, fraud, and privilege. Not to breed security, laudation, complacent indolence, passive acquiescence in the acts of a government protected by the label "home-made," but to beget a wakeful jealousy, a never-ending watchfulness of rulers, a determination to squelch every attempt of those entrusted with power to encroach upon the sphere of individual action—this was the prime motive of the revolutionists in endeavoring to provide for common education.

"Confidence," said the revolutionists who adopted the Kentucky Resolutions[7], "is everywhere the parent of despotism; free government is founded in jealousy, not in confidence; it is jealousy, not confidence, which prescribes limited constitutions to bind down those whom we are obliged to trust with power; our Constitution has accordingly fixed the limits to which, and no further, our confidence may go... In questions of power, let no more be heard of confidence in man, but bind him down from mischief by the chains of the Constitution."

These resolutions were especially applied to the passage of the Alien laws[8] by the monarchist party during John Adams' administration, and were an indignant call from the State of Kentucky to repudiate the right of the general government to assume undelegated powers, for, said they, to accept these laws would be "to be bound by laws made, not with our consent, but by others against our consent—that is, to surrender the form of government we have chosen, and to live under one deriving its powers from its own will, and not from our authority." Resolutions identical in spirit were also passed by Virginia, the following month; in those days the States still considered themselves supreme, the general government subordinate.

To inculcate this proud spirit of the supremacy of the people over their governors was to be the purpose of public education! Pick up today any common school history, and see how much of this spirit you will find therein. On the contrary, from cover to cover you will find nothing but the cheapest sort of patriotism, the inculcation of the most unquestioning acquiescence in the deeds of government, a lullaby of rest, security, confidence—the doctrine that the Law can do no wrong, a Te Deum in praise of the continuous encroachments of the powers of the general government upon the reserved rights of the States, shameless falsification of all acts of rebellion, to put the government in the right and the rebels in the wrong, pyrotechnic glorifications of union, power, and force, and a complete ignoring of the essential liberties to maintain which was the purpose of the revolutionists. The anti-Anarchist law of post-McKinley passage, a much worse law than the Alien and Sedition acts which roused the wrath of Kentucky and Virginia to the point of threatened rebellion, is exalted as a wise provision of our All-Seeing Father in Washington.

Such is the spirit of government-provided schools. Ask any child what he knows about Shays' rebellion[9], and he will answer, "Oh, some of the farmers couldn't pay their taxes, and Shays led a rebellion against the court-house at Worcester, so they could burn up the deeds; and when Washington heard of it he sent over an army quick and taught 'em a good lesson"—"And what was the result of it?" "The result? Why—why—the result was—Oh yes, I remember—the result was they saw the need of a strong federal government to collect the taxes and pay the debts." Ask if he knows what was said on the other side of the story, ask if he knows that the men who had given their goods and their health and their strength for the freeing of the country now found themselves cast into prison for debt, sick, disabled, and poor, facing a new tyranny for the old; that their demand was that the land should become the free communal possession of those who wished to work it, not subject to tribute, and the child will answer "No." Ask him if he ever read Jefferson's letter to Madison about it, in which he says:

> "Societies exist under three forms, sufficiently distinguishable. 1. Without government, as among our Indians. 2. Under government wherein the will of every one has a just influence; as is the case in England in a slight degree, and in our States in a great one. 3. Under government of force, as is the case in all other monarchies, and in most of the other republics. To have an idea of the curse of existence in these last, they must be seen. It is a government of wolves over sheep. It is a

problem not clear in my mind that the first condition is not the best. But I believe it to be inconsistent with any great degree of population. The second state has a great deal of good in it...It has its evils too, the principal of which is the turbulence to which it is subject. ...But even this evil is productive of good. It prevents the degeneracy of government, and nourishes a general attention to public affairs. I hold that a little rebellion now and then is a good thing."

Or to another correspondent:

"God forbid that we should ever be twenty years without such a rebellion!...What country can preserve its liberties if its rulers are not warned from time to time that the people preserve the spirit of resistance? Let them take up arms...The tree of liberty must be refreshed from time to time with the blood of patriots and tyrants. It is its natural manure."

Ask any school child if he was ever taught that the author of the Declaration of Independence, one of the great founders of the common school, said these things, and he will look at you with open mouth and unbelieving eyes. Ask him if he ever heard that the man who sounded the bugle note in the darkest hour of the Crisis, who roused the courage of the soldiers when Washington saw only mutiny and despair ahead, ask him if he knows that this man also wrote, "Government at best is a necessary evil, at worst an intolerable one," and if he is a little better informed than the average he will answer, "Oh well, *he* was an infidel!" Catechize him about the merits of the Constitution which he has learned to repeat like a poll-parrot, and you will find his chief conception is not of the powers withheld from Congress, but of the powers granted.

Such are the fruits of government schools. We, the Anarchists, point to them and say: If the believers in liberty wish the principles of liberty taught, let them never entrust that instruction to any government; for the nature of government is to become a thing apart, an institution existing for its own sake, preying upon the people, and teaching whatever will tend to keep it secure in its seat. As the fathers said of the governments of Europe, so say we of this government also after a century and a quarter of independence: "The blood of the people has become its inheritance, and those who fatten on it will not relinquish it easily."

Public education, having to do with the intellect and spirit of a people, is probably the most subtle and far-reaching engine for molding the course of a nation; but commerce, dealing as it does with material things and producing immediate effects, was the force that bore down soonest upon the paper barriers of constitutional restriction, and shaped the government to its requirements. Here, indeed, we arrive at the point where we, looking over the hundred and twenty five years of independence, can see that the simple government conceived by the revolutionary republicans was a foredoomed failure. It was so because of: 1) the essence of government itself; 2) the essence of human nature; 3) the essence of Commerce and Manufacture.

Of the essence of government, I have already said, it is a thing apart, developing its own interests at the expense of what opposes it; all attempts to make it anything else fail. In this Anarchists agree with the traditional enemies of the Revolution, the monarchists, federalists, strong government believers, the Roosevelts of today, the Jays, Marshalls, and Hamiltons of then—that Hamilton, who, as Secretary of the Treasury, devised a financial system of which we are the unlucky heritors, and whose objects were twofold: To puzzle the people and make public finance obscure to those that paid for it; to serve as a machine for corrupting the legislatures; "for he avowed the opinion that man could be governed by two motives only, force or interest"; force being then out of the question, he laid hold of interest, the greed of the legislators, to set going an association of persons having an entirely separate welfare from the welfare of their electors, bound together by mutual corruption and mutual desire for plunder. The Anarchist agrees that Hamilton was logical, and understood the core of government; the difference is, that while strong governmentalists believe this is necessary and desirable, we choose the opposite conclusion, No GOVERNMENT WHATEVER.

As to the essence of human nature, what our national experience has made plain is this, that to remain in a continually exalted moral condition is not human nature. That has happened which was prophesied: we have gone down hill from the Revolution until now; we are absorbed in "mere money-getting." The desire for material ease long ago vanquished the spirit of '76. What was that spirit? The spirit that animated the people of Virginia, of the Carolinas, of Massachusetts, of New York, when they refused to import goods from England; when they preferred (and stood by it) to wear coarse, homespun cloth, to drink the brew of their own growths, to fit their appetites to the home supply, rather than submit to the taxation of the imperial ministry. Even within the lifetime of the revolutionists, the spirit decayed. The love of material ease has been, in the mass of men and permanently speaking, always greater than the love of liberty. Nine hundred and ninety nine women out of a thousand are more interested in the cut of a dress than in the independence of their sex; nine hundred and ninety nine men out of a thousand are more interested in drinking a glass of beer than in questioning the tax that is laid on it; how many children are not willing to trade the liberty to play for the promise of a new cap or a new dress? That it is which begets the complicated mechanism of society; that it is which, by multiplying the concerns of government, multiplies the strength of government and the corresponding weakness of the people; this it is which begets indifference to public concern, thus making the corruption of government easy.

As to the essence of Commerce and Manufacture, it is this: to establish bonds between every corner of the earth's surface and every other corner, to multiply the needs of mankind, and the desire for material possession and enjoyment.

The American tradition was the isolation of the States as far as possible. Said they: We have won our liberties by hard sacrifice and struggle unto death. We wish now to be let alone and to let others alone, that our principles may have time for trial; that we may become accustomed to the exercise of our rights; that we may be kept free from the contaminating influence of European gauds, pageants, distinctions. So richly did they esteem the absence of these that they could in all fervor write: "We shall see multiplied instances of Europeans coming to America, but no man living will ever see an instance of an American removing to settle in Europe, and continuing there." Alas! In less than a hundred years the highest aim of a "Daughter of the Revolution" was, and is, to buy a castle, a title, and rotten lord, with the money wrung from American servitude! And the commercial interests of America are seeking a world empire!

In the earlier days of the revolt and subsequent independence, it appeared that the "manifest destiny" of America was to be an agricultural people, exchanging food stuffs and raw materials for manufactured articles. And in those days it was written: "We shall be virtuous as long as agriculture is our principal object, which will be the case as long as there remain vacant lands in any part of America. When we get piled upon one another in large cities, as in Europe, we shall become corrupt as in Europe, and go to eating one another as they do there." Which we are doing, because of the inevitable development of Commerce and Manufacture, and the concomitant development of strong government. And the parallel prophecy is likewise fulfilled: "If ever this vast country is brought under a single government, it will be one of the most extensive corruption, indifferent and incapable of a wholesome care over so wide a spread of surface." There is not upon the face of the earth today a government so utterly and shamelessly corrupt as that of the United States of America. There are others more cruel, more tyrannical, more devastating; there is none so utterly venal.

And yet even in the very days of the prophets, even with their own consent, the first concession to this later tyranny was made. It was made when the Constitution was made; and the Constitution was made chiefly because of the demands of Commerce. Thus it was at the outset a merchant's machine, which the other interests of the country, the land and labor interests, even then foreboded would destroy their · liberties. In vain their jealousy of its central power made enact the first twelve amendments. In vain they endeavored to set bounds over which the federal power dare not trench. In vain they enacted into general law the freedom of speech, of the press, of assemblage and petition. All of these things we see ridden roughshod upon every day, and have so seen with more or less intermission since the beginning of the nineteenth century. At this day, every police lieutenant considers himself, and rightly so, as more powerful than the General Law of the Union; and that one who told Robert Hunter[10] that he held in his fist something stronger than the Constitution, was perfectly correct. The right of assemblage is an American tradition which has gone out of fashion; the police club is now the mode. And it is so in virtue of the people's indifference to liberty, and the steady progress of constitutional interpretation towards the substance of imperial government.

It is an American tradition that a standing army is a standing menace to liberty; in Jefferson's presidency the army was reduced to 3,000 men. It is American tradition that we keep out of the affairs of other nations. It is American practice that we meddle with the affairs of everybody else from the West to the East Indies, from Russia to Japan; and to do it we have a standing army of 83,251 men.

It is American tradition that the financial affairs of a nation should be transacted on the same principles of simple honesty that an individual conducts his own business; viz., that debt is a bad thing, and a man's first surplus earning should be applied to his debts; that offices and office holders should be few. It is American practice that the general government should always have millions of debt, even if a panic or a war has to be forced to prevent its being paid off; and as to the application of its income office holders come first. And within the last administration it is reported that 99,000 offices have been created at an annual expense of $63,000,000. Shades of Jefferson! "How are vacancies to be obtained? Those by deaths are few; by resignation none." Roosevelt cuts the knot by making 99,000 new ones! And few will die—and none resign. They will beget sons and daughters, and Taft will have to create 99,000 more! Verily a simple and a serviceable thing is our general government.

It is American tradition that the Judiciary shall act as a check upon the impetuosity of Legislatures, should these attempt to pass the bounds of constitutional limitation. It is American practice that the Judiciary justifies every law which trenches on the liberties of the people and nullifies every act of the Legislature by which the people seek to regain some measure of their freedom. Again, in the words of Jefferson: "The Constitution is a mere thing of wax in the hands of the Judiciary, which they may twist and shape in any form they please." Truly, if the men who fought the good fight for the triumph of simple, honest, free life in that day, were now to look upon the scene of their labors, they would cry out together with him who said:

> "I regret that I am now to die in the belief that the useless sacrifices of themselves by the generation of '76 to acquire self-government and happiness to their country, is to be thrown away by the unwise and unworthy passions of their sons, and that my only consolation is to be that I shall not live to see it."

And now, what has Anarchism to say to all this, this bankruptcy of republicanism, this modern empire that has grown up on the ruins of our early freedom? We say this, that the sin our fathers sinned was that they did not trust liberty wholly. They thought it possible to compromise between liberty and government, believing the latter to be "a necessary evil," and the moment the compromise was made, the whole misbegotten monster of our present tyranny began to grow. Instruments which are set up to safeguard rights become the very whip with which the free are struck.

Anarchism says, Make no laws whatever concerning speech, and speech will be free; so soon as you make a declaration on paper that speech shall be free, you will have a hundred lawyers proving that "freedom does not mean abuse, nor liberty license"; and they will define and define freedom out of existence. Let the guarantee of free speech be in every man's determination to use it, and we shall have no need of paper declarations. On the other hand, so long as the people do not care to exercise their freedom, those who wish to tyrannize will do so; for tyrants are active and ardent, and will devote themselves in the name of any number of gods, religious and otherwise, to put shackles upon sleeping men.

The problem then becomes, Is it possible to stir men from their indifference? We have said that the spirit of liberty was nurtured by colonial life; that the elements of colonial life were the desire for sectarian independence, and the jealous watchfulness incident thereto; the isolation of pioneer communities which threw each individual strongly on his own resources, and thus developed all-around men, yet at the same time made very strong such social bonds as did exist; and, lastly, the comparative simplicity of small communities.

All this has disappeared. As to sectarianism, it is only by dint of an occasional idiotic persecution that a sect becomes interesting; in the absence of this, outlandish sects play the fool's role, are anything but heroic, and have little to do with either the name or the substance of liberty. The old colonial religious parties have gradually become the "pillars of society," their animosities have died out, their offensive peculiarities have been effaced, they are as like one another as beans in a pod, they build churches—and sleep in them.

As to our communities, they are hopelessly and helplessly interdependent, as we ourselves are, save that continuously diminishing proportion engaged in all around farming; and even these are slaves to mortgages. For our cities, probably there is not one that is provisioned to last a week, and certainly there is none which would not be bankrupt with despair at the proposition that it produce its own food. In response to this condition and its correlative political tyranny, Anarchism affirms the economy of self-sustenance, the disintegration of the great communities, the use of the earth.

I am not ready to say that I see clearly that this *will* take place; but I see clearly that this *must* take place if ever again men are to be free. I am so well satisfied that the mass of mankind prefer material possessions to liberty, that I have no hope that they will ever, by means of intellectual or moral stirrings merely, throw off the yoke of oppression fastened on them by the present economic system, to institute free societies. My only hope is in the blind development of the economic system and political oppression itself. The great characteristic looming factor in this gigantic power is Manufacture. The tendency of each nation is to become more and more a manufacturing one, an exporter of fabrics, not an importer. If this tendency follows its own logic, it must eventually circle round to each community producing for itself. What then will become of the surplus product when the manufacturer shall have no foreign market? Why, then mankind must face the dilemma of sitting down and dying in the midst of it, or confiscating the goods.

Indeed, we are partially facing this problem even now; and so far we are sitting down and dying. I opine, however, that men will not do it forever, and when once by an act of general expropriation they have overcome the reverence and fear of property,

31

and their awe of government, they may waken to the consciousness that things are to be used, and therefore men are greater than things. This may rouse the spirit of liberty.

If, on the other hand, the tendency of invention to simplify, enabling the advantages of machinery to be combined with smaller aggregations of workers, shall also follow its own logic, the great manufacturing plants will break up, population will go after the fragments, and there will be seen not indeed the hard, self-sustaining, isolated pioneer communities of early America, but thousands of small communities stretching along the lines of transportation, each producing very largely for its own needs, able to rely upon itself, and therefore able to be independent. For the same rule holds good for societies as for individuals,—those may be free who are able to make their own living.

In regard to the breaking up of that vilest creation of tyranny, the standing army and navy, it is clear that so long as men desire to fight, they will have armed force in one form or another. Our fathers thought they had guarded against a standing army by providing for the voluntary militia. In our day we have lived to see this militia declared part of the regular military force of the United States, and subject to the same demands as the regulars. Within another generation we shall probably see its members in the regular pay of the general government. Since any embodiment of the fighting spirit, any military organization, inevitably follows the same line of centralization, the logic of Anarchism is that the least objectionable form of armed force is that which springs up voluntarily, like the minute men of Massachusetts, and disbands as soon as the occasion which called it into existence is past: that the really desirable thing is that all men—not Americans only—should be at peace; and that to reach this, all peaceful persons should withdraw their support from the army, and require that all who make war shall do so at their own cost and risk; that neither pay nor pensions are to be provided for those who choose to make man-killing a trade.

As to the American tradition of non-meddling, Anarchism asks that it be carried down to the individual himself. It demands no jealous barrier of isolation; it knows that such isolation is undesirable and impossible; but it teaches that by all men strictly minding their own business, a fluid society, freely adapting itself to mutual needs, wherein all the world shall belong to all men, as much as each has need or desire, will result.

And when Modern Revolution has thus been carried to the heart of the whole world—if it ever shall be, as I hope it will,—then may we hope to see a resurrection of that proud spirit of our fathers which put the simple dignity of Man above the gauds of wealth and class, and held that to be an American was greater than to be a king.

In that day there shall be neither kings nor Americans,—only Men; over the whole earth, MEN.

The Dominant Idea

On everything that lives, if one looks searchingly, is limned the shadow line of an idea—an idea, dead or living, sometimes stronger when dead, with rigid, unswerving lines that mark the living embodiment with the stern immobile cast of the non-living. Daily we move among these unyielding shadows, less pierceable, more enduring than granite, with the blackness of ages in them, dominating living, changing bodies, with dead, unchanging souls. And we meet, also, living souls dominating dying bodies—living ideas regnant over decay and death. Do not imagine that I speak of human life alone. The stamp of persistent or of shifting Will is visible in the grass-blade rooted in its clod of earth, as in the gossamer web of being that floats and swims far over our heads in the free world of air.

Regnant ideas, everywhere! Did you ever see a dead vine bloom? I have seen it. Last summer I trained some morning-glory vines up over a second story balcony; and every day they blew and curled in the wind, their white, purple-dashed faces winking at the sun, radiant with climbing life. Higher every day the green heads crept, carrying their train of spreading fans waving before the sun-seeking blossoms. Then all at once some mischance happened, some cut worm or some mischievous child tore one vine off below, the finest and most ambitious one, of course. In a few hours the leaves hung limp, the sappy stem wilted and began to wither; in a day it was dead,—all but the top which still clung longingly to its support, with bright head lifted. I mourned a little for the buds that could never open now, and tied that proud vine whose work in the world was lost. But the next night there was a storm, a heavy, driving storm, with beating rain and blinding lightning. I rose to watch the flashes, and lo! the wonder of the world! In the blackness of the mid-NIGHT, in the fury of wind and rain, the dead vine had flowered. Five white, moon-faced blossoms blew gaily round the skeleton vine, shining back triumphant at the red lightning. I gazed at them in dumb wonder. Dear, dead vine, whose will had been so strong to bloom, that in the hour of its sudden cut-off from the feeding earth, it sent the last sap to its blossoms; and, not waiting for the morning, brought them forth in storm and flash, as white night-glories, which should have been the children of the sun.

In the daylight we all came to look at the wonder, marveling much, and saying, "Surely these must be the last." But every day for three days the dead vine bloomed; and even a week after, when every leaf was dry and brown, and so thin you could see through it, one last bud, dwarfed, weak, a very baby of a blossom, but still white and delicate, with five purple flecks, like those on the live vine beside it, opened and waved at the stars, and waited for the early sun. Over death and decay the Dominant Idea smiled: the vine was in the world to bloom, to bear white trumpet blossoms dashed with purple; and it held its will beyond death.

Our modern teaching is, that ideas are but attendant phenomena, impotent to determine the actions or relations of life, as the image in the glass which should say to the body it reflects: "*I shall shape thee.*" In truth we know that directly the body goes from before the mirror, the transient image is nothingness; but the real body has its being to live, and will live it, heedless of vanished phantoms of itself, in response to the ever-shifting pressure of things without it.

It is thus that the so-called Materialist Conception of History, the modern Socialists, and a positive majority of Anarchists would have us look upon the world of ideas,—shifting, unreal reflections, having naught to do in the determination of Man's life, but so many mirror appearances of certain material relations, wholly powerless to act upon the course of material things. Mind to them is in itself a blank mirror, though in fact never wholly blank, because always facing the reality of the material and bound to reflect some shadow. To-day I am somebody, to-morrow somebody else, if the scenes have shifted; my Ego is a gibbering phantom, pirouetting in the glass, gesticulating, transforming, hourly or momentarily, gleaming with the phosphor light of a deceptive unreality, melting like the mist upon the hills. Rocks, fields, woods, streams, houses, goods, flesh, blood, bone, sinew,—these are realities, with definite parts to play, with essential characters that abide under all changes; but my Ego does not abide; it is manufactured afresh with every change of these.

I think this unqualified determinism of the material is a great and lamentable error in our modern progressive movement; and while I believe it was a wholesome antidote to the long-continued blunder of Middle Age theology, viz., that Mind was an utterly irresponsible entity making laws of its own after the manner of an Absolute Emperor, without logic, sequence, or relation, ruler over matter, and its own supreme determinant, not excepting God (who was himself the same sort of a mind writ large)—while I do believe that the modern re-conception of Materialism has done a wholesome thing in pricking the bubble of such conceit and restoring man and his "soul" to its "place in nature," I nevertheless believe that to this also there is a limit; and that the absolute sway of Matter is quite as mischievous an error as the unrelated nature of Mind; even that in its direct action upon personal conduct, it has the more ill effect of the two. For if the doctrine of free-will has raised up fanatics and persecutors, who, assuming that men may be good under all conditions if they merely wish to be so, have sought to persuade other men's wills with threats, fines, imprisonments, torture, the spike, the wheel, the axe, the fagot, in order to make them good and save them against their obdurate wills; if the doctrine of Spiritualism, the soul supreme, has done this, the doctrine of Materialistic Determinism[1] has produced shifting, self-excusing, worthless, parasitical characters, who are *this* now and *that* at some other time, and anything and nothing upon principle. "My conditions have made me so, they cry, and there is no more to be said; poor mirror-ghosts! how could they help it! To be sure, the influence of such a character rarely reaches so far as that of the principled persecutor; but for every one of the latter, there are a hundred of these easy, doughy characters, who will fit any baking tin, to whom determinist self-excusing appeals; so the balance of evil between the two doctrines is *about* maintained.

What we need is a true appraisement of the power and *rôle* of the Idea. I do not think I am able to give such a true appraisement, I do not think that any one—even *much* greater intellects than mine—will be able to do it for a long time to come. But I am at least able to suggest it, to show its necessity, to give a rude approximation of it.

And first, against the accepted formula of modern Materialism, "Men are what circumstances make them," I set the opposing declaration, "Circumstances are what men make them"; and I contend that both these things are true up to the point where the combating powers are equalized, or one is overthrown. In other words, my conception of mind, or character, is not that it is a powerless reflection of a momentary condition of stuff and form, but an active modifying agent, reacting on its environment and transforming circumstances, sometimes slightly, sometimes greatly, sometimes, though not often, entirely.

All over the kingdom of life, I have said, one may see dominant ideas working, if one but trains his eyes to look for them and recognize them. In the human world there have been many dominant ideas. I cannot conceive that ever, at any time, the struggle of the body before dissolution can have been aught but agony. If the reasoning that insecurity of conditions, the expectation of suffering, are circumstances which make the soul of man uneasy, shrinking, timid, what answer will you give to the challenge of old Ragnar Lodbrog, to that triumphant death-song hurled out, not by one cast to his death in the heat of battle, but under slow prison torture, bitten by serpents, and yet singing: "The goddesses of death invite me away—now end I my song. The hours of my life are run out. I shall smile when I die"? Nor can it be said that this is an exceptional instance, not to be accounted for by the usual operation of general law, for old King Lodbrog the Skalder did only what his fathers did, and his sons and his friends and his enemies, through long generations; they set the force of a dominant idea, the idea of the super ascendant ego, against the force of torture and of death, ending life as they wished to end it, with a smile on their lips. But a few years ago, did we not read how the helpless Kaffirs[2], victimized by the English for the contumacy of the Boers, having been forced to dig the trenches wherein for pleasant sport they were to be shot, were lined up on the edge, and seeing death facing them, began to chant barbaric strains of triumph, smiling as they fell? Let us admit that such exultant defiance was owing to ignorance, to primitive beliefs in gods and hereafters; but let us admit also that it shows the power of an idea dominant.

Everywhere in the shells of dead societies, as in the shells of the sea-slime, we shall see the force of purposive action, of intent *within* holding its purpose against obstacles *without*.

I think there is no one in the world who can look upon the steadfast, far-staring face of an Egyptian carving, or read a description of Egypt's monuments, or gaze upon the mummied clay of its old dead men, without feeling that the dominant idea of that people in that age was to be enduring and to work enduring things, with the immobility of their great still sky upon them and the stare of the desert in them. One must feel that whatever other ideas animated them, and expressed themselves in their lives, this was the dominant idea. *That which was* must remain, no matter at what cost, even if it were to break the ever-lasting hills: an idea which made the live humanity beneath it, born and nurtured in the coffins of caste, groan and writhe and gnaw its bandages, till in the fullness of time it passed away: and still the granite mould of it stares with empty eyes out across the world, the stern old memory of the *Thing-that-was*.

I think no one can look upon the marbles wherein Greek genius wrought the figuring of its soul without feeling an apprehension that the things are going to leap and fly; that in a moment one is like to be set upon by heroes with spears in their hands, by serpents that will coil around him; to be trodden by horses that may trample and flee; to be smitten by these gods that have as little of the idea of stone in them as a dragon-fly, one instant poised upon a wind-swayed petal edge. I think no one can look upon them without realizing at once that those figures came out of the boil of life; they seem like rising bubbles about to float into the air, but beneath them other bubbles rising, and others, and others,—there will be no end of it. When one's eyes are upon one group, one feels that behind one, perhaps, a figure is uptoeing to seize the darts of the air and hurl them on one's head; one must keep whirling to face the miracle that appears about to be wrought—stone leaping! And this though nearly every one is minus some of the glory the old Greek wrought into it so long ago; even the broken stumps of arms and legs live. And the dominant idea is Activity, and the beauty and strength of it. Change, swift, ever-circling Change! The making of things and the casting of them away, as children cast away their toys, not interested that these shall endure, so that they themselves realize incessant activity. Full of creative power, what matter if the creature perished. So there was an endless procession of changing shapes in their schools, their philosophies their dramas, their poems, till at last it wore itself to death. And the marvel passed away from the world. But still their marbles live to show what manner of thoughts dominated them.

And if we wish to know what master-thought ruled the lives of men when the mediæval period had had time to ripen it, one has only at this day to stray into some quaint, out-of-the-way English village, where a strong old towered Church yet stands in the midst of little straw-thatched cottages, like a brooding mother-hen surrounded by her chickens. Everywhere the greatening of God and the lessening of Man: the Church so looming, the home so little. The search for the spirit, for the *enduring* thing (not the poor endurance of granite which in the ages crumbles, but the eternal), the eternal,—and contempt for the body which perishes, manifest in studied uncleanliness, in mortifications of the flesh, as if the spirit should have spat its scorn upon it.

Such was the dominant idea of that middle age which has been too much cursed by modernists. For the men who built the castles and the cathedrals were men of mighty works, though they made no books, and though their souls spread crippled wings, because of their very endeavors to soar too high. The spirit of voluntary subordination for the accomplishment of a great work, which proclaimed the aspiration of the common soul,—that was the spirit wrought into the cathedral stones; and it is not wholly to be condemned.

In waking dream, when the shadow-shapes of world-ideas swim before the vision, one sees the Middle-Age Soul an ill-contorted, half-formless thing, with dragon wings and a great, dark, tense face, strained sunward with blind eyes.

If now we look around us to see what idea dominates our own civilization, I do not know that it is even as attractive as this piteous monster of the old darkness. The relativity of things has altered: Man has risen and God has descended. The modern village has better homes and less pretentious churches. Also, the conception of dirt and disease as much-sought afflictions, the patient suffering of which is a meet offering to win God's pardon, has given place to the emphatic promulgation of cleanliness. We have Public School nurses notifying parents that "pediculosis capitis" is a very contagious and unpleasant disease; we have cancer associations gathering up such cancers as have attached themselves to impecunious persons, and carefully experimenting with a view to cleaning them out of the human race; we have tuberculosis societies attempting the Herculean labor of clearing the Aegean stables of our modern factories of the deadly bacillus, and they have got as far as spittoons with water in them in some factories; and others, and others, and others, which while not yet overwhelmingly successful in their avowed purposes are evidence sufficient that humanity no longer seeks dirt as a means of grace. We laugh at those old superstitions and talk much about exact experimental knowledge. We endeavor to galvanize the Greek corpse, and pretend that we enjoy physical culture. We dabble in many things; but the one great real idea of our age, not copied from any other, not pretended, not raised to life by any conjuration, is the Much Making of Things,—not the making of beautiful things, not the joy of spending living energy in creative work; rather the shameless, merciless driving and over-driving, wasting and draining of the last bit of energy, only to produce heaps and heaps of things,—things ugly, things harmful, things useless, and at the best largely unnecessary. To what end are they produced? Mostly the producer does not know; still less does he care. But he is possessed with the idea that he *must* do it, every one is doing it, and every year the making of things goes on more and faster; there are mountain ranges of things made and making, and still men go about desperately seeking to increase the list of created things, to start fresh heaps and to add to the existing heaps. And with what agony of body, under what stress and strain of danger and fear of danger, with what mutilations and maimings and lamings they struggle on, dashing themselves out against these rocks of wealth! Verily, if the vision of the Mediæval Soul is painful in its blind staring and pathetic striving, grotesque in its senseless tortures, the Soul of the Modern is most amazing with its restless, nervous eyes, ever searching the corners of the universe, its restless, nervous hands ever reaching and grasping for some useless toil.

And certainly the presence of things in abundance, things empty and things vulgar and things absurd, as well as things convenient and useful, has produced the desire for the possession of things, the exaltation of the possession of things. Go through the business street of any city, where the tilted edges of the strata of things are exposed to gaze, and look at the faces of the people as they pass,—not at the hungry and smitten ones who fringe the sidewalks and plaint dolefully for alms, but at the crowd,—and see what idea is written on their faces. On those of the women, from the ladies of the horse-shows to the shop girls out of the factory, there is a sickening vanity, a consciousness of their clothes, as of some jackdaw in borrowed feathers. Look for the pride and glory of the free, strong, beautiful body, lithe-moving and powerful. You will not see it. You will see mincing steps, bodies tilted to show the cut of a skirt, simpering, smirking faces, with eyes cast about seeking admiration for the gigantic bow of ribbon in the overdressed hair. In the caustic words of an acquaintance, to whom I once said, as we walked, "Look at the amount of vanity on all these women's faces," "No: look at the little bit of womanhood showing out of all that vanity!"

And on the faces of the men, coarseness! Coarse desires for coarse things, and lots of them: the stamp is set so unmistakably that "the wayfarer though a fool need not err therein." Even the frightful anxiety and restlessness begotten of the creation of all this, is less distasteful than the abominable expression of lust for the things created.

Such is the dominant idea of the western world, at least in these our days. You may see it wherever you look, impressed plainly on things and on men; very like if you look in the glass, you will see it there. And if some archaeologist of a long future shall some day unbury the bones of our civilization, where ashes or flood shall have entombed it, he will see this frightful idea stamped on the factory walls he shall uncover, with their rows and rows of square lightholes, their tons upon tons of toothed steel, grinning out of the skull of this our life; its acres of silk and velvet, its square miles of tinsel and shoddy. No glorious marbles of nymphs and fawns, whose dead images are yet so sweet that one might wish to kiss them still; no majestic figures of winged horses, with men's faces and lions' paws casting their colossal symbolism in a mighty spell forward upon Time, as those old stone chimeras of Babylon yet do; but meaningless iron giants, of wheels and teeth, whose secret is forgotten, but whose business was to grind men up, and spit them out as housefuls of woven stuffs, bazaars of trash, wherethrough other men might wade. The statues he shall find will bear no trace of mythic dream or mystic symbol; they will be statues of merchants and ironmasters and militiamen, in tailored coats and pantaloons and proper hats and shoes.

But the dominant idea of the age and land does not necessarily mean the dominant idea of any single life. I doubt not that in those long gone days, far away by the banks of the still Nile, in the abiding shadow of the pyramids, under the heavy burden of other men's stolidity, there went to and fro restless, active, rebel souls who hated all that the ancient society stood for, and with burning hearts sought to overthrow it.

I am sure that in the midst of all the agile Greek intellect created, there were those who went about with downbent eyes, caring nothing for it all, seeking some higher revelation, willing to abandon the joys of life, so that they drew near to some distant, unknown perfection their fellows knew not of. I am certain that in the dark ages, when most men prayed and cowered, and beat and bruised themselves, and sought afflictions, like that St. Teresa[3] who still, "Let me suffer, or die," there were some, many, who looked on the world as a chance jest, who despised or pitied their ignorant comrades, and tried to compel the answers of the universe to their questionings, by the patient, quiet searching which came to be Modern Science. I am sure there were hundreds, thousands of them, of whom we have never heard.

And now, to-day, though the Society about us is dominated by Thing-Worship, and will stand so marked for all time, that is no reason any single soul should be. Because the one thing seemingly worth doing to my neighbor, to all my neighbors, is to pursue dollars, that is no reason I should pursue dollars. Because my neighbors conceive they need an inordinate heap of carpets, furniture, clocks, china, glass, tapestries, mirrors, clothes, jewels—and servants to care for them, and detectives to keep an eye on the servants, judges to try the thieves, and politicians to appoint the judges, jails to punish the culprits, and wardens to watch in the jails, and tax collectors to gather support for the wardens, and fees for the tax collectors, and strong houses to hold the fees, so that none but the guardians thereof can make off with them,—and therefore, to keep this host of parasites, need other men to work for them, and make the fees; because my neighbors want all this, is that any reason I should devote myself to such a barren folly? and bow my neck to serve to keep up the gaudy show?

Must we, because the Middle Age was dark and blind and brutal, throw away the one good thing it wrought into the fibre of Man, that the inside of a human being was worth more than the outside? that to conceive a higher thing than oneself and live toward that is the only way of living worthily? The goal strived for should, and must, be a very different one from that which led the mediæval fanatics to despise the body and belabor it with hourly crucifixions. But one can recognize the claims and the importance of the body without therefore sacrificing truth, honor, simplicity, and faith, to the vulgar gauds of body-service, whose very decorations debase the thing they might be supposed to exalt.

I have said before that the doctrine that men are nothing and circumstances all, has been, and is, the bane of our modern social reform movements.

Our youth, themselves animated by the spirit of the old teachers who believed in the supremacy of ideas, even in the very hour of throwing away that teaching, look with burning eyes to the social East, and believe that wonders of revolution are soon to be accomplished. In their enthusiasm they foreread the gospel of Circumstances to mean that very soon the pressure of material development must break down the social system—they give the rotten thing but a few years to last; and then, they themselves shall witness the transformation, partake in its joys. The few years pass away and nothing happens; enthusiasm cools. Behold these same idealists then, successful business men, professionals, property owners, money leaders, creeping into the social ranks they once despised, pitifully, contemptibly, at the skirts of some impecunious personage to whom they have lent money, or done some professional service gratis; behold them lying, cheating, tricking, flattering, buying and selling themselves for any frippery, any cheap little pretense. The Dominant Social Idea has seized them, their lives are swallowed up in it; and when you ask the reason why, they tell you that Circumstances compelled them so to do. If you quote their lies to them, they smile with calm complacency, assure you that when Circumstances demand lies, lies are a great deal better than truth; that tricks are sometimes more effective than honest dealing; that flattering and duping do not matter, if the end to be attained is desirable; and that under existing "Circumstances" life isn't possible without all this; that it is going to be possible whenever Circumstances have made truth-telling easier than lying, but till then a man must look out for himself, by all means. And so the cancer goes on rotting away the moral fibre, and the man becomes a lump, a squash, a piece of slippery slime taking all shapes and losing all shapes, according to what particular hole or corner he wishes to glide into—a disgusting embodiment of the moral bankruptcy begotten by Thing-Worship.

Had he been dominated by a less material conception of life, had his will not been rotted by the intellectual reasoning of it out of its existence, by its acceptance of its own nothingness, the unselfish aspirations of his earlier years would have grown and strengthened by exercise and habit; and his protest against the time might have been enduringly written, and to some purpose.

Will it be said that the Pilgrim fathers did not hew, out of the New England ice and granite, the idea which gathered them together out of their scattered and obscure English villages, and drove them in their frail ships aver the Atlantic in midwinter, to cut their way against all opposing forces? Were they not common men, subject to the operation of common law? Will it be said that Circumstances aided them? When death, disease, hunger, and cold had done their worst, not one of those remaining was willing by an *easy lie* to return to material comfort and the possibility of long days.

Had our modern social revolutionists the vigorous and undaunted conception of their own powers that these had, our social movements would not be such pitiful abortions,—core-rotten even before the outward flecks appear.

"Give a labor leader a political job, and the system becomes all right," laugh our enemies; and they point mockingly to Terence Powderly[4] and his like; and they quote John Burns[5], who as soon as *he* went into Parliament declared: "The time of the agitator is past; the time of the legislator has come." "Let an Anarchist marry an heiress, and the country is safe," they sneer:—and they have the right to sneer. But would they have that right, could they have it, if our lives were not in the first instance dominated by more insistent desires than those we would fain have others think we hold most dear?

It is the old story: "Aim at the stars, and you may hit the top of the gatepost; but aim at the ground and you will hit the ground."

It is not to be supposed that any one will attain to the full realization of what he purposes, even when those purposes do not involve united action with others; he *will* fall short; he will in some measure be overcome by contending or inert opposition. But something he will attain, if he continues to aim high.

What, then, would I have? you ask. I would have men invest themselves with the dignity of an aim higher than the chase for wealth; choose a thing to do in life outside of the making of things, and keep it in mind,—not for a day, nor a year, but for a lifetime. And then keep faith with themselves! Not be a light-o'-love, to-day professing this and to-morrow that, and easily reading oneself out of both whenever it becomes convenient; not advocating a thing to-day and to-morrow kissing its enemies' sleeve, with that weak, coward cry in the mouth, "Circumstances make me." Take a good look into yourself, and if you love Things and the power and the plenitude of Things better than you love your own dignity, human dignity, Oh, say so, say so! Say it to yourself, and abide by it. But do not blow hot and cold in one breath. Do not try to be a social reformer and a respected possessor of Things at the same time. Do not preach the straight and narrow way while going joyously upon the wide one. *Preach the wide one,* or do not preach at all; but do not fool yourself by saying you would like to help usher in a free society, but you cannot sacrifice an armchair for it. Say honestly, "I love armchairs better than free men, and pursue them because I choose; not because circumstances make me. I love hats, large, large hats, with many feathers and great bows; and I would rather have those hats than trouble myself about social dreams that will never be accomplished in my day. The world worships hats, and I wish to worship with them."

But if you choose the liberty and pride and strength of the single soul, and the free fraternization of men, as the purpose which your life is to make manifest, then do not sell it for tinsel. Think that your soul is strong and will hold its way; and slowly, through bitter struggle perhaps the strength will grow. And the foregoing of possessions for which others barter the last possibility of freedom will become easy.

At the end of life you may close your eyes, saying: "I have not been dominated by the Dominant Idea of my Age; I have chosen mine own allegiance, and served it. I have proved by a lifetime that there is that in man which saves him from the absolute tyranny of Circumstance, which in the end conquers and remoulds Circumstance, the immortal fire of Individual Will, which is the salvation of the Future."

Let us have Men, Men who will say a word to their souls and keep it—keep it not when it is easy, but keep it when it is hard—keep it when the storm roars and there is a white-streaked sky and blue thunder before, and one's eyes are blinded and one's ears deafened with the war of opposing things; and keep it under the long leaden sky and the gray dreariness that never lifts. Hold unto the last: that is what it means to have a Dominant Idea, which Circumstance cannot break. And such men make and unmake Circumstance.

Direct Action

From the standpoint of one who thinks himself capable of discerning an undeviating route for human progress to pursue, if it is to be progress at all, who, having such a route on his mind's map, has endeavored to point it out to others; to make them see it as he sees it; who in so doing has chosen what appeared to him clear and simple expressions to convey his thoughts to others,—to such a one it appears matter for regret and confusion of spirit that the phrase "Direct Action" has suddenly acquired in the general mind a circumscribed meaning, not at all implied in the words themselves, and certainly never attached to it by himself or his co-thinkers.

However, this is one of the common jests which Progress plays on those who think themselves able to set metes and bounds for it. Over and over again, names, phrases, mottoes, watchwords, have been turned inside out, and upside down, and hindside before, and sideways, by occurrences out of the control of those who used the expressions in their proper sense; and still, those who sturdily held their ground, and insisted on being heard, have in the end found that the period of misunderstanding and prejudice has been but the prelude to wider inquiry and understanding.

I rather think this will be the case with the present misconception of the term Direct Action, which through the misapprehension, or else the deliberate misrepresentation, of certain journalists in Los Angeles, at the time the McNamaras[1] pleaded guilty, suddenly acquired in the popular mind the interpretation, "Forcible Attacks on Life and Property." This was either very ignorant or very dishonest of the journalists; but it has had the effect of making a good many people curious to know all about Direct Action.

As a matter of fact, those who are so lustily and so inordinately condemning it, will find on examination that they themselves have on many occasion practised direct action, and will do so again.

Every person who ever thought he had a right to assert, and went boldly and asserted it, himself, or jointly with others that shared his convictions, was a direct actionist. Some thirty years ago I recall that the Salvation Army was vigorously practising direct action in the maintenance of the freedom of its members to speak, assemble, and pray. Over and over they were arrested, fined, and imprisoned; but they kept right on singing, praying, and marching, till they finally compelled their persecutors to let them alone. The Industrial Workers are now conducting the same fight, and have, in a number of cases, compelled the officials to let them alone by the same direct tactics.

Every person who ever had a plan to do anything, and went and did it, or who laid his plan before others, and won their co-operation to do it with him, without going to external authorities to please do the thing for them, was a direct actionist. All co-operative experiments are essentially direct action.

Every person who ever in his life had a difference with anyone to settle, and went straight to the other persons involved to settle it, either by a peaceable plan or otherwise, was a direct actionist. Examples of such action are strikes and boycotts; many persons will recall the action of the housewives of New York who boycotted the butchers, and lowered the price of meat; at the present moment a butter boycott seems looming up, as a direct reply to the price-makers for butter.

These actions are generally not due to any one's reasoning overmuch on the respective merits of directness or indirectness, but are the spontaneous retorts of those who feel oppressed by a situation. In other words, all people are, most of the time, believers in the principle of direct action, and practicers of it. However, most people are also indirect or political actionists. And they are both these things at the same time, without making much of an analysis of either. There are only a limited number of persons who eschew political action under any and all circumstances; but there is nobody, nobody at all, who has ever been so "impossible" as to eschew direct action altogether.

The majority of thinking people are really opportunists, leaning, some perhaps more to directness, some more to indirectness as a general thing, but ready to use either means when opportunity calls for it. That is to say, there are those who hold that balloting governors into power is essentially a wrong and foolish thing; but who, nevertheless, under stress of special circumstance, might consider it the wisest thing to do, to vote some individual into office at that particular time. Or there are those who believe that, in general, the wisest way for people to get what they want is by the indirect method of voting into power some one who will make what they want legal; yet who, all the same, will occasionally, under exceptional conditions, advise a strike; and a strike, as I have said, is direct action. Or they may do as the Socialist Party

48

agitators, who are mostly declaiming now against direct action, did last summer, when the police were holding up their meetings. They went in force to the meeting-places, prepared to speak whether-or-no; and they made the police back down. And while that was not logical on their part, thus to oppose the legal executors of the majority's will, it was a fine, successful piece of direct action.

Those who, by the essence of their belief, are committed to Direct Action only are—just who? Why, the non-resistants; precisely those who do not believe in violence at all! Now do not make the mistake of inferring that I say direct action means non-resistance; not by any means. Direct action may be the extreme of violence, or it may be as peaceful as the waters of the Brook of Siloa[2] that go softly. What I say is, that the real non-resistants can believe in direct action only, never in political action. For the basis of all political action is coercion; even when the State does good things, it finally rests on a club, a gun, or a prison, for its power to carry them through.

Now every school child in the United States has had the direct action of certain non-resistants brought to his notice by his school history. The case which everyone instantly recalls is that of the early Quakers who came to Massachusetts. The Puritans had accused the Quakers of "troubling the world by preaching peace to it." They refused to pay church taxes; they refused to bear arms; they refused to swear allegiance to any government. (In so doing, they were direct actionists; what we may call negative direct actionists.) So the Puritans, being political actionists, passed laws to keep them out, to deport, to fine, to imprison, to mutilate, and finally, to hang them. And the Quakers just kept on coming (which was positive direct action); and history records that after the hanging of four Quakers, and the flogging of Margaret Brewster at the cart's tail through the streets of Boston, "the Puritans gave up trying to silence the new missionaries"; that "Quaker persistence and Quaker non-resistance had won the day."

Another example of direct action in early colonial history, but this time by no means of the peaceable sort, was the affair known as Bacon's Rebellion[3]. All our historians certainly defend the action of the rebels in that matter, as reason is, for they were right. And yet it was a case of violent direct action against lawfully constituted authority. For the benefit of those who have forgotten the details, let me briefly remind them that the Virginia planters were in fear of a general attack by the Indians; with reason. Being political actionists, they asked, or Bacon as their leader asked, that the governor grant him a commission to raise volunteers in their own defense. The governor feared that such a company of armed men would be a threat to him; also with reason. He refused the commission. Whereupon the planters resorted to direct

49

action. They raised the volunteers without the commission, and successfully fought off the Indians. Bacon was pronounced a traitor by the governor; but the people being with him, the governor was afraid to proceed against him. In the end, however, it came so far that the rebels burned Jamestown; and but for the untimely death of Bacon, much more might have been done. Of course the reaction was very dreadful, as it usually is where a rebellion collapses, or is crushed. Yet even during the brief period of success, it had corrected a good many abuses. I am quite sure that the political-action-at-all-costs advocates of those times, after the reaction came back into power, must have said: "See to what evils direct action brings us! Behold, the progress of the colony has been set back twenty-five years"; forgetting that if the colonists had not resorted to direct action, their scalps would have been taken by the Indians a year sooner, instead of a number of them being hanged by the governor a year later.

In the period of agitation and excitement preceding the revolution, there were all sorts and kinds of direct action from the most peaceable to the most violent; and I believe that almost everybody who studies United States history finds the account of these performances the most interesting part of the story, the part which dents into his memory most easily.

Among the peaceable moves made, were the non-importation agreements, the leagues for wearing homespun clothing and the "committees of correspondence." As the inevitable growth of hostility progressed, violent direct action developed; e.g., in the matter of destroying the revenue stamps, or the action concerning the tea-ships, either by not permitting the tea to be landed, or by putting it in damp storage, or by throwing it into the harbor, as in Boston, or by compelling a tea-ship owner to set fire to his own ship, as at Annapolis. These are all actions which our commonest text-books record, certainly not in a condemnatory way, not even in an apologetic one, though they are all cases of direct action against legally constituted authority and property rights. If I draw attention to them, and others of like nature, it is to prove to unreflecting repeaters of words that *direct action has always been used, and has the historical sanction of the very people now reprobating it.*

George Washington is said to have been the leader of the Virginia planters' non-importation league: he would now be "enjoined," probably by a court, from forming any such league; and if he persisted, he would be fined for contempt.

When the great quarrel between the North and the South was waxing hot and hotter, it was again direct action which preceded and precipitated political action. And I may remark here that political action is never taken, nor even contemplated, until slumbering minds have first been aroused by direct acts of protest against existing conditions.

The history of the anti-slavery movement and the Civil War is one of the greatest of paradoxes, although history is a chain of paradoxes. Politically speaking, it was the slave-holding States that stood for greater political freedom, for the autonomy of the single State against the interference of the United States; politically speaking, it was the non-slave-holding States that stood for a strong centralized government, which, Secessionists said, and said truly, was bound progressively to develop into more and more tyrannical forms. Which happened. From the close of the Civil War on, there has been continuous encroachment of the federal power upon what was formerly the concern of the States individually. The wage-slaves, in their struggles of today, are continually thrown into conflict with that centralized power, against which the slave-holder protested (with liberty on his lips but tyranny in his heart). Ethically speaking, it was the non-slave-holding States that, in a general way, stood for greater human liberty, while the Secessionists stood for race-slavery. In a general way only; that is, the majority of northerners, not being accustomed to the actual presence of negro slavery about them, thought it was probably a mistake; yet they were in no great ferment of anxiety to have it abolished. The Abolitionists only, and they were relatively few, were the genuine ethicals, to whom slavery itself—not secession or union—was the main question. In fact, so paramount was it with them, that a considerable number of them were themselves for the dissolution of the union, advocating that the North take the initiative in the matter of dissolving, in order that the northern people might shake off the blame of holding negroes in chains.

Of course, there were all sorts of people with all sorts of temperaments among those who advocated the abolition of slavery. There were Quakers like Whittier[4] (indeed it was the peace-at-all-costs Quakers who had advocated abolition even in early colonial days); there were moderate political actionists, who were for buying off the slaves, as the cheapest way; and there were extremely violent people, who believed and did all sorts of violent things.

As to what the politicians did, it is one long record of "how-not-to-do-it," a record of thirty years of compromising, and dickering, and trying to keep what was as it was, and to hand sops to both sides when new conditions demanded that something be done, or be pretended to be done. But "the stars in their courses fought against Sisera"; the system was breaking down from within, and the direct actionists from without, as well, were widening the cracks remorselessly.

Among the various expressions of direct rebellion was the organization of the "underground railroad." Most of the people who belonged to it believed in both sorts of action; but however much they theoretically subscribed to the right of the majority to enact and enforce laws, they didn't believe in it on that point. My grandfather was a member of the "underground"; many a fugitive slave he helped on his way to Canada. He was a very patient, law-abiding man, in most respects, though I have often thought that he respected it because he didn't have much to do with it; always leading a pioneer life, law was generally far from him, and direct action imperative. Be that as it may, and law-respecting as he was, he had no respect whatever for slave laws, no matter if made by ten times of a majority; and he conscientiously broke every one that came in his way to be broken.

There were times when in the operation of the "underground", violence was required, and was used. I recollect one old friend relating to me how she and her mother kept watch all night at the door, while a slave for whom a posse was searching hid in the cellar; and though they were of Quaker descent and sympathies, there was a shot-gun on the table. Fortunately it did not have to be used that night.

When the fugitive slave law was passed with the help of the political actionists of the North who wanted to offer a new sop to the slave-holders, the direct actionists took to rescuing recaptured fugitives. There was the "rescue of Shadrach,"[5] and the "rescue of Jerry,"[6] the latter rescuers being led by the famous Gerrit Smith[7]; and a good many more successful and unsuccessful attempts. Still the politicals kept on pottering and trying to smooth things over, and the Abolitionists were denounced and decried by the ultra-law-abiding pacificators, pretty much as Wm. D. Haywood[8] and Frank Bohn[9] are being denounced by their own party now.

The other day I read a communication in the Chicago *Daily Socialist* from the secretary of the Louisville local, Socialist Party, to the national secretary, requesting that some safe and sane speaker be substituted for Bohn, who had been announced to speak there. In explaining why, Mr. Dobbs, secretary, makes this quotation from Bohn's lecture: "Had the McNamaras been successful in defending the interests of the working class, they would have been right, just as John Brown[10] would have been right, had he been successful in freeing the slaves. Ignorance was the only crime of John Brown, and ignorance was the only crime of the McNamaras."

Upon this Mr. Dobbs comments as follows: "We dispute emphatically the statements here made. The attempt to draw a parallel between the open—if mistaken—

revolt of John Brown on the one hand, and the secret and murderous methods of the McNamaras on the other, is not only indicative of shallow reasoning, but highly mischievous in the logical conclusions which may be drawn from such statements."

Evidently Mr. Dobbs is very ignorant of the life and work of John Brown. John Brown was a man of violence; he would have scorned anybody's attempt to make him out anything else. And when once a person is a believer in violence, it is with him only a question of the most effective way of applying it, which can be determined only by a knowledge of conditions and means at his disposal. John Brown did not shrink at all from conspiratical methods. Those who have read the autobiography of Frederick Douglas[11][sic] and the Reminiscences of Lucy Colman[12], will recall that one of the plans laid by John Brown was to organize a chain of armed camps in the mountains of West Virginia, North Carolina, and Tennessee, send secret emissaries among the slaves inciting them to flee to these camps, and there concert such measures as times and conditions made possible for further arousing revolt among the negroes. That this plan failed was due to the weakness of the desire for liberty among the slaves themselves, more than anything else.

Later on, when the politicians in their infinite deviousness contrived a fresh proposition of how-not-to-do-it, known as the Kansas-Nebraska Act, which left the question of slavery to be determined by the settlers, the direct actionists on both sides sent bogus settlers into the territory, who proceeded to fight it out. The pro-slavery men, who got in first, made a constitution recognizing slavery, and a law punishing with death any one who aided a slave to escape; but the Free Soilers[13], who were a little longer in arriving, since they came from more distant States, made a second constitution, and refused to recognize the other party's laws at all. And John Brown was there, mixing in all the violence, conspiratical or open; he was "a horse-thief and a murderer," in the eyes of decent, peaceable, political actionists. And there is no doubt that he stole horses, sending no notice in advance of his intention to steal them, and that he killed pro-slavery men. He struck and got away a good many times before his final attempt on Harper's Ferry. If he did not use dynamite, it was because dynamite had not yet appeared as a practical weapon. He made a great many more intentional attacks on life than the two brothers Secretary Dobbs condemns for their "murderous methods." And yet, history has not failed to understand John Brown. Mankind knows that though he was a violent man, with human blood upon his hands, who was guilty of high treason and hanged for it, yet his soul was a great, strong, unselfish soul, unable to bear the frightful crime which kept 4,000,000 people like dumb beasts, and thought that making war against it was a sacred, a God-called duty, (for John Brown was a very religious man—a Presbyterian).

It is by and because of the direct acts of the forerunners of social change, whether they be of peaceful or warlike nature, that the Human Conscience, the conscience of the mass, becomes aroused to the need for change. It would be very stupid to say that no good results are ever brought about by political action; sometimes good things do come about that way. But never until individual rebellion, followed by mass rebellion, has forced it. Direct action is always the clamorer, the initiator, through which the great sum of indifferentists become aware that oppression is getting intolerable.

We have now an oppression in the land,—and not only in this land, but throughout all those parts of the world which enjoy the very mixed blessings of Civilization. And just as in the question of chattel slavery, so this form of slavery has been begetting both direct action and political action. A certain per cent of our population (probably a much smaller per cent than politicians are in the habit of assigning at mass meetings) is producing the material wealth upon which all the rest of us live; just as it was the 4,000,000 chattel Blacks who supported all the crowd of parasites above them. These are the *land workers* and the *industrial workers*.

Through the unprophesied and unprophesiable operation of institutions which no individual of us created, but found in existence when he came here, these workers, the most absolutely necessary part of the whole social structure, without whose services none can either eat, or clothe, or shelter himself, are just the ones who get the least to eat, to wear, and to be housed withal—to say nothing of their share of the other social benefits which the rest of us are supposed to furnish, such as education and artistic gratification.

These workers have, in one form or another, mutually joined their forces to see what betterment of their condition they could get; primarily by direct action, secondarily by political action. We have had the Grange[14], the Farmer's Alliance[15], Co-operative Associations, Colonization Experiments, Knights of Labor[16], Trade Unions, and Industrial Workers of the World[17].

All of them have been organized for the purpose of wringing from the masters in the economic field a little better price, a little better conditions, a little shorter hours; or on the other hand to resist a reduction in price, worse conditions, or longer hours. None of them has attempted a final solution of the social war. None of them, except the Industrial Workers, has recognized that there is a social war, inevitable so long as present legal-social conditions endure. They accepted property institutions as they found them. They were made up of average men, with average desires, and they undertook to do what appeared to them possible and very reasonable things. They were not committed to any particular political policy when they were organized, but were associated for direct action of their own initiation, either positive or defensive.

Undoubtedly there were, and are, among all these organizations, members who looked beyond immediate demands; who did see that the continuous development of forces now in operation was bound to bring about conditions to which it is impossible that life continue to submit, and against which, therefore, it will protest, and violently protest; that it will have no choice but to do so; that it must do so, or tamely die; and since it is not the nature of life to surrender without struggle, it will not tamely die. Twenty-two years ago I met Farmers' Alliance people who said so, Knights of Labor who said so, Trade Unionists who said so. They wanted larger aims than those to which their organizations were looking; but they had to accept their fellow members as they were, and try to stir them to work for such things as it was possible to make them see. And what they could see was better prices, better wages, less dangerous or tyrannical conditions, shorter hours. At the stage of development when these movements were initiated, the land workers could not see that their struggle had anything to do with the struggle of those engaged in the manufacturing or transporting service; nor could these latter see that theirs had anything to do with the movement of the farmers. For that matter very few of them see it yet. They have yet to learn that there is one common struggle against those who have appropriated the earth, the money, and the machines.

Unfortunately the great organization of the farmers frittered itself away in a stupid chase after political power. It was quite successful in getting the power in certain States; but the courts pronounced its laws unconstitutional, and there was the burial hole of all its political conquests. Its original program was to build its own elevators, and store the products therein, holding these from the market till they could escape the speculator. Also, to organize labor exchanges, issuing credit notes upon products deposited for exchange. Had it adhered to this program of direct mutual aid, it would, to some extent, for a time at least, have afforded an illustration of how mankind may free itself from the parasitism of the bankers and the middlemen. Of course, it would have been overthrown in the end, unless it had so revolutionized men's minds by the example as to force the overthrow of the legal monopoly of land and money; but at least it would have served a great educational purpose. As it was, it "went after the red herring", and disintegrated merely from its futility.

The Knights of Labor subsided into comparative insignificance, not because of failure to use direct action, nor because of its tampering with politics, which was small, but chiefly because it was a heterogeneous mass of workers who could not associate their efforts effectively.

The Trade Unions grew strong as the K. of L. subsided, and have continued slowly but persistently to increase in power. It is true the increase has fluctuated; that there have been set-backs; that great single organizations have been formed and again dispersed. But on the whole, trade unions have been a growing power. They have been so because, poor as they are, inefficient as they are, they have been a means whereby a certain section of the workers have been able to bring their united force to bear directly upon their masters, and so get for themselves some portion of what they wanted,—of what their conditions dictated to them they must try to get. The strike is their natural weapon, that which they themselves forged. It is the direct blow of the strike which nine times out of ten the boss is afraid of. (Of course there are occasions when he is glad of one, but that's unusual.) And the reason he dreads a strike is not so much because he thinks he cannot win out against it, but simply and solely because he does not want an interruption of his business. The ordinary boss isn't in much dread of a "class-conscious vote"; there are plenty of shops where you can talk Socialism or any other political program all day long; but if you begin to talk Unionism, you may forthwith expect to be discharged, or at best warned to shut up. Why? Not because the boss is so wise as to know that political action is a swamp in which the workingman gets mired, or because he understands that political Socialism is fast becoming a middle-class movement; not at all. He thinks Socialism is a very bad thing; but it's a good way off! But he knows that if his shop is unionized, he will have trouble right away. His hands will be rebellious, he will be put to expense to improve his factory conditions, he will have to keep workingmen that he doesn't like, and in case of strike he may expect injury to his machinery or his buildings.

It is often said, and parrot-like repeated, that the bosses are "class-conscious," that they stick together for their class interest, and are willing to undergo any sort of personal loss rather than be false to those interests. It isn't so at all. The majority of business people are just like the majority of workingmen; they care a whole lot more about their individual loss or gain than about the gain or loss of their class. And it is his individual loss the boss sees, when threatened by a union.

Now everybody knows that a strike of any size means violence. No matter what any one's ethical preference for peace may be, he knows it will not be peaceful. If it's a telegraph strike, it means cutting wires and poles, and getting fake scabs in to spoil the instruments. If it is a steel rolling mill strike, it means beating up the scabs, breaking the windows, setting the gauges wrong, and ruining the expensive rollers together with tons and tons of material. If it's a miners' strike, it means destroying tracks and bridges, and blowing up mills. If it is a garment workers' strike, it means having an unaccountable fire, getting a volley of stones through an apparently inaccessible window, or possibly a brickbat on the manufacturer's own head. If it's a street-car strike, it means tracks torn up or barricaded with the contents of ash-carts and slop-carts, with overturned wagons or stolen fences, it means smashed or incinerated cars and turned switches. If it is a system federation strike, it means "dead" engines, wild engines, derailed freights, and stalled trains. If it is a building trades strike, it means dynamited structures. And always, everywhere, all the time, fights between strike-breakers and scabs against strikers and strike-sympathizers, between People and Police.

On the side of the bosses, it means search-lights, electric wires, stockades, bull-pens, detectives and provocative agents, violent kidnapping and deportation, and every device they can conceive for direct protection, besides the ultimate invocation of police, militia, State constabulary, and federal troops.

Everybody knows this; everybody smiles when union officials protest their organizations to be peaceable and law-abiding, because everybody knows they are lying. They know that violence is used, both secretly and openly; and they know it is used because the strikers cannot do any other way, without giving up the fight at once. Nor do they mistake those who thus resort to violence under stress for destructive miscreants who do what they do out of innate cussedness. The people in general understand that they do these things, through the harsh logic of a situation which they did not create, but which forces them to these attacks in order to make good in their struggle to live, or else go down the bottomless descent into poverty, that lets Death find them in the poorhouse hospital, the city street, or the river-slime. This is the awful alternative that the workers are facing; and this is what makes the most kindly disposed human beings,—men who would go out of their way to help a wounded dog, or bring home a stray kitten and nurse it, or step aside to avoid walking on a worm—resort to violence against their fellow men. They know, for the facts have taught them, that this is the only way to win, if they can win at all. And it has always appeared to me one of the most utterly ludicrous, absolutely irrelevant things that a person can do or say, when approached for relief or assistance by a striker who is dealing with an immediate situation, to respond with "Vote yourself into power!" when the next election is six months, a year, or two years away.

Unfortunately, the people who know best how violence is used in union warfare, cannot come forward and say: "On such a day, at such a place, such and such a specific action was done, and as a result such and such concession was made, or such and such boss capitulated." To do so would imperil their liberty, and their power to go on fighting. Therefore those that know best must keep silent, and sneer in their sleeves, while those that know little prate. Events, not tongues, must make their position clear.

And there has been a very great deal of prating these last few weeks. Speakers and writers, honestly convinced, I believe, that political action, and political action only, can win the workers' battle, have been denouncing what they are pleased to call "direct action" (what they really mean is conspiratical violence) as the author of mischief incalculable. One Oscar Ameringer[18], as an example, recently said at a meeting in Chicago that the Haymarket bomb of '86 had set back the eight-hour movement twenty-five years, arguing that the movement would have succeeded but for the bomb. It's a great mistake. No one can exactly measure in years or months the effect of a forward push or a reaction. No one can demonstrate that the eight-hour movement could have been won twenty-five years ago. We know that the eight-hour day was put on the statute books of Illinois in 1871, by political action, and has remained a dead letter. That the direct action of the workers could have won it, then, can not be proved; but it can be shown that many more potent factors than the Haymarket bomb worked against it. On the other hand, if the reactive influence of the bomb was really so powerful, we should naturally expect labor and union conditions to be worse in Chicago than in the cities where no such thing happened. On the contrary, bad as they are, the general conditions of labor are better in Chicago than in most other large cities, and the power of the unions is more developed there than in any other American city except San Francisco. So if we are to conclude anything for the influence of the Haymarket bomb, keep these facts in mind. Personally I do not think its influence on the labor movement, as such, was so very great.

It will be the same with the present furore about violence. Nothing fundamental has been altered. Two men have been imprisoned for what they did (twenty-four years ago they were hanged for what they did not do); some few more may yet be imprisoned. But the forces of life will continue to revolt against their economic chains.

There will be no cessation in that revolt, no matter what ticket men vote or fail to vote, until the chains are broken.

How will the chains be broken?

Political actionists tell us it will be only by means of working-class party action at the polls; by voting themselves into possession of the sources of life and the tools; by voting that those who now command forests, mines, ranches, waterways, mills and factories, and likewise command the military power to defend them, shall hand over their dominion to the people.

And meanwhile?

Meanwhile be peaceable, industrious, law-abiding, patient, and frugal (as Madero[19] told the Mexican peons to be, after he sold them to Wall Street)! Even if some of you are disenfranchised, don't rise up even against that, for it might "set back the party."

Well, I have already stated that some good is occasionally accomplished by political action,—not necessarily working-class party action either. But I am abundantly convinced that the occasional good accomplished is more than counterbalanced by the evil; just as I am convinced that though there are occasional evils resulting from direct action, they are more than counterbalanced by the good.

Nearly all the laws which were originally framed with the intention of benefiting the workers, have either turned into weapons in their enemies' hands, or become dead letters, unless the workers through their organizations have directly enforced their observance. So that in the end, it is direct action that has to be relied on anyway. As an example of getting the tarred end of a law, glance at the anti-trust law, which was supposed to benefit the people in general, and the working class in particular. About two weeks since, some 250 union leaders were cited to answer to the charge of being trust formers, as the answer of the Illinois Central[20] to its strikers.

But the evil of pinning faith to indirect action is far greater than any such minor results. The main evil is that it destroys initiative, quenches the individual rebellious spirit, teaches people to rely on someone else to do for them what they should do for themselves, what they alone can do for themselves; finally renders organic the anomalous idea that by massing supineness together until a majority is acquired, then, through the peculiar magic of that majority, this supineness is to be transformed into energy. That is, people who have lost the habit of striking for themselves as individuals, who have submitted to every injustice while waiting for the majority to grow, are going to become metamorphosed into human high-explosives by a mere process of packing!

I quite agree that the sources of life, and all the natural wealth of the earth, and the tools necessary to co-operative production, must become free of access to all. It is a positive certainty to me that unionism must widen and deepen its purposes, or it will go under; and I feel sure that the logic of the situation will force them to see it gradually. They must learn that the workers' problem can never be solved by beating up scabs, so long as their own policy of limiting their membership by high initiation fees and other restrictions helps to make scabs. They must learn that the course of growth is not so much along the line of higher wages, but shorter hours, which will enable them to increase membership, to take in everybody who is willing to come into the union. They must learn that if they want to win battles, all allied workers must act together, act quickly (serving no notice on bosses), and retain their freedom so to do at all times. And finally they must learn that even then (when they have a complete organization), they can win nothing permanent unless they strike for everything,—not for a wage, not for a minor improvement, but for the whole natural wealth of the earth. And proceed to the direct expropriation of it all!

They must learn that their power does not lie in their voting strength, that their power lies in their ability to stop production. It is a great mistake to suppose that the wage-earners constitute a majority of the voters. Wage-earners are here to-day and there to-morrow, and that hinders a large number from voting; a great percentage of them in this country are foreigners without a voting right. The most patent proof that Socialist leaders know this is so, is that they are compromising their propaganda at every point to win the support of the business class, the small investor. Their campaign papers proclaimed that their interviewers had been assured by Wall Street bond purchasers that they would be just as ready to buy Los Angeles bonds from a socialist as a capitalist administration; that the present Milwaukee administration has been a boon to the small investor; their reading notices assure their readers in this city that we need not go to the great department stores to buy,—buy rather of So-and-so on Milwaukee Avenue, who will satisfy us quite as well as a "big business" institution. In short, they are making every desperate effort to win the support, and to prolong the life, of that middle-class which socialist economy says must be ground to pieces, because they know they cannot get a majority without them.

The most that a working-class party could do, even if its politicians remained honest, would be to form a strong faction in the legislatures, which might, by combining its vote with one side or the other, win certain political or economic palliatives.

But what the working-class can do, when once they grow into a solidified organization, is to show the possessing classes, through a sudden cessation of all work, that the whole social structure rests on them; that the possessions of the others are absolutely worthless to them without the workers' activity; that such protests, such strikes, are inherent in the system of property, and will continually recur until the whole thing is abolished,—and having shown that, effectively, proceed to expropriate.

"But the military power," says the political actionist; "we must get political power, or the military will be used against us!"

Against a real General Strike, the military can do nothing. Oh, true, if you have a Socialist Briand in power, he may declare the workers "public officials" and try to make them serve against themselves! But against the solid wall of an immobile working-mass, even a Briand would be broken.

Meanwhile, until this international awakening, the war will go on as it has been going, in spite of all the hysteria which well-meaning people, who do not understand life and its necessities, may manifest; in spite of all the shivering that timid leaders have done; in spite of all the reactionary revenges that may be taken; in spite of all the capital that politicians make out of the situation. It will go on because Life cries to live, and Property denies its freedom to live; and Life will not submit.

And should not submit.

It will go on until that day when a self-freed Humanity is able to chant Swinburne's Hymn of Man[21]

> "Glory to Man in the highest,
> For Man is the master of Things."

The Economic Tendency of Freethought

F riends,—On page 286, Belford-Clarke edition, of the "Rights of Man," the words which I propose as a text for this discourse may be found. Alluding to the change in the condition of France brought about by the Revolution of '93, Thomas Paine says:

"The mind of the nation had changed beforehand, and a new order of things had naturally followed a new order of thoughts."

Two hundred and eighty-nine years ago, a man, a student, a scholar, a thinker, a philosopher, was roasted alive for the love of God and the preservation of the authority of the Church; and as the hungry flames curled round the crisping flesh of martyred Bruno[1], licking his blood with their wolfish tongues, they shadowed forth the immense vista of "a new order of things": they lit the battle-ground where Freedom fought her first successful revolt against authority.

That battle-ground was eminently one of thought. Religious freedom was the rankling question of the day. "Liberty of conscience! Liberty of conscience! Non-interference between worshipper and worshipped!" That was the voice that cried out of dungeons and dark places, from under the very foot of prince and ecclesiastic. And why? Because the authoritative despotisms of that day were universally ecclesiastic despotisms; because Church aggression was grinding every human right beneath its heel, and every other minor oppressor was but a tool in the hands of the priesthood; because Tyranny was growing towards its ideal and crushing out of existence the very citadel of Liberty,—individuality of thought; Ecclesiasticism had a corner on ideas.

But individuality is a thing that cannot be killed. Quietly it may be, but just as certainly, silently, perhaps, as the growth of a blade of grass, it offers its perpetual and unconquerable protest against the dictates of Authority. And this silent, unconquerable, menacing thing, that balked God, provoked him to the use of rack, thumb-screw, stock, hanging, drowning, burning, and other instruments of "infinite mercy," in the seventeenth century fought a successful battle against that authority which sought to control this fortress of freedom. It established its right to be. It overthrew that portion of government which attempted to guide the brains of men. It "broke the corner." It declared and maintained the anarchy, or non-rulership, of thought.

Now you who so fear the word an-arche, remember! the whole combat of the seventeenth century, of which you are justly proud, and to which you never tire of referring, was waged for the sole purpose of realizing anarchism in the realm of thought.

It was not an easy struggle,—this battle of the quiet thinkers against those who held all the power, and all the force of numbers, and all of the strength of tortures! It was not easy for them to speak out of the midst of faggot flames, "We believe differently, and we have the right". But on their side stood Truth! And there lies more inequality between her and Error, more strength for Truth, more weakness for Falsehood, than all the fearful disparity of power that lies between the despot and the victim. So theirs was the success. So they paved the way for the grand political combat of the eighteenth century.

Mark you! The seventeenth century made the eighteenth possible, for it was the "new order of thoughts," which gave birth to a "new order of things". Only by deposing priests, only by rooting out their authority, did it become logical to attack the tyranny of kings: for, under the old regime, kingcraft had ever been the tool of priestcraft, and in the order of things but a secondary consideration. But with the downfall of the latter, kingcraft rose into prominence as the pre-eminent despot, and against the pre-eminent despot revolt always arises.

The leaders of that revolt were naturally those who carried the logic of their freethought into the camp of the dominant oppressor; who thought, spoke, wrote freely of the political fetich, as their predecessors had of the religious mockery; who did not waste their time hugging themselves in the camps of dead enemies, but accepted the live issue of the day, pursued the victories of Religion's martyrs, and carried on the war of Liberty in those lines most necessary to the people at the time and place. The result was the overthrow of the principle of kingcraft. (Not that all kingdoms have been overthrown, but find me one in a hundred of the inhabitants of a kingdom who will not laugh at the farce of the "divine appointment" of monarchs.) So wrought the new order of thoughts.

I do not suppose for a moment that Giordano Bruno or Martin Luther[2] foresaw the immense scope taken in by their doctrine of individual judgment. From the experience of men up to that date it was simply impossible that they could foresee its tremendous influence upon the action of the eighteenth century, much less upon the nineteenth. Neither was it possible that those bold writers who attacked the folly of "hereditary government" should calculate the effects which certainly followed as their thoughts took form and shape in the social body. Neither do I believe it possible that any brain that lives can detail the working of a thought into the future, or push its logic to an ultimate. But that many who think, or think they think, do not carry their syllogisms even to the first general conclusion, I am also forced to believe. If they did, the freethinkers of today would not be digging, mole-like, through the substratum of dead issues; they would not waste their energies gathering the ashes of fires burnt out two centuries ago; they would not lance their shafts at that which is already bleeding at the arteries; they would not range battalions of brains against a crippled ghost that is "laying" itself as fast as it decently can, while a monster neither ghostly nor yet like the rugged Russian bear, the armed rhinoceros, or the Hyrcan tiger, but rather like a terrible anaconda, steel-muscled and iron-jawed, is winding its horrible folds around the human bodies of the world, and breathing its devouring breath into the faces of children. If they did, they would understand that the paramount question of the day is not political, is not religious, but is economic. That the crying-out demand of today is for a circle of principles that shall forever make it impossible for one man to control another by controlling the means of his existence. They would realize that, unless the freethought movement has a practical utility in rendering the life of man more bearable, unless it contains a principle which, worked out, will free him from the all-oppressive tyrant, it is just as complete and empty a mockery as the Christian miracle or Pagan myth. Eminently is this the age of utility; and the freethinker who goes to the Hovel of Poverty with metaphysical speculations as to the continuity of life, the transformation of matter, etc.; who should say, "My dear friend, your Christian brother is mistaken; you are not doomed to an eternal hell; your condition here is your misfortune and can't be helped, but when you are dead, there's an end of it," is of as little use in the world as the most irrational religionist. To him would the hovel justly reply: "Unless you can show me something in freethought which commends itself to the needs of the race, something which will adjust my wrongs, 'put down the mighty from his seat,' then go sit with priest and king, and wrangle out your metaphysical opinions with those who mocked our misery before."

The question is, does freethought contain such a principle? And right here permit me to introduce a sort of supplementary text, taken, I think, from a recent letter of Cardinal Manning[3], but if not Cardinal Manning, then some other of the various dunce-capped gentlemen who recently "biled" over the Bruno monument.

Says the Cardinal: "Freethought leads to Atheism, to the destruction of social and civil order, and to the overthrow of government." I accept the gentleman's statement; I credit him with much intellectual acumen for perceiving that which many freethinkers have failed to perceive: accepting it, I shall do my best to prove it, and then endeavor to show that this very iconoclastic principle is the salvation of the economic slave and the destruction of the economic tyrant.

First: does freethought lead to Atheism?

Freethought, broadly defined, is the right to believe as the evidence, coming in contact with the mind, forces it to believe. This implies the admission of any and all evidence bearing upon any subject which may come up for discussion. Among the subjects that come up for discussion, the moment so much is admitted, is the existence of a God.

Now, the idea of God is, in the first place, an exceeding contradiction. The sign God, so Deists[4] tell us, was invented to express the inexpressible, the incomprehensible and infinite! Then they immediately set about defining it. These definitions prove to be about as self-contradictory and generally conflicting as the original absurdity. But there is a particular set of attributes which form a sort of common ground for all these definitions. They tell us that God is possessed of supreme wisdom, supreme justice, and supreme power. In all the catalogue of creeds, I never yet heard of one that had not for its nucleus unlimited potency.

Now, let us take the deist upon his own ground and prove to him either that his God is limited as to wisdom, or limited as to justice, or limited as to power, or else there is no such thing as justice.

First, then, God, being all-just, wishes to do justice; being all-wise, knows what justice is; being all-powerful, can do justice. Why then injustice? Either your God can do justice and won't or doesn't know what justice is, or he can not do it. The immediate reply is: "What appears to be injustice in our eyes, in the sight of omniscience may be justice. God's ways are not our ways."

Oh, but if he is the all-wise pattern, they should be; what is good enough for God ought to be good enough for man; but what is too mean for man won't do in a God. Else there is no such thing as justice or injustice, and every murder, every robbery, every lie, every crime in the calendar is right and upon that one premise of supreme authority you upset every fact in existence.

What right have you to condemn a murderer if you assume him necessary to "God's plan"? What logic can command the return of stolen property, or the branding of a thief, if the Almighty decreed it? Yet here, again, the Deist finds himself in a dilemma, for to suppose crime necessary to God's purpose is to impeach his wisdom or deny his omnipotence by limiting him as to means. The whole matter, then, hinges upon the one attribute of authority of the central idea of God.

But, you say, what has all this to do with the economic tendency of freethought? Everything. For upon that one idea of supreme authority is based every tyranny that was ever formulated. Why? Because, if God is, no human being no thing that lives, ever had a right! He simply had a privilege, bestowed, granted, conferred, gifted to him, for such a length of time as God sees fit.

This is the logic of my textator, the logic of Catholicism, the only logic of Authoritarianism. The Catholic Church says: "You who are blind, be grateful that you can hear: God could have made you deaf as well. You who are starving, be thankful that you can breathe; God could deprive you of air as well as food. You who are sick, be grateful that you are not dead: God is very merciful to let you live at all. Under all times and circumstances take what you can get, and be thankful." These are the beneficences, the privileges, given by Authority.

Note the difference between a right and a privilege. A right, in the abstract, is a fact; it is not a thing to be given, established, or conferred; it is. Of the exercise of a right power may deprive me; of the right itself, never. Privilege, in the abstract, does not exist; there is no such thing. Rights recognized, privilege is destroyed.

But, in the practical, the moment you admit a supreme authority, you have denied rights. Practically the supremacy has all the rights, and no matter what the human race possesses, it does so merely at the caprice of that authority. The exercise of the respiratory function is not a right, but a privilege granted by God; the use of the soil is not a right, but a gracious allowance of Deity; the possession of product as the result of labor is not a right, but a boon bestowed. And the thievery of pure air, the withholding of land from use, the robbery of toil, are not wrongs (for if you have no rights, you cannot be wronged), but benign blessings bestowed by "the Giver of all Good" upon the air-thief, the landlord, and the labor-robber.

Hence the freethinker who recognizes the science of astronomy, the science of mathematics, and the equally positive and exact science of justice, is logically forced to the denial of supreme authority. For no human being who observes and reflects can admit a supreme tyrant and preserve his self-respect. No human mind can accept the dogma of divine despotism and the doctrine of eternal justice at the same time; they contradict each other, and it takes two brains to hold them. The cardinal is right: freethought does logically lead to atheism, if by atheism he means the denial of supreme authority.

I will now take his third statement, leaving the second for the present; freethought, he says, leads to the overthrow of government. I am sensible that the majority of you will be ready to indignantly deny the cardinal's asseveration; I know that the most of my professedly atheistic friends shrink sensitively from the slightest allusion that sounds like an attack on government; I am aware that there are many of you who could eagerly take this platform to speak upon "the glorious rights and privileges of American citizenship"; to expatiate upon that "noble bulwark of our liberties—the constitution"; to defend "that peaceful weapon of redress, the ballot"; to soar off rhapsodically about that "starry banner that floats 'over the land of the free and the home of the brave.'" We are so free! and so brave! We don't hang Brunos at the stake any more for holding heretical opinions on religious subjects. No! But we imprison men for discussing the social question, and we hang men for discussing the economic question! We are so very free and so very brave in this country! "Ah"! we say in our nineteenth century freedom and bravery, " it was a weak God, a poor God, a miserable, quaking God, whose authority had to be preserved by the tortuous death of a creature!" Aye! the religious question is dead, and the stake is no longer fashionable. But is it a strong State, a brave State, a conscience-proud State, whose authority demands the death of five creatures? Is the scaffold better than the faggot? Is it a very free mind which will read that infamous editorial in the Chicago "Herald": "It is not necessary to hold that Parsons[5] was legally, rightfully, or wisely hanged: he was mightily hanged. The State, the sovereign, need give no reasons; the State need abide by no law; the State is the law!"—to read that and applaud, and set the Cain-like curse upon your forehead and the red "damned spot" upon your hand? Do you know what you do?—Craven, you worship the fiend, Authority, again! True, you have not the ghosts, the incantations, the paraphernalia and mummery of the Church. No: but you have the "precedents," the "be it enacted," the red-tape, the official uniforms of the State; and you are just as bad a slave to statecraft as your Irish Catholic neighbor is to popecraft. Your Government becomes your God, from whom you accept privileges, and in whose hands all rights are vested. Once more the individual has no rights; once more intangible, irresponsible authority assumes the power of deciding what is right and what is wrong. Once more the race must labor under just such restricted conditions as the law—the voice of the Authority, the governmentalist's bible-shall dictate. Once more it says: "You who have not meat, be grateful that you have bread; many are not allowed even so much. You who work sixteen hours a day, be glad it is not twenty; many have not the privilege to work. You who have not fuel, be thankful that you have shelter; many walk the street! And you, street-walkers, be grateful that there are well-lighted dens of the city; in the country you might die upon the roadside. Goaded human race! Be thankful for your goad. Be submissive to the Lord, and kiss the hand that lashes you!" Once more misery is the diet of the many, while the few receive, in addition to their rights, those rights of their fellows which government has wrested from them. Once more the hypothesis is that the Government, or Authority, or God in his other form, owns all the rights, and grants privileges according to its sweet will.

The freethinker who should determine to question it would naturally suppose that one difficulty in the old investigation was removed. He would say, "at least this thing Government possesses the advantage of being of the earth,—earthy. This is something I can get hold of, argue, reason, discuss with. God was an indefinable, arbitrary, irresponsible something in the clouds, to whom I could not approach nearer than to his agent, the priest. But this dictator surely I shall be able to meet it on something like possible ground." Vain delusion! Government is as unreal, as intangible, as unapproachable as God. Try it, if you don't believe it. Seek through the legislative halls of America and find, if you can, the Government. In the end you will be doomed to confer with the agent, as before. Why, you have the statutes! Yes, but the statutes are not the government; where is the power that made the statutes? Oh, the legislators! Yes, but the legislator, per se, has no more power to make a law for me than I for him. I want the power that gave him the power. I shall talk with him; I go to the White House; I say: "Mr. Harrison, are you the government?" "No, madam, I am its representative." "Well, where is the principal?—Who is the government?" "The people of the United States." "The whole people?" "The whole people." "You, then, are the representative of the people of the United States. May I see your certificate of authorization?" "Well, no; I have none. I was elected." "Elected by whom? the whole people?" "Oh, no. By some of the people,—some of the voters." (Mr. Harrison being a pious Presbyterian, he would probably add: "The majority vote of the whole was for another man, but I had the largest electoral vote.") "Then you are the representative of the electoral college, not of the whole people, nor the majority of the people, nor even a majority of the voters. But suppose the largest number of ballots cast had been for you: you would represent the majority of the voters, I suppose. But the majority, sir, is not a tangible thing; it is an unknown quantity. An agent is usually held accountable to his principals. If you do not know the individuals who voted for you, then you do not know for whom you are acting, nor to whom you are accountable. If any body of persons has delegated to you any authority, the disposal of any right or part of a right (supposing a right to be transferable), you must have received it from the individuals composing that body; and you must have some means of learning who those individuals are, or you cannot know for whom you act, and you are utterly irresponsible as an agent.

"Furthermore, such a body of voters cannot give into your charge any rights but their own; by no possible jugglery of logic can they delegate the exercise of any function which they themselves do not control. If any individual on earth has a right to delegate his powers to whomsoever he chooses, then every other individual has an equal right; and if each has an equal right, then none can choose an agent for another, without that other's consent. Therefore, if the power of government resides in the whole people, and out of that whole all but one elected you as their agent, you would still have no authority whatever to act for the one. The individuals composing the minority who did not appoint you have just the same rights and powers as those composing the majority who did; and if they prefer not to delegate them at all, then neither you, nor any one, has any authority whatever to coerce them into accepting you, or any one, as their agent—for upon your own basis the coercive authority resides, not in the majority, not in any proportion of the people, but in the whole people."

Hence "the overthrow of government" as a coercive power, thereby denying God in another form.

Upon this overthrow follows, the Cardinal says, the disruption of social and civil order!

Oh! it is amusing to hear those fellows rave about social order! I could laugh to watch them as they repeat the cry, "Great is Diana of the Ephesians!" "Down on your knees and adore this beautiful statue of Order," but that I see this hideous, brainless, disproportion idol come rolled on the wheels of Juggernaut over the weak and the helpless, the sorrowful and the despairing. Hate burns, then, where laughter dies.

Social Order! Not long ago I saw a letter from a young girl to a friend; a young girl whose health had been broken behind a counter, where she stood eleven and twelve hours a day, six days in the week, for the magnificent sum of $5. The letter said: "Can't you help me to a position? My friends want me to marry a man I do not like, because he has money. Can't you help me? I can sew, or keep books. I will even try clerking again rather than that!" Social Order! When the choice for a young girl lies between living by inches and dying by yards at manual labor, or becoming the legal property of a man she does not like because he has money!

Walk up Fifth Avenue in New York some hot summer day, among the magnificent houses of the rich; hear your footsteps echo for blocks with the emptiness of it! Look at places going to waste, space, furniture, draperies, elegance,—all useless. Then take a car down town; go among the homes of the producers of that idle splendor; find six families living in a five-room house,—the sixth dwelling in the cellar. Space is not wasted here,—these human vermin rub each other's elbows in the stifling narrows; furniture is not wasted,—these sit upon the floor; no echoing emptiness, no idle glories! No—but wasting, strangling, choking, vicious human life! Dearth of vitality there—dearth of space for it here! This is social order!

Next winter, when the 'annual output' of coal has been mined, when the workmen are clenching their hard fists with impotent anger, when the coal in the ground lies useless, hark to the cry that will rise from the freezing western prairies, while the shortened commodity goes up, up, up, eight, nine, ten, eleven dollars a ton; and while the syndicate's pockets are filing, the grave-yards fill, and fill. Moralize on the preservation of social order!

Go back to President Grant's administration,—that very "pure republican" administration;—see the settlers of the Mussel Slough compelled to pay thirty-five, forty dollars an acre for the land reclaimed from almost worthlessness by hard labor,— and to whom? To a corporation of men who never saw it! whose "grant" lay a hundred miles away, but who, for reasons of their own, saw fit to hire the "servants of the people" to change it so. See those who refused to pay it shot down by order of "the State"; watch their blood smoke upward to the heavens, sealing the red seal of justice against their murderers; and then—watch a policeman arrest a shoeless tramp for stealing a pair of boots. Say to your self, this is civil order and must be preserved, Go talk with political leaders, big or little, on methods of "making the slate," and "railroading" it through the ward caucus or the national convention. Muse on that "peaceful weapon of redress," the ballot. Consider the condition of the average "American sovereign" and of his "official servant," and prate then of civil order.

Subvert the social and civil order! Aye, I would destroy, to the last vestige, this mockery of order, this travesty upon justice! Break up the home? Yes, every home that rests on slavery! Every marriage that represents the sale and transfer of the individuality of one of its parties to the other! Every institution, social or civil, that stands between man and his right; every tie that renders one a master, another a serf; every law, every statute, every be-it-enacted that represents tyranny; everything you call American privilege that can only exist at the expense of international right. Now cry out, "Nihilist—disintegrationist!" Say that I would isolate humanity, reduce society to its elemental state, make men savage! It is not true. But rather than see this devastating, cankering, enslaving system you call social order go on, rather than help to keep alive the accursed institutions of Authority, I would help to reduce every fabric in the social structure to its native element.

But is it true that freedom means disintegration? Only to that which is bad. Only to that which ought to disintegrate.

What is the history of free thought?

Is it not so, that since we have Anarchy there, since all the children of the brain are legitimate, that there has been less waste of intellectual energy, more cooperation in the scientific world, truer economy in utilizing the mentalities of men, than there ever was, or ever could be, under authoritative dominion of the church? Is it not true that with the liberty of thought, Truth has been able to prove herself without the aid of force? Does not error die from want of vitality when there is no force to keep it alive? Is it not true that natural attractions have led men into associative groups, who can best follow their chosen paths of thought, and give the benefit of their studies to mankind with better economy than if some coercive power had said, "You think in this line—you in that"; or what the majority had by ballot decided it was best to think about?

I think it is true. Follow your logic out; can you not see that true economy lies in Liberty,—whether it be in thought or action? It is not slavery that has made men unite for cooperative effort. It is not slavery that produced the means of transportation, communication, production, and exchange, and all the thousand and one economic, or what ought to be economic, contrivances of civilization. No—nor is it government. It is Self-interest. And would not self-interest exist if that institution which stands between man and his right to the free use of the soil were annihilated? Could you not see the use of a bank if the power which renders it possible for the national banks to control land, production and everything else, were broken down?

Do you suppose the producers of the east and west couldn't see the advantage of a railroad, if the authority which makes a systematizer like Gould[6] or Vanderbilt[7] a curse were swept away? Do you imagine that government has a corner on ideas, now that the Church is overthrown; and that the people could not learn the principles of economy, if this intangible giant which has robbed and slaughtered them, wasted their resources and distributed opportunities so unjustly, were destroyed? I don't think so. I believe that legislators as a rule have been monuments of asinine stupidity, whose principal business has been to hinder those who were not stupid, and get paid for doing it. I believe that the so-called brainy financial men would rather buy the legislators than be the legislators; and the real thinkers, the genuine improvers of society, have as little to do with law and politics as they conveniently can.

I believe that "Liberty is the mother, not the daughter, of Order."[8]

"But," some one will say, "what of the criminals? Suppose a man steals." In the first place, a man won't steal, ordinarily, unless that which he steals is something he can not as easily get without stealing; in liberty the cost of stealing would involve greater difficulties than producing, and consequently he would not be apt to steal. But suppose a man steals. Today you go to a representative of that power which has robbed you of the earth, of the right of free contract of the means of exchange, taxes you for everything you eat or wear (the meanest form of robbery),—you go to him for redress from a thief! It is about as logical as the Christian lady whose husband had been "removed" by Divine Providence, and who thereupon prayed to said Providence to "comfort the widow and the fatherless." In freedom we would not institute a wholesale robber to protect us from petty larceny. Each associative group would probably adopt its own methods of resisting aggression, that being the only crime. For myself, I think criminals should be treated as sick people.

"But suppose you have murderers, brutes, all sorts of criminals. Are you not afraid to lose the restraining influence of the law?" First, I think it can be shown that the law makes ten criminals where it restrains one. On that basis it would not, as a matter of policy merely, be an economical institution. Second, this is not a question of expediency, but of right. In antebellum days the proposition was not, Are the blacks good enough to be free? but, Have they the right? So today the question is not, Will outrages result from freeing humanity? but, Has it the right to life, the means of life, the opportunities of happiness?

In the transition epoch, surely crimes will come. Did the seed of tyranny ever bear good fruit? And can you expect Liberty to undo in a moment what Oppression has been doing for ages? Criminals are the crop of despots, as much a necessary expression of the evil in society as an ulcer is of disease in the blood; and so long as the taint of the poison remains, so long there will be crimes.

"For it must needs that offences come, but woe to him through whom the offence cometh." The crimes of the future are the harvests sown of the ruling classes of the present. Woe to the tyrant who shall cause the offense!

Sometimes I dream of this social change. I get a streak of faith in Evolution, and the good in man. I paint a gradual slipping out of the now, to that beautiful then, where there are neither kings, presidents, landlords, national bankers, stockbrokers, railroad magnates, patentright monopolists, or tax and title collectors; where there are no over-stocked markets or hungry children, idle counters and naked creatures, splendor and misery, waste and need. I am told this is farfetched idealism, to paint this happy, povertyless, crimeless, diseaseless world; I have been told I "ought to be behind the bars" for it.

Remarks of that kind rather destroy the white streak of faith. I lose confidence in the slipping process, and am forced to believe that the rulers of the earth are sowing a fearful wind, to reap a most terrible whirlwind. When I look at this poor, bleeding, wounded World, this world that has suffered so long, struggled so much, been scourged so fiercely, thorn-pierced so deeply, crucified so cruelly, I can only shake my head and remember:

The giant is blind, but he's thinking: and his locks are growing, fast.

Francisco Ferrer[1]

In all unsuccessful social upheavals there are two terrors: the Red—that is, the people, the mob; the White—that is, the reprisal.

When a year ago to-day the lightning of the White Terror[2] shot out of that netherest blackness of Social Depth, the Spanish Torture House, and laid in the ditch of Montjuich[3] a human being who but a moment before had been the personification of manhood, in the flower of life, in the strength and pride of a balanced intellect, full of the purpose of a great and growing undertaking,—that of the Modern Schools,—humanity at large received a blow in the face which it could not understand.

Stunned, bewildered, shocked, it recoiled and stood gaping with astonishment. How to explain it? The average individual—certainly the average individual in America—could not believe it possible that any group of persons calling themselves a government, let it be of the worst and most despotic, could slay a man for being a teacher, a teacher of modern sciences, a builder of hygienic schools, a publisher of text-books. No: they could not believe it. Their minds staggered back and shook refusal. It was not so; it could not be so. The man was shot,—that was sure. He was dead, and there was no raising him out of the ditch to question him. The Spanish government had certainly proceeded in an unjustifiable manner in court-martialing him and sentencing him without giving him a chance at defense. But surely he had been guilty of something; surely he must have rioted, or instigated riot, or done some desperate act of rebellion; for never could it be that in the twentieth century a country of Europe could kill a peaceful man whose aim in life was to educate children in geography, arithmetic, geology, physics, chemistry, singing, and languages.

No: it was not possible!—And, for all that, it was possible; it was done, on the 13th of October, one year ago to-day, in the face of Europe, standing with tied hands to look on at the murder.

And from that day on, controversy between the awakened who understood, the reactionists who likewise understood, and their followers on both sides who have half understood, has surged up and down and left confusion pretty badly confounded in the mind of him who did not understand, but sought to.

The men who did him to death, and the institutions they represent have done all in their power to create the impression that Ferrer was a believer in violence, a teacher

75

of the principles of violence, a doer of acts of violence, and an instigator of widespread violence perpetrated by a mass of people. In support of the first they have published reports purporting to be his own writings, have pretended to reproduce seditious pictures from the walls of his class-rooms, have declared that he was seen mingling with the rebels during the Catalonian uprising of last year, and that upon trial he was found guilty of having conceived and launched the Spanish rebellion against the Moroccan war. And that his death was a just act of reprisal.

On the other hand, we have had a storm of indignant voices clamoring in his defense, alternately admitting and denying him to be a revolutionist, alternately contending that his schools taught social rebellion and that they taught nothing but pure science; we have had workmen demonstrating and professors and litterateurs protesting on very opposite grounds; and almost none were able to give definite information for the faith that was in them.

And indeed it has been very difficult to obtain exact information, and still is so. After a year's lapse, it is yet not easy to get the facts disentangled from the fancies,— the truths from the lies, and above all from the half-lies.

And even when we have the truths as to the facts, it is still difficult to valuate them, because of American ignorance of Spanish ignorance. Please understand the phrase. America has not too much to boast of in the way of its learning; but yet it has that much of common knowledge and common education that it does not enter into our minds to conceive of a population 68% of which are unable to read and write, and a good share of the remaining 32% can only read, not write; neither does it at all enter our heads to think that of this 32% of the better informed, the most powerful contingent is composed of those whose distinct, avowed, and deliberate purpose it is to keep the ignorant ignorant.

Whatever may be the sins of Government in this country, or of the Churches— and there are plenty of such sins—at least they have not (save in the case of negro slaves) constituted themselves a conspiratical force to keep out enlightenment,—to prevent the people from learning to read and write, or to acquire whatever scientific knowledge their economic circumstances permitted them to. What the unconscious conspiracy of economic circumstance has done, and what conscious manipulations the Government school is guilty of, to render higher education a privilege of the rich and a maintainer of injustice is another matter. But it cannot be charged that the rulers of America seek to render the people illiterate. People, therefore, who have grown up in a general atmosphere of thought which regards the government as a provider of education, even as a compeller of education, do not, unless their attention is drawn to the facts, conceive of a state of society in which government is a hostile force, opposed to the enlightenment of the people,—its politicians exercising all their ingenuity to sidetrack the demand of the people for schools. How much less do they conceive the hostile force and power of a Church, having behind it an unbroken descent from feudal ages, whose direct interest it is to maintain a closed monopoly of learning, and to keep out of general circulation all scientific information which would tend to destroy the superstitions whereby it thrives.

I say that the American people in general are not informed as to these conditions, and therefore the phenomenon of a teacher killed for instituting and maintaining schools staggers their belief. And when they read the assertions of those who defend the murder, that it was because his schools were instigating the overthrow of social order in Spain, they naturally exclaim: "Ah, that explains it! The man taught sedition, rebellion, riot, in his schools! That is the reason."

Now the truth is, that what Ferrer was teaching in his schools was really instigating the overthrow of the social order of Spain; furthermore it was not only instigating it, but it was making it as certain as the still coming of the daylight out of the night of the east. But not by the teaching of riot; of the use of dagger, bomb, or knife; but by the teaching of the same sciences which are taught in our public schools, through a generally diffused knowledge of which the power of Spain's despotic Church must crumble away. Likewise it was laying the primary foundation for the overthrow of such portions of the State organization as exist by reason of the general ignorance of the people.

The Social Order of Spain ought to be overthrown; must be overthrown, will be overthrown; and Ferrer was doing a mighty work in that direction. The men who killed him knew and understood it well. And they consciously killed him for what he really did; but they have let the outside world suppose they did it, for what he did not do. Knowing there are no words so hated by all governments as "sedition and rebellion," knowing that such words will make the most radical of governments align itself with the most despotic at once, knowing there is nothing which so offends the majority of conservative and peace-loving people everywhere as the idea of violence unordered by authority, they have willfully created the impression that Ferrer's schools were places where children and youths were taught to handle weapons, and to make ready for armed attacks on the government.

They have, as I said before, created this impression in various ways; they have pointed to the fact that the man who in 1906 made the attack on Alfonso's life, had acted as a translator of books used by Ferrer in his schools; they have scattered over Europe and America pictures purporting to be reproductions of drawings in prominent wall-spaces in his schools, recommending the violent overthrow of the government.

As to the first of these accusations, I shall consider it later in the lecture; but as to the last, it should be enough to remind any person with an ordinary amount of reflection, that the schools were public places open to any one, as our schools are; and that if any such pictures had existed, they would have been sufficient cause for shutting up the schools and incarcerating the founder within a day after their appearance on the walls. The Spanish Government has that much sense of how to preserve its own existence, that it would not allow such pictures to hang in a public place for one day. Nor would books preaching sedition have been permitted to be published or circulated.—All this is foolish dust sought to be thrown in foolish eyes.

No; the real offense was the real thing that he did. And in order to appreciate its enormity, from the Spanish ruling force's standpoint, let us now consider what that ruling force is, what are the economic and educational conditions of the Spanish people, why and how Ferrer founded the Modern Schools, and what were the subjects taught therein.

Up to the year 1857 there existed no legal provision for general elementary education in Spain. In that year, owing to the liberals having gotten into power in Madrid, after a bitter contest aroused partially by the general political events of Europe, a law making elementary education compulsory was passed. This was two years before Ferrer's birth.

Now it is one thing for a political party, temporarily in possession of power, to pass a law. It is quite another thing to make that law effective, even when wealth and general sentiment are behind it. But when joined to the fact that there is a strong opposition is added the fact that this opposition is in possession of the greatest wealth of the country, that the people to be benefited are often quite as bitterly opposed to their own enlightenment as those who profit by their ignorance, and that those who do ardently desire their own uplift are extremely poor, the difficulty of practicalizing this educational law is partially appreciated.

78

Ferrer's own boyhood life is an illustration of how much benefit the children of the peasantry reaped from the educational law. His parents were vine dressers; they were eminently orthodox and believed what their priest (who was probably the only man in the little village of Alella[4] able to read) told them: that the Liberals were the emissaries of Satan and that whatever they did was utterly evil. They wanted no such evil thing as popular education about, and would not that their children should have it. Accordingly, even at 13 years of age, the boy was without education,—a circumstance which in after years made him more anxious that others should not suffer as he had.

It is self-understood that if it was difficult to found schools in the cities where there existed a degree of popular clamor for them, it was next to impossible in the rural districts where people like Ferrer's parents were the typical inhabitants. The best result obtained by this law in the 20 years from 1857 to 1877 was that, out of 16,000,000 people, 4,000,000 were then able to read and write,—75% remaining illiterate. At the end of 1907 the proportion was altered to 6,000,000 literate out of 18,500,000 population, which may be considered as a fairly correct approximate of the present condition.

One of the very great accounting causes for this situation is the extreme poverty of the mass of the populace. In many districts of Spain a laborer's wages are less than $1.00 a week, and nowhere do they equal the poorest workman's wages in America. Of course, it is understood that the cost of living is likewise low; but imagine it as low as you please, it is still evident that the income of the workers is too small to permit them to save anything, even from the most frugal living. The dire struggle to secure food, clothing and shelter is such that little energy is left wherewith to aspire to anything, to demand anything, either for themselves or their children. Unless, therefore, the government provided the buildings, the books, and appliances, and paid the teachers' salaries, it is easy to see that the people most in need of education are least able, and least likely, to provide it for themselves. Furthermore the government itself, unless it can tax the wealthier classes for it, cannot out of such an impoverished source wring sufficient means to provide adequate schools and school equipments.

Now, the wealthiest classes are just the religious orders. According to the statement of Monsignor José Valeda de Gunjado, these orders own two-thirds of the money of the country and one-third of the wealth in property. These orders are utterly opposed to all education except such as they themselves furnish—a lamentable travesty on learning.

As a writer who has investigated these conditions personally, observes, in reply to the question, "Does not the Church provide numbers of schools, day and night, at its own expense?—'It does,—unhappily for Spain.'" It provides schools whose principal aim is to strengthen superstition, follow a mediaeval curriculum, *keep out* scientific light,—and prevent other and better schools from being established.

A Spanish educational journal *(La Escuela Espanola)*, not Ferrer's journal, declared in 1907 that these schools were largely "without light or ventilation, dens of death, ignorance, and bad training." It was estimated that 50,000 children died every year in consequence of the mischievous character of the school rooms. And even to schools like these, there were half a million children in Spain who could gain no admittance.

As to the teachers, they are allowed a salary ranging from $50.00 to $100.00 a year; but this is provided, not by the State, but through voluntary donations from the parents. So that a teacher, in addition to his legitimate functions, must perform those of collector of his own salary.

Now conceive that he is endeavoring to collect it from parents whose wages amount to two or three dollars a week; and you will not be surprised at the case reported by a Madrid paper in 1903 of a master's having canvassed a district to find how many parents would contribute if he opened a school. Out of one hundred families, three promised their support!

Is it any wonder that the law of compulsory education is a mockery? How could it be anything else?

Now let us look at the products of this popular ignorance, and we shall presently understand why the Church fosters it, why it fights education; and also why the Catalonian[5] insurrection of 1909, which began as a strike of workers in protest against the Moroccan war, ended in mob attacks upon convents, monasteries, and churches.

I have already quoted the statement of a high Spanish prelate that the religious orders of Spain own two-thirds of the money of Spain, and one-third of the wealth in property. Whether this estimate is precisely correct or not, it is sufficiently near correctness to make us aware that at least a great portion of the wealth of the country has passed into their hands,—a state not widely differing from that existing in France prior to the great Revolution. Before the insurrection of last year, the city of Barcelona alone had 165 convents, many of which were exceedingly rich. The province of Catalonia maintained 2,300 of these institutions. Aside from these religious orders with their accumulations of wealth, the Church itself, the united body of priests not in orders, is immensely wealthy. Conceive that in the Cathedral at Toledo[6] there is an image of the Virgin whose wardrobe alone would be sufficient to build hundreds of schools. Imagine that this doll, which is supposed to symbolize the forlorn young woman who in her pain and sorrow and need was driven to seek shelter in a stable, whose life was ever lowly, and who is called the Mother of Sorrows[7],—imagine that this image of her has become a vulgar coquette sporting a robe where into are sown 85,000 pearls, besides as many more sapphires, amethysts, and diamonds!

Oh, what a decoration for the mother of the Carpenter of Nazareth! What a vision for the dying eyes on the Cross to look forward to! What an outcome of the gospel of salvation free to the poor and lowly, taught by the poorest and the lowliest,—that the humble keeper of the humble household of the despised little village of Judea should be imaged forth as a Queen of Gauds, bedizened with a crown worth $25,000 and bracelets valued at $10,000 more. The Virgin Mary, the Daughter of the Stable, transformed into a diamond merchant's showcase!

And this in the midst of men and women working for just enough to keep the skin upon the bone; in the midst of children who are denied the primary necessities of childhood.

Now I ask you, when the fury of these people burst, as under the provocation they received it was inevitable that it should burst, was it any wonder that it manifested itself in mob violence against the institutions which mock their suffering by this useless, senseless, criminal waste of wealth in the face of utter need?

Will some one now whisper in our ears that there are women in America who decorate themselves with more jewels than the Virgin of Toledo, and throw away the price of a school on a useless decoration in a single night; while within a radius of five miles from them there are also uneducated children, for whom our School Boards can provide no place?

Yes, it is so; let them remember the mobs of Barcelona!

And let me remember I am talking about Spain!

The question naturally intrudes, How does the Church, how do the religious orders manage to accumulate such wealth? Remember first that they are old, and of unbroken continuance for hundreds of years. That various forms of acquisition, in operation for centuries, would produce immense accumulations, even supposing nothing but legitimate purchases and gifts. But when we consider the actual means whereby money is daily absorbed from the people by these institutions we receive a shock which sets all our notions of the triumph of Modern Science topsy-turvy.

It is almost impossible to realize, and yet it is true, that the Spanish Church still deals in that infamous "graft" against which Martin Luther hurled the splendid force of his wrath four hundred years ago. The Church of Spain still sells indulgences. Every Catholic bookstore, and every priest, has them for sale. They are called "bulas." Their prices range from about 15 to 25 cents, and they constitute an elastic excuse for doing pretty much what the possessor pleases to do, providing it is not a capital crime, for a definitely named period.

Probably there is no one in America so little able to believe this condition to exist, as the ordinary well-informed Roman Catholic. I have myself listened to priests of the Roman faith giving the conditions on which pardon for venal offenses might be obtained; and they had nothing to do with money. They consisted in saying a certain number of prayers at stated periods, with specified intent. While that may be a very illogical way of putting things together that have no connection, there is nothing in it to offend one's ideas of honesty. The enlightened conscience of an entire mass of people has demanded that a spiritual offense be dealt with by spiritual means. It would revolt at the idea that such grace could be written out on paper and sold either to the highest bidder or for a fixed price.

But now conceive what happens where a people are illiterate, regarding written documents with that superstitious awe which those who cannot read always have for the mysterious language of learning; regarding them besides with the combination of fear and reverence which the ignorant believer entertains for the visible sign of Supernatural Power, the Power which holds over him the threat of eternal punishment,—and you will have what goes on in Spain. Add to this that such a condition of fear and gullibility on the side of the people, is the great opportunity of the religious "grafter." Whatever number of honest, self-sacrificing, devoted people may be attracted to the service of the Church, there will certainly be found also, the cheat, the impostor, the searcher for ease and power.

These indulgences, which for 15 or 25 cents pardon the buyer for his past sins, but are good only till he sins again, constitute a species of permission to do what otherwise is forbidden; the most expensive one, the 25¢-one, is practically a license to hold stolen property up to a certain amount.

Both rich and poor buy these things, the rich of course paying a good deal more than the stipulated sum. But it hardly requires the statement that an immense number of the very poor buy them also. And from this horrible traffic the Church of Spain annually draws millions.

There are other sources of income such as the sale of scapulars, agnus-deis, charms, and other pieces of trumpery, which goes on all over the Catholic world also, but naturally to no such extent as in Spain, Portugal, and Italy, where popular ignorance may be again measured by the materialism of its religion.

Now, is it reasonable to suppose that the individuals who are thriving upon these sales, want a condition of popular enlightenment? Do they not know how all this traffic would crumble like the ash of a burnt-out fire, once the blaze of science were to flame through Spain? *They* EDUCATE! Yes; they educate the people to believe in these barbaric relics of a dead time,—for *their own material interest*. Spain and Portugal are the last resort of the mediaeval church; the monasticism and the Jesuitry which have been expelled from other European countries, and compelled to withdraw from Cuba and the Philippines, have concentrated there; and there they are making their last fight. There they will go down into their eternal grave; but not till Science has invaded the dark corners of the popular intellect.

The political condition is parallel with the religious condition of the people, with the exception that the State is poor while the Church is rich.

There are some elements in the government which are opposed to the Church religiously, which nevertheless do not wish to see its power as an institution upset, because they foresee that the same people who would overthrow the Church, would later overthrow them. These, too, wish to see the people kept ignorant.

Nevertheless, there have been numerous political rebellions in Spain, having for their object the establishment of a republic.

In 1868 there occurred such a rebellion, under the leadership of Ruiz Zorilla[8]. At that time, Ferrer was not quite 20 years old. He had acquired an education by his own efforts. He was a declared Republican, as it seems that every young, ardent, bright-minded youth, seeing what the condition of his country was, and wishing for its betterment, would be. Zorilla was for a short time Minister of Public Instruction, under the new government, and very zealous for popular education.

Naturally he became an object of admiration and imitation to Ferrer.

In the early eighties, after various fluctuations of political power, Zorilla, who had been absent from Spain, returned to it, and began the labor of converting the soldiers to republicanism. Ferrer was then a director of railways, and of much service to Zorilla in the practical work of organization. In 1885 this movement culminated in an abortive revolution, wherein both Ferrer and Zorilla took active part, and were accordingly compelled to take refuge in France upon the failure of the insurrection.

It is therefore certain that from his entrance into public agitation till the year 1885, Ferrer was an active revolutionary republican, believing in the overthrow of Spanish tyranny by violence.

There is no question that at that time he said and wrote things which, whether we shall consider them justifiable or not, were openly in favor of forcible rebellion. Such utterances charged against him at the alleged trial in 1909, which were really his, were quotations from this period. Remember he was then 26 years old. When the trial occurred, he was 50 years old. What had been his mental evolution during those 24 years?

In Paris, where, with the exception of a short intermission in 1889 when he visited Spain, he remained for about fifteen years, he naturally drifted into a method of making a living quite common to educated exiles in a foreign land; viz., giving private lessons in his native language. But while this is with most a mere temporary makeshift, which they change for something else as soon as they are able, to Ferrer it revealed what his real business in life should be; he found teaching to be his genuine vocation; so much so that he took part in several movements for popular education in Paris, giving much free service.

This participation in the labor of training the mind, which is always a slow and patient matter, began to have its effect on his conceptions of political change. Slowly the idea of a Spain regenerated through the storm blasts of revolution, mightily and suddenly, faded out of his belief, being replaced, probably almost insensibly, by the idea that a thorough educational enlightenment must precede political transformation, if that transformation were to be permanent. This conviction he voiced with strange power and beauty of expression, when he said to his old revolutionary Republican friend, Alfred Naquet[9]: "Time respects those works alone which Time itself has helped to build."

Naquet himself, old and sinking man as he is, is at this day and hour heart and soul for forcible revolution; admitting all the evils which it engenders and all the dangers of miscarriage which accompany it, he still believes, to quote his own words, that "Revolutions are not only the marvelous accoucheurs of societies; they are also fecundating forces. They fructify men's intelligences; and if they determine the final realization of matured evolutions, they also become, through their action on human minds, points of departure for newer evolutions." Yet he, who thus sings the paean of the uprisen people, with a fire of youth and an ardor of love that sound like the singing of some strong young blacksmith marching at the head of an insurgent column, rather than the quavering voice of an old spent man; he, who was the warm personal friend of Ferrer for many years, and who would surely have wished that his ideal love should also have been his friend's love, he expressly declares that Ferrer was of those who feel themselves drawn to the field of preparative labor, making sure the ground over which the Revolution may march to enduring results.

This then was the ripened condition of his mind, especially after the death of Zorilla, and all his subsequent life and labor is explicable only with this understanding of his mental attitude.

In the confusion of deafening voices, it has been declared that not only did he not take part in last year's manifestations, nor instigate them; but that he in fact had become a Tolstoyan, a non-resistant.

This is not true: he undoubtedly understood that the introduction of popular education into Spain means revolt, sooner or later. And he would certainly have been glad to see a successful revolt overthrow the monarchy at Madrid. He did not wish the people to be submissive; it is one of the fundamental teachings of the schools he founded that the assertive spirit of the child is to be encouraged; that its will is not to be broken; that the sin of other schools is the forcing of obedience. He hoped to help to form a young Spain which would not submit; which would resist, resist consciously, intelligently, steadily. He did not wish to enlighten people merely to render them more sensitive to their pains and deprivations, but that they might so use their enlightenment as to rid themselves of the system of exploitation by Church and State which is responsible for their miseries. By what means they would choose to free themselves, he did not make his affair.

How and when were these schools founded? It was during his long sojourn in Paris, that he had as a private pupil in Spanish, a middle-aged, wealthy, unmarried, Catholic lady. After much conflict over religion between teacher and pupil, the latter modified her orthodoxy greatly; and especially after her journeys to Spain, where she herself saw the condition of public instruction.

Eventually she became interested in Ferrer's conceptions of education, and his desire to establish schools in his own country. And when she died in 1900 (she was then somewhat over 50 years old) she devised a certain part of her property to Ferrer, to be used as he saw fit, feeling assured no doubt that he would see fit to use it not for his personal advantage, but for the purpose so dear to his heart. Which he did.

The bequest amounted to about $150,000; and the first expenditure was for the establishment of the Modern School of Barcelona, in the year 1901.

It should be said that this was not the first of the Modern School movement in Spain; for previous to that, and for several years, there had sprung up, in various parts of the country, a spontaneous movement towards self-education; a very heroic effort, in a way, considering that the teachers were generally workingmen who had spent their day in the shops, and were using the remainder of their exhausted strength to enlighten their fellow-workers and the children. These were largely night-schools. As there were no means behind these efforts, the buildings in which they were held were of course unsuitable; there was no proper plan of work; no sufficient equipment, and little co-ordination of labor. A considerable percentage of these schools were already on the decline, when Ferrer, equipped with his splendid organizing ability, his teacher's experience, and Mlle. Meunier's[10] endowment, opened the Barcelona School, having as pupils eighteen boys and twelve girls.

So proper to the demand was this effort, that at the end of four years' earnest activity, fifty schools had been established, ten in Barcelona, and forty in the provinces.

In 1906, that is, after five years' work, a banquet was held on Good Friday, at which 1,700 pupils were present.

From 30 to 1,700,—that is something. And a banquet in Catholic Spain on Good Friday! A banquet of children who have bade good-bye to the salvation of the soul by the punishment of the stomach! We here may laugh; but in Spain it was a triumph and a menace, which both sides understood.

I have said that Ferrer brought to his work splendid organizing ability. This he speedily put to purpose by enlisting the co-operation of a number of the greatest scientists of Europe in the preparation of text-books embodying the discoveries of science, couched in language comprehensible to young minds.

So far, I am sorry to say, I have not succeeded in getting copies of these manuals; the Spanish government confiscated most of them, and has probably destroyed them. Still there are some uncaptured sets (one is already in the British Museum) and I make no doubt that within a year or so we shall have translations of most of them.

There were thirty of these manuals all told, comprising the work of the three sections, primary, intermediate, and superior, into which the pupils were divided.

From what I have been able to find out about these books, I believe the most interesting of them all would be the First Reading Book. It was prepared by Dr. Odon de Buen[11], and is said to be at the same time "a speller, a grammar and an illustrated manual of evolution," "the majestic story of the evolution of the cosmos from the atom to the thinking being, related in a language simple, comprehensible to the child."

20,000 copies of this book were rapidly sold.

Imagine what that meant to Catholic schools! That the babies of Spain should learn nothing about eternal punishment for their deadly sins, and *should* learn that they are one in a long line of unfolding life that started in the lowly sea-slime!

The books on geography, physics, and minerology were written in like manner and with like intent by the same author; on anthropology, Dr. Enguerrand wrote, and on evolution, Dr. Letourneau of Paris.

Among the very suggestive works was one on "The Universal Substance," a collaborate production of Albert Bloch and Paraf Javal[12], in which the mysteries of existence are resolved into their chemical equivalents, so that the foundations for magic and miracle are unceremoniously cleared out of the intellectual field.

This book was prepared at Ferrer's special request, as an antidote to ancestral leanings, inherited superstitions, the various outside influences counteracting the influences of the school.

The methods of instruction were modeled after earlier attempts in France, and were based on the general idea that physical and intellectual education must continually supplement each other. That no one is really educated, so long as his knowledge is merely the recollection of what he has read or seen in a book. Accordingly a lesson often consisted of a visit to a factory, a workshop, a studio, or a laboratory, where things were explained and illustrated; or in a class journey to the hills, or the sea, or the open country, where the geological or topographical conditions were studied, or botanical specimens collected and individual observation encouraged.

Very often even book classes were held out of doors, and the children insensibly put in touch with the great pervading influences of nature, a touch too often lost, or never felt at all, in our city environments.

How different was all this from the incomprehensible theology of the Catholic schools to be learned and believed but not understood, the impractical rehearsing of strings of words characteristic of mediaeval survivals! No wonder the Modern Schools grew and grew, and the hatred of the priests waxed hotter and hotter.

Their opportunity came; indeed, they did not wait long.

In the year 1906, on the 31st day of May, not so very long after that Good Friday banquet, occurred the event which they seized upon to crush the Modern School and its founder.

I am not here to speak either for or against Mateo Morral[13]. He was a wealthy young man, of much energy and considerable learning. He had helped to enrich the library of the Modern School and being an excellent linguist, he had offered to make translations of text-books. Ferrer had accepted the offer. That is all Morral had to do with the Modern School.

But on the day of royal festivities, Morral had it in his head to throw a bomb where it would do some royal hurt. He missed his calculations, and the hurt intended did not take place; but after a short interval, finding himself about to be captured, he killed himself.

Think of him as you please: think that he was a madman who did a madman's act; think that he was a generous enthusiast who in an outburst of long chafing indignation at his country's condition wanted to strike a blow at a tyrannical monarchy, and was willing to give his own life in exchange for the tyrant's; or better than this, reserve your judgment, and say that you know not the man nor his personal condition, nor the special external conditions that prompted him; and that without such knowledge he cannot be judged. But whatever you think of Morral, pray why was Ferrer arrested and the Modern School of Barcelona closed? Why was he thrown in prison and kept there for more than a year? Why was it sought to railroad him before a Court Martial, and that attempt failing, the civil trial postponed for all that time?

WHY? WHY?

Because Ferrer taught science to the children of Spain,—and for no other thing. His enemies would have killed him then; but having been compelled to yield an open trial, by the outcry of Europe, they were also compelled to release him. But I imagine I hear, yea hear, the resolute mutter behind the closed walls of the monasteries, the day Ferrer went free. "Go, then; we shall get you again. And then—"

And then they would do what three years later they did,—*damn him to the ditch of* MONTJUICH.

Yea, they shut their lips together like the thin lips of Fate and—waited. The hatred of an order has something superb in it,—it hates so relentlessly, so constantly, so transcendently; its personnel changes, its hate never alters; it wears one priest's face or another's; itself is identical, inexorable; it pursues to the end.

Did Ferrer know this? Undoubtedly in a general way he did. And yet he was so far from conceiving its appalling remorselessness, that even when he found himself in prison again, and utterly in their power, he could not believe that he would not be freed.

What was this opportunity for which the Jesuitry of Spain waited with such terrible security? The Catalonian uprising. How did they know it would come? As any sane man, not over-optimistic, knows that uprising must come in Spain. Ferrer hoped to sap away the foundations of tyranny through peaceful enlightenment. He was right. But they are also right who say that there are other forces hurling towards those foundations; the greatest of these,—*Starvation.*

Now it was plain and simple Starvation that rose to rend its starvers when the Catalonian women rose in mobs to cry against the command that was taking away their fathers and sons to their death in Morocco. The Spanish people did not want the Moroccan war; the Government, in the interest of a number of capitalists, did; but like all governments and all capitalists, it wanted workingmen to do the dying. And they did not want to die, and leave their wives and children to die too. So they rebelled. At first it was the conscious, orderly protest of organized workingmen. But Starvation no more respects the commands of workingmen's unions, than the commands of governments, and other orderly bodies. It has nothing to lose: and it gets away, in its fury, from all management; and it riots.

Where Churches and Monasteries are offensively rich and at ease in the face of Hunger, Hunger takes its revenge. It has long fangs, it rends, and tears, and tramples— the innocent with the guilty—always. It is very horrible! But remember,—remember how much more horrible is the long, slow systematic crushing, wasting, drying of men upon their bones, which year after year, century after century, has begotten the Monster, Hunger. Remember the 50,000 innocent children annually slaughtered, the blinded and the crippled children, maimed and forsaken by social power; and behind the smoke and flame of the burning convents of July, 1909, see the staring of those sightless eyes.

Ferrer instigate that mad frenzy! Oh, no; it was a mightier than Ferrer!

"Our Lady of Pain"—Our Lady of Hunger—Our Lady with uncut nails and wolf-like teeth—Our Lady who bears the Man-flesh in her body that cannon are to tear— Our Lady the Workingwoman of Spain, ahungered. She incarnated the Red Terror.

And the enemies of Ferrer in 1906, as in 1909, knew that such things would come; and they bided their time.

It is one of those pathetic things which destiny deals, that it was only for love's sake—and most for the love of a little child—who died moreover—that the uprising found Ferrer in Spain at all. He had been in England, investigating schools and methods there from April until the middle of June. Word came that his sister-in-law and his niece were ill, so the 19th of June found him at the little girl's bedside. He intended soon after to go to Paris, but delayed to make some inquiries for a friend concerning the proceedings of the Electrical Society of Barcelona. So the storm caught him as it caught thousands of others.

He went about the business of his publishing house as usual, making the observations of an interested spectator of events. To his friend Naquet he sent a postal card on the 26th of July, in which he spoke of the heroism of the women, the lack of co-ordination in the people's movements, and the total absence of leaders, as a curious phenomenon. Hearing soon after that he was to be arrested, he secluded himself for five weeks. The "White Terror" was in full sway; 3,000 men, women, and children had been arrested, incarcerated, inhumanly treated Then the Chief Prosecutor issued the statement that Ferrer was "the director of the revolutionary movement."

Too indignant to listen to the appeals of his friends, he started to Barcelona to give himself up and demand trial. He was arrested on the way.

And they court-martialed him.

The proceedings were utterly infamous. No chance to confront witnesses against him; no opportunity to bring witnesses; not even the books accused of sedition allowed to offer their mute testimony in their own defense; no opportunity given to his defender to prepare; letters sent from England and France to prove what had been the doomed man's purposes and occupations during his stay there, "lost in transit"; the old articles of twenty-four years before, made to appear as if recent utterances; forgeries imposed; and with all this, nothing but hearsay evidence even from his accusers; and yet—he was sentenced to death.

Sentenced to death and shot.

And all Modern Schools closed, and his property sequestrated.

And the Virgin of Toledo may wear her gorgeous robes in peace, since the shadow of the darkness has stolen back over the circle of light he lit.

Only,—somewhere, somewhere, down in the obscurity—hovers the menacing figure of her rival, "Our Lady of Pain." She is still now,—but she is not dead. And if all things be taken from her, and the light not allowed to come to her, nor to her children,—then—some day—she will set her own lights in the darkness.

Ferrer—Ferrer is with the immortals. His work is spreading over the world; it will yet return, and rid Spain of its tyrants.

Sex Slavery

Night in a prison cell! A chair, a bed, a small washstand, four blank walls, ghastly in the dim light from the corridor without, a narrow window, barred and sunken in the stone, a grated door! Beyond its hideous iron latticework, within the ghastly walls,—a man! An old man, gray-haired and wrinkled, lame and suffering. There he sits, in his great loneliness, shut in from all the earth. There he walks, to and fro, within his measured space, apart from all he loves! There, for every night in five long years to come, he will walk alone, while the white age-flakes drop upon his head, while the last years of the winter of life gather and pass, and his body draws near the ashes. Every night, for five long years to come, he will sit alone, this chattel slave, whose hard toil is taken by the State,—and without recompense save that the Southern planter gave his negroes,—every night he will sit there so within those four white walls. Every night, for five long years to come, a suffering woman will lie upon her bed, longing, longing for the end of those three thousand days; longing for the kind face, the patient hand, that in so many years had never failed her. Every night, for five long years to come, the proud spirit must rebel, the loving heart must bleed, the broken home must lie desecrated. As I am speaking now, as you are listening, there within the cell of that accursed penitentiary whose stones have soaked up the sufferings of so many victims, murdered, as truly as any outside their walls, by that slow rot which eats away existence inch-meal,—as I am speaking now, as you are listening, *there sits Moses Harman*[1]*!*

Why? Why, when murder now is stalking in your streets, when dens of infamy are so thick within your city that competition has forced down the price of prostitution to the level of the wages of your starving shirt-makers; when robbers sit in State and national Senate and House, when the boasted "bulwark of our liberties," the elective franchise, has become a U.S. dice-box, wherewith great gamblers play away your liberties; when debauchees of the worst type hold all your public offices and dine off the food of fools who support them, why, then, sits Moses Harman there within his prison cell? If he is so *great* a criminal, why is he not with the rest of the spawn of crime, dining at Delmonico's[2] or enjoying a trip to Europe? If he is so bad a man, why in the name of wonder did he ever get in the penitentiary?

Ah, no; it is not because he has done any evil thing; but because he, a pure enthusiast, searching, searching always for the cause of misery of the kind which he loved with that broad love of which only the pure soul is capable, searched for the data of evil. And searching so he found the vestibule of life to be a prison cell; the holiest and purest part of the temple of the body, if indeed one part can be holier or purer than another, the altar where the most devotional love in truth should be laid, he found this altar ravished, despoiled, trampled upon. He found little babies, helpless, voiceless little things, generated in lust, cursed with impure moral natures, cursed, prenatally, with the germs of disease, forced into the world to struggle and to suffer, to hate themselves, to hate their mothers for bearing them, to hate society and to be hated by it in return,— a bane upon self and race, draining the lees of crime. And he said, this felon with the stripes upon his body, "Let the mothers of the race go free! Let the little children be pure love children, born of the mutual desire for parentage. Let the manacles be broken from the shackled slave, that no more slaves be born, no more tyrants conceived."

He looked, this obscenist, looked with clear eyes into this ill-got thing you call morality, sealed with the seal of marriage, and saw in it the consummation of *im*morality, impurity, and injustice. He beheld every married woman what she is, a bonded slave, who takes her master's name, her master's bread, her master's commands, and serves her master's passion; who passes through the ordeal of pregnancy and the throes of travail at *his* dictation,—not at her desire; who can control no property, not even her own body, without his consent, and from whose straining arms the children she bears may be torn at his pleasure, or willed away while they are yet unborn. It is said the English language has a sweeter word than any other,—*home*. But Moses Harman looked beneath the word and saw the fact,—a prison more horrible than that where he is sitting now, whose corridors radiate over all the earth, and with so many cells, that none may count them.

Yes, our Masters! The earth is a prison, the marriage-bed is a cell, women are the prisoners, and you are the keepers!

He saw, this corruptionist, how in those cells are perpetrated such outrages as are enough to make the cold sweat stand upon the forehead, and the nails clench, and the teeth set, and the lips grow white in agony and hatred. And he saw too how from those cells might none come forth to break her fetters, how no slave dare cry out, how all these murders are done quietly, beneath the shelter-shadow of home, and sanctified by the angelic benediction of a piece of paper, within the silence-shade of a marriage certificate, Adultery and Rape stalk freely and at ease.

94

Yes, for that is adultery where woman submits herself sexually to man, without desire on her part, for the sake of "keeping him virtuous," "keeping him at home," the women say. (Well, if a man did not love me and respect himself enough to be "virtuous" without prostituting me, he might go, and welcome. He has no virtue to keep.) And that is rape, where a man forces himself sexually upon a woman whether he is licensed by the marriage law to do it or not. And that is the vilest of all tyranny where a man compels the woman he says he loves, to endure the agony of bearing children that she does not want, and for whom, as is the rule rather than the exception, they cannot properly provide. It is worse than any other human oppression; it is fairly *God*-like! To the sexual tyrant there is no parallel upon earth; one must go to the skies to find a fiend who thrusts life upon his children only to starve and curse and outcast and damn them! And only through the marriage law is such tyranny possible. The man who deceives a woman outside of marriage (and mind you, such a man will deceive *in* marriage too) may deny his own child, if he is mean enough. He cannot tear it from her arms—he cannot touch it! The girl he wronged, thanks to your very pure and tender morality-standard, may die in the street for want of food. *He* cannot force his hated presence upon her again. But his wife, gentlemen, his wife, the woman he respects so much that he consents to let her merge her individuality into his, lose her identity and become his chattel, his wife he may not only force unwelcome children upon, outrage at his own good pleasure, and keep as a general cheap and convenient piece of furniture, but if she does not get a divorce (and she cannot for such cause) he can follow her wherever she goes, come into her house, eat her food, force her into the cell, *kill* her by virtue of his sexual authority! And she has no redress unless he is indiscreet enough to abuse her in some less brutal but unlicensed manner. I know a case in your city where a woman was followed so for ten years by her husband. I believe he finally developed grace enough to die; please applaud him for the only decent thing he ever did.

Oh, is it not rare, all this talk about the preservation of morality by marriage law! O splendid carefulness to preserve that which you have not got! O height and depth of purity, which fears so much that the children will not know who their fathers are, because, forsooth, they must rely upon their mother's word instead of the hired certification of some priest of the Church, or the Law! I wonder if the children would be improved to know what their fathers have done. I would rather, much rather, not know who my father was than know he had been a tyrant to my mother. I would rather, much rather, be illegitimate according to the statutes of men, than illegitimate according to the unchanging law of Nature. For what is it to be legitimate, born "according to law"? It is to be, nine cases out of ten, the child of a man who acknowledges his fatherhood simply because he is forced to do so, and whose conception of virtue is realized by the statement that "a woman's duty is to keep her husband at home"; to be the child of a woman who cares more for the benediction of Mrs. Grundy³ than the simple honor of her lover's word, and conceives prostitution to be purity and duty when exacted of her by her husband. It is to have Tyranny as your progenitor, and slavery as your prenatal cradle. It is to run the risk of unwelcome birth, "legal" constitutional weakness, morals corrupted before birth, possibly a murder instinct, the inheritance of excessive sexuality or no sexuality, either of which is disease. It is to have the value of a piece of paper, a rag from the tattered garments of the "Social Contract," set above health, beauty, talent or goodness; for I never yet had difficulty in obtaining the admission that illegitimate children are nearly always prettier and brighter than others, even from conservative women. And how supremely disgusting it is to see them look from their own puny, sickly, lust-born children, upon whom lie the chain-traces of their own terrible servitude, look from these to some healthy, beautiful "natural" child, and say, "What a pity its *mother* wasn't virtuous!" Never a word about *their* children's fathers' virtue, they know too much! Virtue! Disease, stupidity, criminality! What an *obscene* thing "virtue" is!

What is it to be illegitimate? To be despised, or pitied, by those whose spite or whose pity isn't worth the breath it takes to return it. To be, possibly, the child of some man contemptible enough to deceive a woman; the child of some woman whose chief crime was belief in the man she loved. To be free from the prenatal curse of a slave mother, to come into the world without the permission of any law-making set of tyrants who assume to corner the earth, and say what terms the unborn must make for the privilege of coming into existence. This is legitimacy and illegitimacy! Choose.

The man who walks to and fro in his cell in Lansing penitentiary to-night, this vicious man, said: "The mothers of the race are lifting their dumb eyes to me, their sealed lips to me, their agonizing hearts to me. They are seeking, seeking for a voice! The unborn in their helplessness, are pleading from their prisons, pleading for a voice! The criminals, with the unseen ban upon their souls, that has pushed them, pushed them to the vortex, out of their whirling hells, are looking, waiting for a voice! *I will be their voice.* I will unmask the outrages of the marriage-bed. I will make known how criminals are born. I will make one outcry that shall be heard, and let what will be, *be!*" He cried out through the letter of Dr. Markland⁴, that a young mother lacerated by unskillful surgery in the birth of her babe, but recovering from a subsequent successful operation, had been stabbed, remorselessly, cruelly, brutally stabbed, not with a knife, but with the procreative organ of her husband, stabbed to the doors of death, and yet there was no redress!

And because he called a spade a spade, because he named that organ by its own name, so given in Webster's dictionary and in every medical journal in the country, because of this Moses Harman walks to and fro in his cell to-night. He gave a concrete example of the effect of sex slavery, and for it he is imprisoned. It remains for us now to carry on the battle, and lift the standard where they struck him down, to scatter broadcast the knowledge of this crime of society against a man and the reason for it; to inquire into this vast system of licensed crime, its cause and its effect, broadly upon the race. The Cause! Let woman ask herself, "Why am I the slave of Man? Why is my brain said not to be the equal of his brain? Why is my work not paid equally with his? Why must my body be controlled by my husband? Why may he take my labor in the household, giving me in exchange what he deems fit? Why may he take my children from me? Will them away while yet unborn?" Let every woman ask.

There are two reasons why, and these ultimately reducible to a single principle— the authoritarian, supreme power, *God*-idea, and its two instruments, the Church— that is, the priests—and the State—that is, the legislators.

From the birth of the Church, out of the womb of Fear and the fatherhood of Ignorance, it has taught the inferiority of woman. In one form or another through the various mythical legends of the various mythical creeds, runs the undercurrent of the belief in the fall of man through the persuasion of woman, her subjective condition as punishment, her natural vileness, total depravity, etc.; and from the days of Adam until now the Christian Church, with which we have specially to deal, has made *woman* the excuse, the scapegoat for the evil deeds of *man*. So thoroughly has this idea permeated Society that numbers of those who have utterly repudiated the Church, are nevertheless soaked in this stupefying narcotic to true morality. So pickled is the male creation with the vinegar of Authoritarianism, that even those who have gone further and repudiated the State still cling to the god, Society as it is, still hug the old theological idea that they are to be "heads of the family"—to that wonderful formula "of simple proportion" that "Man is the head of the Woman even as Christ is the head of the Church." No longer than a week since, an Anarchist (?) said to me, "I will be boss in my own house"—a "Communist-Anarchist," if you please, who doesn't believe in "*my* house." About a year ago a noted libertarian speaker said, in my presence, that his sister, who possessed a fine voice and had joined a concert troupe, should "stay at home with her children; that is *her place.*" The old Church idea! This man was a Socialist, and since an Anarchist; yet his highest idea for woman was serfhood to husband and children, in the present mockery called "home." Stay at home, ye malcontents! Be patient, obedient, submissive! Darn our socks, mend our shirts, wash our dishes, get our meals, wait on us and *mind the children!* Your fine voices are not to delight the public nor yourselves; your inventive genius is not to work, your fine art taste is not to be cultivated, your business faculties are not to be developed; you made the great mistake of being born with them, suffer for your folly! You are *women!* therefore housekeepers, servants, waiters, and child's nurses!

At Macon, in the sixth century, says August Bebel[5], the fathers of the Church met and proposed the decision of the question, "has woman a soul?" Having ascertained that the permission to own a nonentity wasn't going to injure any of their parsnips, a small majority vote decided the momentous question in our favor. Now, holy fathers, it was a tolerably good scheme on your part to offer the reward of your pitiable "salvation or damnation" (odds in favor of the latter) as a bait for the hook of earthly submission; it wasn't a bad sop in those days of Faith and Ignorance. But fortunately fourteen hundred years have made it stale. You, tyrant radicals (?), have no heaven to offer,—you have no delightful chimeras in the form of "merit cards"; you have (save the mark) the respect, the good offices, the smiles—of a slave-holder! This in return for our chains! Thanks!

The question of souls is old—we demand our bodies, now. We are tired of promises, God is deaf, and his church is our worst enemy. Against it we bring the charge of being the moral (or immoral) force which lies behind the tyranny of the State. And the State has divided the loaves and fishes with the Church, the magistrates, like the priests take marriage fees; the two fetters of Authority have gone into partnership in the business of granting patent-rights to parents for the privilege of reproducing themselves, and the State cries as the Church cried of old, and cries now: "See how we protect women!" The State has done more. It has often been said to me, by women with decent masters, who had no idea of the outrages practiced on their less fortunate sisters, "Why don't the wives leave?"

Why don't you run, when your feet are chained together? Why don't you cry out when a gag is on your lips? Why don't you raise your hands above your head when they are pinned fast to your sides? Why don't you spend thousands of dollars when you haven't a cent in your pocket? Why don't you go to the seashore or the mountains, you fools scorching with city heat? If there is one thing more than another in this whole accursed tissue of false society, which makes me angry, it is the asinine stupidity which with the true phlegm of impenetrable dullness says, "Why don't the women leave!" Will you tell me where they will go and what they shall do? When the State, the legislators, has given to itself, the politicians, the utter and absolute control of the opportunity to live; when, through this precious monopoly, already the market of labor is so overstocked that workmen and workwomen are cutting each others' throats for the dear privilege of serving their lords; when girls are shipped from Boston to the south and north, shipped in carloads, like cattle, to fill the dives of New Orleans or the lumber-camp hells of my own state (Michigan), when seeing and hearing these things reported every day, the proper prudes exclaim, "Why don't the women leave," they simply beggar the language of contempt.

When America passed the fugitive slave law compelling men to catch their fellows more brutally than runaway dogs, Canada, aristocratic, unrepublican Canada, still stretched her arms to those who might reach her. But there is no refuge upon earth for the enslaved sex. Right where we are, there we must dig our trenches, and win or die.

This, then, is the tyranny of the State; it denies, to both woman and man, the right to earn a living, and grants it as a privilege to a favored few who for that favor must pay ninety per cent toll to the granters of it. These two things, the mind domination of the Church, and the body domination of the State are the causes of Sex Slavery.

First of all, it has introduced into the world the constructed crime of obscenity: it has set up such a peculiar standard of morals that to speak the names of the sexual organs is to commit the most brutal outrage. It reminds me that in your city you have a street called "Callowhill." Once it was called Gallows' Hill, for the elevation to which it leads, now known as "Cherry Hill," has been the last touching place on earth for the feet of many a victim murdered by the Law. But the sound of the word became too harsh; so they softened it, though the murders are still done, and the black shadow of the Gallows still hangs on the City of Brotherly Love. Obscenity has done the same; it has placed virtue in the shell of an idea, and labelled all "good" which dwells within the sanction of Law and respectable (?) custom; and all bad which contravenes the usage of the shell. It has lowered the dignity of the human body, below the level of all other animals. Who thinks a dog is impure or obscene because its body is not covered with suffocating and annoying clothes? What would you think of the meanness of a man who would put a skirt upon his horse and compel it to walk or run with such a thing impeding its limbs? Why, the "Society for the Prevention of Cruelty to Animals" would arrest him, take the beast from him, and he would be sent to a lunatic asylum for treatment on the score of an *impure* mind. And yet, gentlemen, you expect your wives, the creatures you say you respect and love, to wear the longest skirts and the highest necked clothing, in order to conceal the *obscene human body*. There is no society for the prevention of cruelty to women. And you, yourselves, though a little better, look at the heat you wear in this roasting weather! How you curse your poor body with the wool you steal from the sheep! How you punish yourselves to sit in a crowded house with coats and vests on, because dead Mme. Grundy is shocked at the "vulgarity" of shirt sleeves, or the naked arm!

Look how the ideal of beauty has been marred by this obscenity notion. Divest yourselves of prejudice for once. Look at some fashion-slaved woman, her waist surrounded by a high-board fence called a corset, her shoulders and hips angular from the pressure above and below, her feet narrowest where they should be widest, the body fettered by her everlasting prison skirt, her hair fastened tight enough to make her head ache and surmounted by a thing of neither sense nor beauty, called a hat, ten to one a hump upon her back like a dromedary,—look at her, and then imagine such a thing as that carved in marble! Fancy a statue in Fairmount Park with a corset and bustle on. Picture to yourselves the image of the equestrienne. We are permitted to ride, providing we sit in a position ruinous to the horse; providing we wear a riding-habit long enough to hide the obscene human foot, weighed down by ten pounds of gravel to cheat the Wind in its free blowing, so running the risk of disabling ourselves completely should accident throw us from the saddle. Think how we swim! We must even wear clothing in the water, and run the gauntlet of derision, if we dare battle in the surf minus stockings! Imagine a fish trying to make headway with a water-soaked flannel garment upon it. Nor are you yet content. The vile standard of obscenity even kills the little babies with clothes. The human race is murdered, horribly, "in the name of" Dress.

And in the name of Purity what lies are told! What queer morality it has engendered. For fear of it you dare not tell your own children the truth about their birth; the most sacred of all functions, the creation of a human being, is a subject for the most miserable falsehood. When they come to you with a simple, straightforward question, which they have a right to ask, you say, "Don't ask such questions," or tell some silly hollowlog story; or you explain the incomprehensibility by another—God! You say "God made you." You know you are lying when you say it. You know, or you ought to know, that the source of inquiry will not be dammed up so. You know that what you could explain purely, reverently, rightly (if you have any purity in you), will be learned through many blind gropings, and that around it will be cast the shadow-thought of wrong, embryo'd by your denial and nurtured by this social opinion everywhere prevalent. If you do not know this, then you are blind to facts and deaf to Experience.

Think of the double social standard the enslavement of our sex has evolved. Women considering themselves very pure and very moral, will sneer at the street-walker, yet admit to their homes the very men who victimized the street-walker. Men, at their best, will pity the prostitute, while they themselves are the worst kind of prostitutes. Pity yourselves, gentlemen—you need it!

How many times do you see where a man or woman has shot another through jealousy! The standard of purity has decided that it is right, "it shows spirit," "it is justifiable" to—murder a human being for doing exactly what you did yourself,—love the same woman or same man! Morality! Honor! Virtue!! Passing from the moral to the physical phase; take the statistics of any insane asylum, and you will find that, out of the different classes, unmarried women furnish the largest one. To preserve your cruel, vicious, indecent standard of purity (?) you drive your daughters insane, while your wives are killed with excess. Such is marriage. Don't take my word for it; go through the report of any asylum or the annals of any graveyard.

Look how your children grow up. Taught from their earliest infancy to curb their love natures—restrained at every turn! Your blasting lies would even blacken a child's kiss. Little girls must not be tomboyish, must not go barefoot, must not climb trees, must not learn to swim, must not do anything they desire to do which Madame Grundy has decreed "improper." Little boys are laughed at as effeminate, silly girl-boys if they want to make patchwork or play with a doll. Then when they grow up, "Oh! Men don't care for home or children as women do!" Why should they, when the deliberate effort of your life has been to crush that nature out of them. "Women can't rough it like men." Train any animal, or any plant, as you train your girls, and it won't be able to rough it either. Now *will* somebody tell me why either sex should hold a corner on athletic sports? Why any child should not have free use of its limbs?

These are the effects of your purity standard, your marriage law. This is your work—look at it! Half your children dying under five years of age, your girls insane, your married women walking corpses, your men so bad that they themselves often admit *Prostitution holds against Purity a bond of indebtedness*. This is the beautiful

101

effect of your god, Marriage, before which Natural Desire must abase and belie itself. Be proud of it!

Now for the remedy. It is in one word, the only word that ever brought equity anywhere—LIBERTY! Centuries upon centuries of liberty is the only thing that will cause the disintegration and decay of these pestiferous ideas. Liberty was all that calmed the bloodwaves of religious persecution! You cannot cure serfhood by any other substitution. Not for you to say "in this way shall the race love." Let the race *alone*.

Will there not be atrocious crimes? Certainly. He is a fool who says there will not be. But you can't stop them by committing the arch-crime and setting a block between the spokes of Progress-wheels. You will never get right until you start right.

As for the final outcome, it matters not one iota. I have my ideal, and it is very pure, and very sacred to me. But yours, equally sacred, may be different and we may both be wrong. But certain am I that with free contract, that form of sexual association will survive which is best adapted to time and place, thus producing the highest evolution of the type. Whether that shall be monogamy, variety, or promiscuity matters naught to us; it is the business of the future, to which we dare not dictate.

For freedom spoke Moses Harman, and for this he received the felon's brand. For this he sits in his cell to-night. Whether it is possible that his sentence be shortened, we do not know. We can only try. Those who would help us try, let me ask to put your signatures to this simple request for pardon addressed to Benjamin Harrison. To those who desire more fully to inform themselves before signing, I say: Your conscientiousness is praiseworthy—come to me at the close of the meeting and I will quote the exact language of the Markland letter. To those extreme Anarchists who cannot bend their dignity to ask pardon for an offense not committed, and of an authority they cannot recognize, let me say: Moses Harman's back is bent, low bent, by the brute force of the Law, and though I would never ask anyone to bow for himself, I can ask it, and easily ask it, for him who fights the slave's battle. Your dignity is criminal; every hour behind the bars is a seal to your partnership with Comstock[6]. No one can hate petitions worse than I; no one has less faith in them than I. But for *my* champion I am willing to try any means that invades no other's right, even though I have little hope in it.

If, beyond these, there are those here to-night who have ever forced sexual servitude from a wife, those who have prostituted themselves in the name of Virtue, those who have brought diseased, immoral or unwelcome children to the light, without the means of provision for them, and yet will go from this hall and say, "Moses Harman is an unclean man—a man rewarded by just punishment," then to *you* I say, and may the words ring deep within your ears UNTIL YOU DIE: Go on! Drive your sheep to the shambles! Crush that old, sick, crippled man beneath your Juggernaut! In the name of Virtue, Purity and Morality, do it! In the name of God, Home, and Heaven, do it! In the name of the Nazarene who preached the golden rule, do it! In the name of Justice, Principle, and Honor, do it! In the name of Bravery and Magnanimity put yourself on the side of the robber in the government halls, the murderer in the political convention, the libertine in public places, the whole brute force of the police, the constabulary, the court, and the penitentiary, to persecute one poor old man who stood alone against your licensed crime! Do it. And if Moses Harman dies within your "Kansas Hell," be satisfied *when you have murdered him!* Kill him! And you hasten the day when the Future shall bury you ten thousand fathoms deep beneath its curses. Kill him! And the stripes upon his prison clothes shall lash you like the knout! Kill him! And the insane shall glitter hate at you with their wild eyes, the unborn babes shall cry their blood upon you, and the graves that you have filled in the name of Marriage, shall yield food for a race that will pillory you, until the memory of your atrocity has become a nameless ghost, flitting with the shades of Torquemada, Calvin and Jehovah over the horizon of the World!

Would you smile to see him dead? Would you say, "We are rid of this obscenist"? Fools! The corpse would laugh at you from its cold eyelids! The motionless lips would mock, and the solemn hands, the pulseless, folded hands, in their quietness would write the last indictment, which neither Time nor you can efface. Kill him! And you write his glory and your shame! Moses Harman in his felon stripes stands far above you now, and Moses Harman *dead* will live on, immortal in the race he died to free! Kill him!

The Making of an Anarchist

"Here was one guard, and here was the other at this end; I was here opposite the gate. You know those problems in geometry of the hare and the hounds—they never run straight, but always in a curve, so, see? And the guard was no smarter than the dogs; if he had run straight to the gate he would have caught me."

I t was Peter Kropotkin[1] telling of his escape from the Petro-Paulovsky fortress[2]. Three crumbs on the table marked the relative position of the outwitted guards and the fugitive prisoner; the speaker had broken them from the bread on which he was lunching and dropped them on the table with an amused smile. The suggested triangle had been the starting-point of the life-long exile of the greatest man, save Tolstoy[3] alone, that Russia has produced; from that moment began the many foreign wanderings and the taking of the simple, love-given title "Comrade," for which he had abandoned the "Prince," which he despises.

We were three together in the plain little home of a London workingman—Will Wess[4], a one-time shoemaker—Kropotkin, and I. We had our "tea" in homely English fashion, with thin slices of buttered bread; and we talked of things nearest our hearts, which, whenever two or three Anarchists are gathered together, means present evidences of the growth of liberty and what our comrades are doing in all lands. And as what they do and say often leads them into prisons, the talk had naturally fallen upon Kropotkin's experience and his daring escape, for which the Russian government is chagrined unto this day.

Presently the old man glanced at the time and jumped briskly to his feet: "I am late. Good-by, Voltairine; good-by, Will. Is this the way to the kitchen? I must say good-by to Mrs. Turner and Lizzie[5]." And out to the kitchen he went, unwilling, late though he was, to leave without a hand-clasp to those who had so much as washed a dish for him. Such is Kropotkin, a man whose personality is felt more than any other in the Anarchist movement—at once the gentlest, the most kindly, and the most

105

invincible of men. Communist as well as Anarchist, his very heart-beats are rhythmic with the great common pulse of work and life.

Communist am not I, though my father was, and his father before him during the stirring times of '48, which is probably the remote reason for my opposition to things as they are: at bottom convictions are mostly temperamental. And if I sought to explain myself on other grounds, I should be a bewildering error in logic; for by early influences and education I should have been a nun, and spent my life glorifying Authority in its most concentrated form, as some of my schoolmates are doing at this hour within the mission houses of the Order of the Holy Names of Jesus and Mary. But the old ancestral spirit of rebellion asserted itself while I was yet fourteen, a schoolgirl at the Convent of Our Lady of Lake Huron, at Sarnis, Ontario[6]. How I pity myself now, when I remember it, poor lonesome little soul, battling solitary in the murk of religious superstition, unable to believe and yet in hourly fear of damnation, hot, savage, and eternal, if I do not instantly confess and profess! How well I recall the bitter energy with which I repelled my teacher's enjoinder, when I told her that I did not wish to apologize for an adjudged fault, as I could not see that I had been wrong, and would not *feel* my words. "It is not necessary," said she, "that we should feel what we say, but it is always necessary that we obey our superiors." "I will not lie," I answered hotly, and at the same time trembled lest my disobedience had finally consigned me to torment!

I struggled my way out at last, and was a freethinker when I left the institution, three years later, though I had never seen a book or heard a word to help me in my loneliness. It had been like the Valley of the Shadow of Death, and there are white scars on my soul yet, where Ignorance and Superstition burnt me with their hell-fire in those stifling days. Am I blasphemous? It is their word, not mine. Beside that battle of my young days all others have been easy, for whatever was without, within my own Will was supreme. It has owed no allegiance, and never shall; it has moved steadily in one direction, the knowledge and the assertion of its own liberty, with all the responsibility falling thereon.

This, I am sure, is the ultimate reason for my acceptance of Anarchism, though the specific occasion which ripened tendencies to definition was the affair of 1886–7, when five innocent men were hanged in Chicago for the act of one guilty who still remains unknown[7]. Till then I believed in the essential justice of the American law and trial by jury. After that I never could. The infamy of that trial has passed into history, and the question it awakened as to the possibility of justice under law has passed into clamorous crying across the world. With this question fighting for a hearing at a time when, young and ardent, all questions were pressing with a force which later life would in vain hear again, I chanced to attend a Paine Memorial Convention in an out-of-the-way corner of the earth among the mountains and the snow-drifts of Pennsylvania. I was a freethought lecturer at this time, and had spoken in the afternoon on the lifework of Paine[8]; in the evening I sat in the audience to hear Clarence Darrow[9] deliver an address on Socialism. It was my first introduction to any plan for bettering the condition of the working-classes which furnished some explanation of the course of economic development, and I ran to it as one who has been turning about in darkness runs to the light. I smile now at how quickly I adopted the label "Socialist" and how quickly I cast it aside. Let no one follow my example; but I was young. Six weeks later I was punished for my rashness, when I attempted to argue for my faith with a little Russian Jew named Mozersky, at a debating club in Pittsburgh. He was an Anarchist, and a bit of a Socrates. He questioned me into all kinds of holes, from which I extricated myself most awkwardly, only to flounder into others he had smilingly dug while I was getting out of the first ones. The necessity of a better foundation became apparent: hence began a course of study in the principles of sociology and of modern Socialism and Anarchism as presented in their regular journals. It was Benjamin Tucker's *Liberty*[10], the exponent of Individualist Anarchism, which finally convinced me that "Liberty is not the Daughter but the Mother of Order." And though I no longer hold the particular economic gospel advocated by Tucker, the doctrine of Anarchism itself, as then conceived, has but broadened, deepened, and intensified itself with years.

To those unfamiliar with the movement, the various terms are confusing. Anarchism is, in truth, a sort of Protestantism, whose adherents are a unit in the great essential belief that all forms of external authority must disappear to be replaced by self-control only, but variously divided in our conception of the form of future society. Individualism supposes private property to be the cornerstone of personal freedom; asserts that such property should consist in the absolute possession of one's own product and of such share of the natural heritage of all as one may actually use. Communist-Anarchism, on the other hand, declares that such property is both unrealizable and undesirable; that the common possession and use of all the natural sources and means of social production can alone guarantee the individual against a recurrence of inequality, and its attendants, government and slavery. My personal conviction is that both forms of society, as well as many intermediations, would, in the absence of government, be tried in various localities, according to the instincts and material condition of the people, but that well founded objections may be offered to both. Liberty and experiment alone can determine the best forms of society. Therefore I no longer label myself otherwise than as "Anarchist" simply.

I would not, however, have the world think that I am an "Anarchist by trade." Outsiders have some very curious notions about us, one of them being that Anarchists never work. On the contrary, Anarchists are nearly always poor, and it is only the rich who live without work. Not only this, but it is our belief that every healthy human being will, by the laws of his own activity, choose to work, though certainly not as now, for at present there is little opportunity for one to find his true vocation. Thus I, who in freedom would have selected otherwise, am a teacher of language. Some twelve years since, being in Philadelphia and without employment, I accepted the proposition of a small group of Russian Jewish factory workers to form an evening class in the common English branches. I know well enough that behind the desire to help me to make a living lay the wish that I might thus take part in the propaganda of our common cause. But the incidental became once more the principal, and a teacher of working men and women I have remained from that day. In those twelve years that I have lived and loved and worked with foreign Jews I have taught over a thousand, and found them, as a rule, the brightest, the most persistent and sacrificing students, and in youth dreamers of social ideals. While the "intelligent American" has been cursing him as the "ignorant foreigner," while the short-sighted workingman has been making life for the "sheeny" as intolerable as possible, silent and patient the despised man has worked his way against it all. I have myself seen such genuine heroism in the cause of education practiced by girls and boys, and even by men and women with families, as would pass the limits of belief to the ordinary mind. Cold, starvation, self-isolation, all endured for years in order to obtain the means for study; and, worse than all, exhaustion of body even to emaciation—this is common. Yet in the midst of all this, so fervent is the social imagination of the young that most of them find time besides to visit the various clubs and societies where radical thought is discussed, and sooner or later ally themselves either with the Socialist Sections, the Liberal Leagues, the Single Tax Clubs, or the Anarchist Groups[11]. The greatest Socialist daily in America is the Jewish *Vorwaerts*[12], and the most active and competent practical workers are Jews. So they are among the Anarchists.

I am no propagandist at all costs, or I would leave the story here; but the truth compels me to add that as the years pass and the gradual filtration and absorption of American commercial life goes on, my students become successful professionals, the golden mist of enthusiasm vanishes, and the old teacher must turn for comradeship to the new youth, who still press forward with burning eyes, seeing what is lost forever to those whom common success has satisfied and stupefied. It brings tears sometimes, but as Kropotkin says, "Let them go; we have had the best of them." After all, who are the really old? Those who wear out in faith and energy, and take to easy chairs and soft living; not Kropotkin, with his sixty years upon him, who has bright eyes and the eager interest of a little child; not fiery John Most[13], "the old warhorse of the revolution," unbroken after his ten years of imprisonment in Europe and America; not grey-haired Louise Michel[14], with the aurora of the morning still shining in her keen look which peers from behind the barred memories of New Caledonia[15]; not Dyer D. Lum[16], who still smiles in his grave, I think; nor Tucker, nor Turner, nor Theresa Clairmunt[17], nor Jean Grave[18]—not these. I have met them all, and felt the springing life pulsating through heart and hand, joyous, ardent, leaping into action. Not such are the old, but your young heart that goes bankrupt in social hope, dry-rotting in this stale and purposeless society. Would you always be young? Then be an Anarchist, and live with the faith of hope, though you be old.

I doubt if any other hope has the power to keep the fire alight as I saw it in 1897, when we met the Spanish exiles released from the fortress of Montjuich.[19] Comparatively few persons in America ever knew the story of that torture, though we distributed fifty thousand copies of the letters smuggled from the prison, and some few newspapers did reprint them. They were the letters of men incarcerated on mere suspicion for the crime of an unknown person, and subjected to tortures the bare mention of which makes one shudder. Their nails were torn out, their heads compressed in metal caps, the most sensitive portions of the body twisted between guitar strings, their flesh burned with red hot irons; they had been fed on salt codfish after days of starvation, and refused water; Juan Ollé, a boy nineteen years old, had gone mad; another had confessed to something he had never done and knew nothing of. This is no horrible imagination. I who write have myself shaken some of those scarred hands. Indiscriminately, four hundred people of all sorts of beliefs— Republicans, trade unionists, Socialists, Free Masons, as well as Anarchists—had been cast into dungeons and tortured in the infamous "zero." Is it a wonder that most of them came out Anarchists? There were twenty-eight in the first lot that we met at Euston Station that August afternoon,—homeless wanderers in the whirlpool of London, released without trial after months of imprisonment, and ordered to leave Spain in forty-eight hours! They had left it, singing their prison songs; and still across their dark and sorrowful eyes one could see the eternal Maytime bloom. They drifted away to South America chiefly, where four or five new Anarchist papers have since arisen, and several colonizing experiments along Anarchist lines are being tried. So tyranny defeats itself, and the exile becomes the seed-sower of the revolution.

And not only to the heretofore unaroused does he bring awakening, but the entire character of the world movement is modified by this circulation of the comrades of all nations among themselves. Originally the American movement, the native creation which arose with Josiah Warren in 1829, was purely individualistic; the student of economy will easily understand the material and historical causes for such development. But within the last twenty years the communist idea has made great progress, owing primarily to that concentration in capitalist production which has driven the American workingman to grasp at the idea of solidarity, and, secondly, to the expulsion of active communist propagandists from Europe. Again, another change has come within the last ten years. Till then the application of the idea was chiefly narrowed to industrial matters, and the economic schools mutually denounced each other; to-day a large and genial tolerance is growing. The young generation recognizes the immense sweep of the idea through all the realms of art, science, literature, education, sex relations, and personal morality, as well as social economy, and welcomes the accession to the ranks of those who struggle to realize the free life, no matter in what field. For this is what Anarchism finally means, the whole unchaining of life after two thousand years of Christian asceticism and hypocrisy.

Apart from the question of ideals, there is the question of method. "How do you propose to get all this?" is the question most frequently asked us. The same modification has taken place here. Formerly there were "Quakers" and "Revolutionists"; so there are still. But while they neither thought well of the other, now both have learned that each has his own use in the great play of world forces. No man is in himself a unit, and in every soul Jove still makes war on Christ. Nevertheless, the spirit of Peace grows; and while it would be idle to say that Anarchists in general believe that any of the great industrial problems will be solved without the use of force, it would be equally idle to suppose that they consider force itself a desirable thing, or that it furnishes a final solution to any problem. From peaceful experiment alone can come final solution, and that the advocates of force know and believe as well as the Tolstoyans. Only they think that the present tyrannies provoke resistance. The spread of Tolstoy's "War and Peace" and "The Slavery of Our Times," and the growth of numerous Tolstoy clubs having for their purpose the dissemination of the literature of non-resistance, is an evidence that many receive the idea that it is easier to conquer war with peace. I am one of these. I can see no end of retaliation unless someone ceases to retaliate. But let no one mistake this for servile submission or meek abnegation; my right shall be asserted no matter at what cost to me, and none shall trench upon it without my protest.

Good-natured satirists often remark that "the best way to cure an Anarchist is to give him a fortune." Substituting "corrupt" for "cure," I would subscribe to this; and believing myself to be no better than the rest of mortals, I earnestly hope that as so far it has been my lot to work, and work hard, and for no fortune, so I may continue to the end; for let me keep the intensity of my soul, with all the limitations of my material conditions, rather than become the spineless and ideal-less creation of material needs. My reward is that I live with the young; I keep step with my comrades; I shall die in the harness with my face to the east—the East and the Light.

The Heart of Angiolillo[1]

Some women are born to love stories as the sparks fly upward. You see it every time they glance at you, and you feel it every time they lay a finger on your sleeve. There was a party the other night, and a four-year old baby who couldn't sleep for the noise crept down into the parlor half frightened to death and transfixed with wonderment at the crude performances of an obtuse visitor who was shouting out the woes of Othello. One kindly little woman took the baby in her arms and said: "What would they do to you, if you made all that noise."—"Whip me," whispered the child, her round black eyes half admiration and half terror, and altogether coquettish, as she hid and peered round the woman's neck. And every man in the room forthwith fell in love with her, and wanted to smother his face in the bewitching rings of dark hair that crowned the dainty head, and carry her about on his shoulders, or get down on his hands and knees to play horse for her, or let her walk on his neck, or obliterate his dignity in any other way she might prefer. The boys tolerated their fathers with a superior "huh!" Fourteen or fifteen years from now they will be playing the humble cousin of the horse before the same little ringed-haired lady, and having sported Nick Bottom's ears[2] to no purpose, half a dozen or so will go off and hang themselves, or turn monk, or become "bold, bad men," and revenge themselves on the sex. But her conquests will go on, and when those gracious rings are white as snow, the children of those boys will follow in their grandfathers' and fathers' steps and dangle after her, and make drawings on their fly leaves of that sweet kiss-cup of a mouth of hers, and call her their elder sister, and other devotional names. And the other girls of her generation, who were not born with that marvelous entangling grace in every line and look, will dread her and spite her, and feel mean satisfaction when some poor fool does swallow laudanum on her account. Smiles of glacial virtue will creep over their faces like slippery sunshine, when one by one her devotees come trailing off to them to say that such a woman could never fill a man's heart nor become the ornament of

113

his hearthstone; the quiet virtues that wear, are all their desire; of course they have just been studying her character and that of the foolish men who dance her attendance, but even those are not doing it with any serious motives. And the neglected girls will serve him with home-made cake and wine which he will presently convert into agony in that pearl shell ear of hers. And all the while the baby will have done nothing but be what she was born to be through none of her own choosing, which is her lot and portion; and that is another thing the gods will have to explain when the day comes that they go on trial before men; which is the real day of judgment.

But this isn't the baby's story, which has yet to be made, but the story of one who somehow received a wrong portion. Some inadvertent little angel in the destiny shop took down her name when the heroine of a romance was called for, and put her where she shouldn't have been, and then ran off to play no doubt, not stopping to look twice. For even the most insouciant angel that looked twice would have seen that Effie was no woman to play the game of hearts, and there's only one thing more undiscerning than an angel, and that is a social reformer. Effie ran up against both.

They say she had blood in her girlhood, that it shone red and steady through that thin, pure skin of hers; but when I saw her, with her nursing baby in her arms, down in the smutching grime of London, there was only a fluctuant blush, a sort of pink ghost of blood, hovering back and forth on her face. And that was for shame of the poverty of her neat bare room. Not that she had ever known riches. She was the daughter of Scotch peasants, and had gone out to service when she was still a child; her chest was hollowed in and her back bowed with that unnatural labor. There was no gloss on the pale sandy hair, no wilding tendrils clinging round the straight smooth forehead, no light of coquetry or grace in the glimmering blue eyes, no beauty in her at all, unless it lay in the fine, hard sculptured line of her nose and mouth and chin when she turned her head sideways. You could read in that line that having spoken a word to her heart, she would not forget it nor unsay it; and if it took her down into Gethsemane, she would never cry out though by all forsaken.

And that was where it had taken her then. Some ready condemner of all that has been tried for less than a thousand years, will say it was because she had the just reward of those who, holding that love is its own sanction and that it cannot be anything but degraded by seeking permissions from social authorities, live their love lives without

114

the consent of Church and State. But you and I know that the same dark garden has awaited the woman whose love has been blessed by both, and that many such a life lamp has flickered out in a night as profound as poverty and utter loneliness could make it. So if it was justice to Effie, what is it to that other woman? In truth, justice had nothing to do with it; she loved the wrong man, that was all; and married or unmarried, it would have been the same, for a formula doesn't make a man, nor the lack of it unmake him. The fellow was superior in intellect. It is honesty only which can wring so much from those who knew them both, for as to any other thing she sat as high over him as the stars are. Not that he was an actively bad man; just one of those weak, uncertain, tumbling about characters, having sense enough to know it is a fine thing to stand alone, and vanity enough to want the name without the game, and cowardice enough to creep around anything stronger than itself, and hang there, and spread itself about, and say, "Lo, how straight am I!" And if the stronger thing happens to be a father or a brother or some such tolerant piece of friendly, self-sufficient energy, he amuses himself awhile, and finally gives the creeper a shake and says, "Here, now, go hang on somebody else if you can't stand alone", and the world says he should have done it before. But if it happens to be a mother or a sister or a wife or a sweetheart, she encourages him to think he is a wonderful person, that all she does is really his own merit, and she is proud and glad to serve him. If after a while she doesn't exactly believe it any more, she says and does the same; and the world says she is a fool,— which she is. But if, in some sudden spurt of masculine self-assertiveness, she decides to fling him off, the world says she is an un-womanly woman,—which again she is; so much the better.

Effie's creeper dabbled in literature. He wanted to be a translator and several other things. His appearance was mild and gentlemanly, even super-modest. He always spoke respectfully of Effie, and as if momentously impressed with a sense of duty towards her. They had started out to realize the free life together, and the glory of the new ideal had beckoned them forward. So no doubt he believed, for a pretender always deceives himself worse than anybody else. But still, at that particular period, he used to droop his head wearily and admit that he had made a great mistake. It was nobody's fault but his own, but of course—Effie and he were hardly fitted for each other. She could not well enter into his hopes and ambitions, never having had the opportunity to develop when she was younger. He had hoped to stimulate her in that direction, but he feared it was too late. So he said in a delicate and gentlemanly way, as he went from one house to the other, and was invited to dinner and supper and made himself believe he was looking for work. Effie, meanwhile, was taking home boys' caps to make, and worrying along incredibly on bread and tea, and walking the streets with the baby in her arms when she had no caps to make.

Of course when a man drinks other people's teas a great many times, and sits in their houses, and borrows odd shillings now and then, and assumes the gentleman, he is ultimately brought to the necessity of asking some one to tea with him; so one spring night the creeper approached Effie rather dubiously with the statement that he had asked two or three acquaintances to come in the next evening, and he supposed she would need to prepare tea. The girl was just fainting from starvation then, and she asked him wearily where he thought she was to get it. He cast about a while in his pusillanimous way for things that *she* might do, and finally proposed that she pawn the baby's dress,—the white dress she had made from one of her own girlhood dresses, and the only thing it had to wear when she took it out for air. That was the limit, even for Effie. She said she would take anything of her own if she had it, but not the baby's; and she turned her face to the wall and clung to the child.

When the tea-time came next day she went out with the baby and walked up and down the surging London streets looking in the windows and crushing back tears. What the creeper did with his guests she never knew, for she did not return till long after dusk, when she was too weary to wander any more, and she found no one there but himself and a dark stranger, who spoke little and with an Italian accent, but who measured her with serious, intense eyes. He listened to the creeper, but he looked at her; she was quite fagged out and more bloodless than ever as she sat motionless on the edge of the bed. When he went away he lifted his hat to her with the grace of an old time courtier, and begged her pardon if he had intruded. Some days after that he came in again, and brought a toy for the baby, and asked her if he might carry the child out a little for her; it looked sickly shut up there, but he knew it must be heavy for her to carry. The creeper suddenly discovered that he could carry the baby.

All this happened in the days when a pious queen sat on the throne of Spain. With eyes turned upward in much holiness, she failed to see the things done in her prisons, or hear the groans that rose up from the "zero" chamber in the fortress of Montjuich[3], though all Europe heard, and even in America the echo rang. While she told her beads her minister gave the order to "torture the Anarchists"; and scarred with red-hot irons, maimed and deformed and maddened with the nameless horrors that the good devise to correct the bad, even unto this day the evidences of that infamous order live. But two men do not live,—the one who gave the order, and the one who revenged it.

It happened one night, in April, that Effie and the creeper and their sometime visitor met all three in one of those long low smothering London halls where many movements have originated, which in their developed proportions have taken possession of the House of Commons, and even stirred the dust in the House of Lords. There was a crowd of excited people talking all degrees of sense and nonsense in every language of the continent. Letters smuggled from the prison had been received; new tales of torture were passing from mouth to mouth; fresh propositions to arouse a general protest from civilization were bubbling up with the anger of every indignant man and woman. Drifting to the buzzing knots Effie heard some one translating: it was the letter of the tortured Noguès[4], who a month later was shot beneath the fortress wall. The words smote her ears like something hot and stinging:

"You know I am one of the three accusers (the other two are Ascheri and Molas) who figure in the trial. I could not bear the atrocious tortures of so many days. On my arrest I spent eight days without food or drink, obliged to walk continually to and fro or be flogged; and as if that did not suffice, I was made to trot as though I were a horse trained at the riding school, until worn with fatigue I fell to the ground. Then the hangmen burnt my lips with red-hot irons, and when I declared myself the author of the attempt they replied, 'You do not tell the truth. We know that the author is another one, but we want to know your accomplices. Besides you still retain six bombs, and along with little Oller you deposited two bombs in the Rue Fivaller. Who are your accomplices?'

"In spite of my desire to make an end of it I could not answer anything. Whom should I accuse since all are innocent? Finally six comrades were placed before me, whom I had to accuse, and of whom I beg pardon. Thus the declarations and the accusations that I made.... I cannot finish; the hangmen are coming. Noguès."

Sick with horror Effie would have gone away, but her feet were like lead. She heard the next letter, the pathetic prayer of Sebastian Sunyer, indistinctly; the tortures had already seared her ears, but the crying for help seemed to go up over her head like great sobs; she felt herself washed round, sinking, in the desperate pain of it. The piteous reiteration, "Listen you with your honest hearts," "you with your pure souls," "good and right-minded people," "good and right-feeling people," wailed through her like the wild pleading of a child who, shrieking under the whip "Dear papa, good, sweet papa, please don't whip me, please, please," seeks terror-wrung flattery to escape the lash. The last cry, "Aid us in our helplessness; think of our misery," made her quiver like a reed. She walked away and sat down in a corner alone; what could she do, what

117

could any one do? Miserable creature that she was herself, her own misery seemed so worthless beside that prison cry. And she thought on, "Why does he want to live at all, why does any one want to live, why do I want to live myself?"

After a while the creeper and his friend came to her, and the latter sat down beside her, undemonstrative as usual. At the next buzz in the room they two were left alone. She looked at him once as she said, "What do you think the people will do about it?"

He glanced at the crowd with a thin smile: "Do? Talk."

In a little time he said quietly: "It does you no good here. I will take you home and come back for David afterward." She had no idea of contradicting him; so they went out together. At the threshold of her room he said firmly, "I will come in for a few minutes; I have to speak to you."

She struck a light, put the baby on the bed, and looked at him questioningly. He had sat down with his back against the wall, and with rigidly folded arms stared straight ahead of him. Seeing that he did not speak, she said softly, falling into her native dialect, as all Scotch women do when they feel most: "I canna get thae poor creetyer's cries oot o' ma head. It's no human."

"No," he said shortly, and then with a sudden look at her, "Effie, what do you think love is?"

She answered him with surprised eyes and said nothing. He went on: "You love the child, don't you? You do for it, you serve it. That shows you love it. But do you think it's love that makes David act as he does to you? If he loved you, would he let you work as you work? Would he live off you? Wouldn't he wear the flesh off his fingers instead of yours? He doesn't love you. He isn't worth you. He isn't a bad man, but he isn't worth you. And you make him less worth. You ruin him, you ruin yourself, you kill the child. I can't see it any more. I come here, and I see you weaker every time, whiter, thinner. And I know if you keep on you'll die. I can't see it. I want you to leave him; let me work for you. I don't make much, but enough to let you rest. At least till you are well. I would wait till you left him of yourself, but I can't wait when I see you dying like this. I don't want anything of you, except to serve you, to serve the child because it's yours. Come away, to-night. You can have my room; I'll go somewhere else. To-morrow I'll find you a better place. You needn't see him any more. I'll tell him myself. He won't do anything, don't be afraid. Come." And he stood up.

Effie had sat astonished and dumb. Now she looked up at the dark tense eyes above her, and said quietly, "I dinna understand."

A sharp contraction went across the strong bent face: "No? You don't understand what you are doing with yourself? You don't understand that I love you, and I can't see it? I don't ask you to love me; I ask you to let me serve you. Only a little, only so much as to give you health again; is that too much? You don't know what you are to me. Others love beauty, but I—I see in you the eternal sacrifice; your thin fingers that always work, your face—when I look at it, it's just a white shadow; you are the child of the people, that dies without crying. Oh, let me give myself for you. And leave this man, who doesn't care for you, doesn't know you, thinks you beneath him, uses you. I don't want you to be his slave any more."

Effie clasped her hands and looked at them; then she looked at the sleeping baby, smoothed the quilt, and said quietly: "I didna take him the day to leave him the morra. It's no my fault if ye're daft aboot me."

The dark face sharpened as one sees the agony in a dying man, but his voice was very gentle, speaking always in his blurred English: "No, there is no fault in you at all. Did I accuse you?"

The girl walked to the window and looked out. Some way it was a relief from the burning eyes which seemed to fill the room, no matter that she did not look at them. And staring off into the twinkling London night, she heard again the terrible sobs of Sebastian Sunyer's letter rising up and drowning her with its misery. Without turning around she said, low and hard, "I wonder ye can thenk aboot thae things, an' yon deils burnin' men alive."

The man drew his hand across his forehead. "Would you like to hear that they,—one,—the worst of them, was dead?"

"I thenk the worl' wadna be muckle the waur o't," she answered, still looking away from him. He came up and laid his hand on her shoulder. "Will you kiss me once? I'll never ask again." She shook him off: "I dinna feel for't." "Good-bye then. I'll go back for David." And he returned to the hall and got the creeper and told him very honestly what had taken place; and the creeper, to his credit be it said, respected him for it, and talked a great deal about being better in future to the girl. The two men parted at the foot of the stairs, and the last words that echoed through the hallway were: "No, I am going away. But you will hear of me some day."

Now, what went on in his heart that night no one knows; nor what indecision still kept him lingering fitfully about Effie's street a few days more; nor when the indecision finally ceased; for no one spoke to him after that, except as casual acquaintances meet, and in a week he was gone. But what he did the whole world knows; for even the Queen of Spain came out of her prayers to hear how her torturing prime minister had been shot at Santa Agueda, by a stern-faced man, who, when the widow, grief-mad, spit in his face, quietly wiped his cheek, saying, "Madam, I have no quarrel with women." A few weeks later they garrotted him, and he said one word before he died,— one only, "Germinal."[5]

Over there in the long low London hall the gabbling was hushed, and some one murmured how he had sat silent in the corner that night when all were talking. The creeper passed round a book containing the history of the tortures, watching it jealously all the while, for said he, "Angiolillo gave it to me himself; he had it in his own hands."

Effie lay beside the baby in her room, and hid her face in the pillow to keep out the stare of the burning eyes that were dead; and over and over again she repeated, "Was it my fault, was it my fault?" The hot summer air lay still and smothering, and the immense murmur of the city came muffled like thunder below the horizon. Her heart seemed beating against the walls of a padded room. And gradually, without losing consciousness, she slipped into the world of illusion; around her grew the stifling atmosphere of the torture-chamber of Montjuich, and the choked cries of men in agony. She was sure that if she looked up she should see the demoniac face of Portas, the torturer. She tried to cry, "Mercy, mercy," but her dry lips clave. She had a whirling sensation, and the illusion changed; now there was the clank of soldiers' arms, a moment of insufferable stillness as the garrotte shaped itself out of the shadows in her eyes, then loud and clear, breaking the sullen quiet like the sharp ringing of a storm-bringing wind, "Germinal." She sprang up: the long vibration of the bell of St. Pancras was waving through the room; but to her it was the prolongation of the word, "Germ-inal-l-l—germ-inal-l-l—" Then suddenly she threw out her arms in the darkness, and whispered hoarsely, "Ay, I'll kiss ye the noo."

An hour later she was back at the old question, "Was it my fault?"

Poor girl, it is all over now, and all the same to the grass that roots in her bone, whether it was her fault or not. For the end that the man who had loved her foresaw, came, though it was slow in the coming. Let the creeper get credit for all that he did.

He stiffened up in a year or so, and went to Paris and got some work; and there the worn little creature went to him, and wrote to her old friends that she was better off at last. But it was too late for that thin shell of a body that had starved so much; at the first trial she broke and died. And so she sleeps and is forgotten. And the careless boy-angel who mixed all these destinies up so unobservantly has never yet whispered her name in the car of the widowed Lady Canovas del Castillo.

Nor will the birds that fly thither carry it now; for *it was not "Effie."*

The Mexican Revolt

At last we see a genuine awakening of a people, not to political demands alone, but to economic ones,—fundamentally economic ones. And in the brief period of a few months, some millions of human beings have sprung to a full consciousness of a system of wrong, beginning where all slaveries begin, in the sources of life. They have struck for LAND AND LIBERTY. And even if their revolt shall be crushed by the mailed hand of the United States Government (for I do not believe the present nondescript thing calling itself a government, in Mexico, has craft or power to pacify or crush all the seething elements of rebellion), yet it has set a foremost mark upon the record of human demand, from which hereafter there will be no retreat. From now on, when an oppressed people revolt, they will not demand less.

"Events are the true Schoolmasters," I hear the justified voice of my dead Comrade Lum[1] calling triumphantly from his grave. For years and years the brothers Magon[2] and their coworkers in and out of Mexico have been voices crying in the wilderness which some few thousands at best have heard. But in the storm-wind of popular revolt, rising, no prophet could have foretold when, nor gazer at the aftermath just why it was the chosen hour, in that strong clean-sweeping of the psychic atmosphere, millions of unlettered and otherwise ignorant people saw, as with lightning sharpness cutting a black night, the foundation of all their wrong, and heard the slogan "Land and Liberty" to which their ears were so long deaf,—heard it, raised it, acted on it, are acting on it. With that clear and direct perception of the needful thing to do which lettered men, men of complex lives, nearly always lack, being befogged by too many lights, they move straight upon their purpose, hew down the landmarks, burn the records of the title-deeds.

So do the plain people. Temporizing men, sophisticated men, men of books and theories, men made timid with much mind, Hamlets all,—*they* devise solemn indirections; they figure on compensation schemes, on taxation fooleries, on how-to-do and how-not-to-do at the same time. The simple man says, "No: you have told us, and truly, that this land was filched away from us by a paper-title scheme. Its power lay in our admitting its right. Well, we no longer admit it; we destroy it. The land is ours; we take it." And they have driven off the paper-title men, and are working the ground on hundreds of ranches.

It is true there were other millions asleep in the storm; true that many of the awakened have been quieted with political hocus-pocus; true that a hundred and one reactionary forces are battling on the same ground. It is true that the world at large, outside of Mexico, is but little informed as to the real struggle. But that does not alter or diminish the truth that the Slaves of Our Times, in a nation-wide revolt, have smitten the Beast of Property in Land. And once a great human demand is so made, it is never let go again. Future revolts will go on from there; they will never fall behind it.

At present the great press is saying little of the chaos in the Mexican situation, though for the last few days, since as news purveyors they cannot keep entirely silent, small hinting editorials are creeping in, pointing interventionwards, "in case disturbances are not pacified." No doubt the United States Government would prefer to preserve its hypocritical pretense of abstinent impartiality. It hopes its catspaw will safely pull the chestnuts out of the fire. It is comfortable to pose as the disinterested friend of peace in our sister republic, so long as American landlord powers in Mexico are undisturbed, or so long as the Mexican branch of the Capitalistic Defense Association is able to tend to its division. But one thing has been pretty plain since the provisional government assumed its functions: "Barkis is willin',"—but not effulgently able. People who have once taken up arms and felt the satisfaction of ridding themselves of one tyrant, of doing rude justice in opening prison doors, of seeing a whole confraternity of office-holders and office-seekers in anxiety to placate them, are not so unready to take up arms again; especially when the whole mass of discontent is leavened with conscious revolutionists who are crying the means of social regeneration in their ears.

It is very plain now that the provisional governors are treading on thin crust, and the elections instead of steadying the human subsoil down to mortuary rigidity, may prove the prelude to more violent eruptions. In that case, the reluctant (?) hand at Washington may be forced to play—clubs! on its own responsibility.

Meanwhile, what have the revolutionary elements of the United States to say about it? I almost sneered as I wrote "revolutionary elements," for candor compels us to inquire where they are. Time was when some people thought the Single Tax³ was based on a fundamentally revolutionary idea, the final expropriation of the landlord by the people. The Single Tax papers, however, have said as little as possible about the great Land cry of the Mexican revolutionists, have laid all stress upon the political mirage-chasing by which Madero[4] and his coadjutors side-tracked the uprising of May, and have refused to print the Manifestoes and Appeals of the Mexican Liberal Party, to afford the publicity of their columns to the real demands of the revolutionists, that their readers might give their sympathy and support, and the influence of their understanding. They were waiting, they said, for Madero to pronounce himself upon the land question! I opine they have still quite some wait coming.

From all which, it seriously appears that the expropriation of the landlords by the people, the restoration of the land to the people, is not the object of the single tax movement; on the contrary, the object is the establishment of the single tax itself,—not as a working means to a great end, the establishment of the equal right of all to the use of natural resources, but as a neat sleight-of-hand method for collecting revenue; at best, a way of getting rid of landlords by fooling them into getting rid of themselves, not because they are robbers to be got rid of, but because it's such a clever trick to play! Men are to demand the land, not that they may get the land, but that the demand may serve as an excuse for instituting the Single Tax!

If this is not the interpretation we are to put upon it, then how else are we to read the conspicuous silence of the Single Tax press concerning this great agrarian revolt? Millions of people have been demonstrating their appreciation that The Land for All the People is the primary foundation for a better economic structure. They have taken a more direct route than the single tax. And the land agitators are silent!

Time was when Socialism was a revolutionary word. And there are still some Socialists who are international revolutionists. But the official political Socialist Party,—bah! If ever the vitiating influence of the marriage of Socialism with Politics (that old Bluebeard husband of so many fine young wives) was demonstrated beyond disputation, it has been in the official attitude of Socialists towards this spontaneous manifestation of the Mexican people.

The utterances of Victor Berger[5], "the Socialist Congressman" (we receive this information as to his status with painful reiteration at least once a column in every issue of the Chicago *Daily Socialist*), concerning "the bandits of Mexico" were enough to make the authors of the Communist Manifesto repudiate their name. Those strong souls who asserted that "the Communists everywhere support every revolutionary movement against the existing social and political order of things," and appealed to "Workingmen of All Countries to unite,"—what would they have in common with a smug occupier of a congressional seat, who in a strongly marked German accent makes anti-immigration speeches against Slavs and Italians in the name of protection to American labor (?) and who directs his secretary to say, concerning the Mexican revolt, that "the Socialist Party can afford to have no connection with this movement" (?). In the light of this and similar utterances in the Socialist press (I have even learned on good authority that one Socialist editor really desires United States annexation of Mexico, but dares not advocate it yet, "because it would be unpopular" with Socialist readers) it would appear that the distribution of the Communist Manifesto by the Socialist Party is about of a piece with the distribution of the Christian Gospels by the Christian Church; in both cases, it is traditional literature, which nobody is supposed to take seriously.

Instead of giving even the news of international revolutionary movements (often one looks in vain for any), or the economic ground-plan of Socialism, we have columns of vice-crusading, sporting pages, and veritable hot-air balloons of self-inflation for having assisted in some relatively trivial petition. Only in their correspondence columns is there some occasional evidence of the indignant spirit of a true Socialist, outraged by all this trimming to suit the wind, this flunkeying to the respectable element, this suffocation of revolutionary principle and sentiment under a time-serving mantle of political prudence and cheap catering. Yes; Politics is nicely bluebearding Socialism. How far away is all this from the serious, intent spirit which watches and welcomes the manifestations of the people themselves—no matter what their degree of development or enlightenment—as the real indications of how the Race will come into its own! Not according to any men's preconcerted program, not by any little platform-prescription, not by any carefully selected route, not by anybody's plan of campaign to make an "educated, class-conscious," etc. *ad nauseam* vote-casting machine; but in their own unforeseen and unforseeable, unpredetermined, by-the-hour-and-circumstance-decided way, as the peoples always move,—as Life, which is greater than the peoples, always moves.

And the business of the revolutionist, the Seeker for the Changes of Old Forms, the dreamer of Liberty and Plenty, is to be with them in their struggle, in their victory, in their defeat, whenever, wherever, the people rise.

Hail to our brothers, the Mexican peons, who are too unlettered to read Henry George's gospel[6], but who have discharged their landlords and set to working the ground for themselves.

Hail to the Mexican strikers, who likely are too ignorant to pursue a course in the "Evolution of Class-consciousness," but who are apparently very alive to the fact that Now is the hour to Strike for better conditions,—the hour of governmental weakness and popular strength.

Hail to the Mexican Revolution, victorious or defeated. And hail to the next that rises!

The Drama of the Nineteenth Century

The passions of men are actors, events are their motions, all history is their speech. In the long play of the ages a human being sometimes becomes an event; a nation's passion takes a *personnel*. Such beings are the expression of the gathered mind-force of millions.

He only who keeps himself aloof from all feeling can remain the spectator of the hour. All that humanity which is held within the beating, coiling, surging tides of passion, it has no individuality; it sinks its personality to become a vein in the limb of this giant, a pulse in the heart of that Titan. Only when out of the spirit of the times the event is born, only when the act is complete, the curtain rung down, only then does the intellectuality of the vein, the pulse, rise to the level of the dispassionate. Only then can it survey a tragedy and say, "this was necessary"—a reaction, and say, "this was inevitable."

Yet as a drop of blood is a quivering, living, flashing ruby beside the dead, pale pearl of a stagnant pool, so is one drop of feeling a shining thing, a living thing, beside the deadness of the intellect which judges while the heart is stone; beside those quiet bayous of brain which reflect back the images before them very purely, very stilly, giving no heed to the great rushing river of heart that rolls on, hurries on so close beside them. Bye and bye, bye and bye, the river reaches the grand, great sea, and the waters spread out calm and deep, so deep that the stars of the upper sea, the lights of the higher life, shine far up from them as a babe smiles up into its mother's eyes, and up still to the distant source of the light within the eyes.

It is to men and women of feeling that I speak, men and women of the millions, men and women in the hurrying current! Not to the shallow egotist who holds himself apart and with the phariseeism of intellectuality exclaim, "I am more just than thou;" but to those whose every fiber of being is vibrating with emotion as aspen leaves quiver in the breath of Storm! To those whose hearts swell with a great pity at the pitiful toil of women, the weariness of young children, the handcuffed helplessness of strong men! To those whose blood runs quick along the veins like wild-fire on the dry grass of prairies when the wind whirls aside the smokings of the holocaust, and, courting the teeth of the flame, the black priestess, Injustice, beckons it on while her feet stamp on the cinders of the sacrifice! To those whose heart-strings thrill at the touch of Love like the sweet, low musical laugh of childhood, or thrum with hate like the singing vibration of the bowstring speeding the arrow of Death! I speak to those whose eyes behold all things through a haze of gray, or rose, or gold born of their surroundings, and which mist slips away only when the gaze is leveled on that dead Past whose passions and whose deeds are ended: to whom the present is always a morning with the dimness of morning around it—the past clear and still—no vail [sic] on its face, for the vail has been shredded asunder.

For he only who intensely perceives the nature of his surroundings, he, and he only, who has felt, and keenly felt, all the throbs and throes of life, can judge with any degree of truth of the action of that which is past. You, you who have loved, you who have joyed, you who have suffered, it belongs to you to people the silent streets of the silent cities with forms now vanished, to comprehend something of the passions which animated their action; it belongs to you to understand how the fury of a great energy, striking terrible aimless blows in the dark, may yet, across the chasm of awful mistake, touch the hand of a greater Justice.

If from a panoramic survey of the past some wisdom may be gathered, then let the dramas of old ages tell us what have been the mainsprings of their motions; so we shall understand what action ushered in the drama of the nineteenth century.

"Westward the Star of Empire holds its way." Following the course of those majestic spheres of fire which whirl each in his vast ellipse, trending away in a long, southwesterly path athwart the heavens, obedient to that superior attraction which through all the universe holds good, the attraction of greater for lesser things, the tide of life upon our world has risen and swelled and rolled away to the south and west. Away in the orient source of the sunlight, away where the glitter of ice shines up to meet the morning, nations have risen and plunged down impetuously over the sleeping regions of darkness and of heat, bearing with them the breeze-stirring life of the north and the on-trending light of the east. And out of this conquered earth have arisen the mixed passions of another life and another race. Still the governing stars wheel on, and the tide of life which paused only to gather strength rolls up again;

and once more a nation is born, and new passions dictate the action of the peoples. Down, down it sweeps over the Altaian hills, over the Himalayan ranges, over the land of the Euphrates and Tigris, over the deserts of Arabia the barren, the fields of Arabia the stony, and the grasses and waters of Arabia the happy, to those low shores, the home of dark mausoleums and darker pyramids, on to the now classic land of Greece, and golden Italy and the home of the dark-eyed Moors. Sweeps till it touches the frothing sea, and brightly borne upon its upper crest shines the glory, the splendor, the magnificence of the warring powers which dictated the action of Greece and Rome. For centuries their hosted spears send back the burnished glitter of the sun, and then—the light dies out; down rushing from the North-land again the tide of vigor pours, and the health and strength of barbarism conquers the weakness of a tottering civilization! Far away—away over the miles of sparkling sea, in the darkness and the silence a continent lies waiting; waiting for the coming of the light, waiting for the swelling of the tide. Slowly at last a ripple creeps up over the strange beach, and the flood rolls on, and again a continent becomes a cradle, and the Empire Star sends on its rays to kiss the forehead of the rising world. Over the breadth of all our continent that mighty wave is flowing still.

Standing to-day almost upon the threshold of another world, and looking back down this long-vista'd past, gradually there dawns upon Reflection's vision, gradually there grows out of the confusion of forms and the Babel of sounds, a clearer perception of the motor powers which have dictated the action of this past, a better idea of the grand plot which, driven by these motor powers, the passions are working out. For, above the long procession of scenes and events, above the monster massings of happiness and woe, above the War and Peace of centuries, above the nations that have risen and fallen, above the life and above the grave, the winged and shadowy embodiments of two great ideas float and rest. And those two principles are called Authority and Liberty; or, if it please you better, *God* and Liberty. The one is all clad in the purple and scarlet of pomp and of power, while the other stands a glorious shining center in the white radiance of Freedom.

Yet not always; far back in time Authority stood on thrones and altars, with the plumed sables of despotism waving on his brow, while in his hands he held two iron gyves, the one to fetter thought, the other to fetter action; and these two gyves were called *the Church and State.*

Liberty! Ah, Liberty was then a name scarcely to pass the lips; dreamed of only in solitude, spoken of only in dungeons! Yet out of the blackest mire the whitest lily blooms! Out of the dungeon, out of the sorrow, out of the sacrifice, out of the pain, grew this child of the heart; and pure and strong she grew until the sabled plumes have tottered on the despot's brow, and a great palsy shakes the hands that once so firmly held the gyves of Church and State. For, ever seeking to overthrow each other, the one for the aggrandizement of self, the other for the love of all mankind, these two powers have contended; and every energy, every passion, every desire, good or evil, has been ranged on this side or on that, blunderingly or wisely, and nations have swung to and fro in their breath as upon a hinge. And one by one the powers of Authority have been crippled, and step by step Liberty has advanced, until to-day mankind is beginning to measure the forces that, struggling blindly together, are yet evolving light, to drink in the sublime ideal of freedom. Yet, oh, how long the struggle with vested ignorance, with greed in power!

When upon the Drama of the Nineteenth Century the curtain rose, Liberty, triumphant on the younger shores, lay prone and hurled in Europe. Against fifteen centuries of crowned and throned and tithed curse and woe unutterable, she had risen with such a fearful convulsive strength that when she had mown down king, priest and throne, and gorged the guillotine with blood, she sank back, exhausted from the struggle, and the hated tyrant rose again. The wild desire to conquer, to possess, to control, to hold in subjection, seemed to dominate with an unconquerable strength, and the gathered mind-force of millions of people wrought itself into the single brain of Napoleon Bonaparte. This human being became an event—this nation's passion took a *personnel!* The spirit of the times produced this man, and Authority smiled as one after another the despots of Europe plotted and planned only to be overthrown by this incarnation of Ambition, while the scenes were shifted from the Vine-land to the Rhine-land, from the sun-land to the snow-land, and through them all the great event glowed out, lit high by the rust-red light.

How well the plot was working! The Empire triumphant, nations subjected, the fetter of action closing its terrible teeth! Liberty manacled on the left! The armies of God massing their forces—advancing—preparing to close down the iron jaw of the iron gyve upon the right; to imprison thought, to re-establish the union of fetters, to link up the broken chains, to burden human hope and human will and human life once more with the awful oppression of Church and State!

But Liberty will not, cannot die! Wounded and bruised and pinioned sore, condemned to the use of instruments that were none of hers, she wrought with England's jealousy, with Wellington's emulation, with fear, with love, with hate!

Impelled by one motive or another the nations of the coalition moved in concert. Napoleon had been Marengo—he had been Austerlitz! He became *Waterloo!* And when across that awful field rolled the last long cannon boom, when the silence settled, when the Quick and the Dead lay sleeping and the Wounded died, Justice and Suffering touched hands across the gulf of blood, and Liberty heard them whisper, "*Sic semper tyrannis.*" In the tableau that followed, she, the ideal of our dreams, still stood pale and fettered; but a smile lit up her face and a light gleamed in her eyes as she saw Authority reel and stagger from the blow which, though it did not sever, yet shattered half the strength of both its fetters.

For the strength of God lies in a vast unity, an ownership of ideas backed up by the brute force under the command of the individual in whom that ownership of ideas is vested; while the strength of Liberty lies in the very essence of things themselves, the fact that no law or force ever *can* destroy the individualities of existence; and of necessity the natural tendency to break all bonds which seek to control thought, and all force which locks up those bonds entailing liberty of action as the outcome of liberty of thought. And just in proportion as Churches have been dismembered and States have been broken up, no matter that each new Church and each new State were but another form of despotism, just in that proportion has the principle of liberty been served; for each new religious establishment has been an assertion of the right to think differently from the fashionable creed, each change has been a movement away from the centralization of power.

So with Waterloo in the background, with Authority lashed to impotent rage before it, and Liberty pinioned, yet with the lit smile still upon her countenance, the tableau light flames up and dies, and the curtain falls upon the first great act. Those who think, those who feel, those who hope, know why that smile was there. For looking away over the long blue roll of water that swelled like an interlude between, she beheld the sublime opening scene of the act that followed.

Far up the wonderful stage the distant mountains lift their circling crests, at their feet the waters sweep like a march of music, vast acres of untrodden grass-land shower their emerald wealth, nearer the front the lower hills rise up, and then, the short Atlantic slope, all rife with busy life, bends down to meet the sea. On the right the hoar-frost sheens and shines on the majestic northern forests, while the glittering earth, dipped in its bath of frozen crystal, spreads like a field of diamonds; on the left the white flakes of the orange bloom fall like a shimmering bridal vail [sic], the wind floats up like a perfume, and the hazy, lazy languor of warmth creeps all about. Behind it all, behind the hills and the prairies and the lifted summits, the mystical golden light of the west drops down, filling the dim-lit distance with the glory of promise. The silver light of the Empire Star glides over the Atlantic slope, and its rays, like guiding fingers, point onward to the gathering shadows.

Now the Passions of men begin to move upon this vast platform with an energy never before witnessed. Diverted from their old-time channels of struggle against the oppression of Gods and kings and the bitterness of birth-hatred, with a freedom of opportunity denied in the old world, and with such unstinted natural resources waiting for the magic transformer, the genius of humanity, Ambition of power, Avarice, Pride, Jealousy, all those motors born out of the old *regime* of a State propped God, bred and multiplied through generations till they have come to be looked upon as natural laws of human existence, begin to work together to plant this untrodden earth, to sow in its furrows the seed of a newer race—and, paradoxical as it may sound, to work for their own destruction, their final elimination from the human brain. Or perhaps it were more correct to say, that, with the barriers of old institutions taken away they naturally begin their retransformation into those beautiful sentiments from which they were originally warped, distorted, misshapen by that warped, distorted, misshapen idea called God. So do they inaugurate the grand era of development; so do they answer the oft-repeated question, "What incentive would there be for labor or genius if the institutions that compel them to struggle were broken down?" Look at the stage of the past and see! Never before had thought been so free, never before had ability been less cramped, or starved or less compelled! And never before did genius dare so much for purposes so great; never before did the engines which drive the tide of life along a continent send forth a stream of so much vigor. A new light breaks along the pathway of the star, and swells and rolls and floods the great scene with a dawn-burst so magnificent that the very hills blush in its rising splendor. It is the dawn which the night of God so long held shrouded; it is that which is born when Superstition dies; it is that Phoenix which rises from the ashes of religion; it is that clear blent flame of all the great forces of nature, brought to the knowledge of mankind by delving Reason, and shot like northern streamers from the heart of her the Church of God so long held throttled—Science! It is that which shone reflected in the eyes of Liberty when pale and manacled she stood before the field of Waterloo! The ray of the under earth came up to join the ray of the clouds shot down, the energies of sky and mine and sea were clasped to bring down the wealth of the mountains to the shore, and to transport the life of the now populous strip of slope to the unclaimed regions of the west.

In the broad blaze of light the scene is shifted, the golden effulgence melts and flows round that sea-girdled kingdom, where quietly but surely the two great engines of Authority are being shriven apart. The dynasties of kings are growing dusty—much of their power is but a legend; the Church is shrinking in her garments. The desires of this people are slow to move, but deeply rooted and strong; and so far as they have moved forward, they have never moved back. There have been no gigantic strides, no reactions. Little by little the idea of divinely-delegated power has been crippled till the English bishop and the English lord have become mere titled mockeries in comparison with their ancient feudal meaning. But stop! Close lying there, almost beneath her stretching shadows, another island flashes like a green star in its sea-blue setting. And from that island there rises up the cry of a great devotion, clinging blindly to its greatest curse, its priest-hedged God, while persecuted even unto death by the fanaticism of another faith; and the pleading of Hunger while day long and night long the shuttle flies in the flax loom, and the earth yields her golden fruition, only to lade the ships that bear it away from the famine-white lips and the toil-hardened hands that produced it. Blindly Devotion prays to its God, that God whom it calls all-wise, all-powerful and all-just, and the English lord, who cannot thus subdue his own countrymen, reaches out the long arm of the law across the channel for his rent—and, with God looking on, it is given; and still while the hollow-eyed women kneel at the altar for help, the scene widens out, and away in the distance the seven-hilled city lifts up from the sea, and from the dome of the Vatican, from that great mortared hill of God, the Vicar of Christ calls out, "My tribute, my Peter pence!" And with God looking on, it is given! And then from the foot of that tear-stained altar, where so many lips of Woe have pressed, where so many helpless hands have clasped, where so many hearts have broken, comes the ironical promise of Jehovah, "Ask and thou shalt receive."

Oh, God is a very promising personage indeed—very promising, but, like some of his disciples, very poor pay.

Liberty! Shadowed, invisible! Yet a muffled voice is repeating the words which not so long ago rang from the lips of one who stood almost beneath the shadow of the scaffold, who walks to-day in prison gloom:

> *"Ye see me only in your cells, ye see me only in the grave,*
> *Ye see me only wand'ring lone beside the exile's sullen wave!*
> *Ye fools! Do I not also live where you have sought to pierce in vain?*
> *Rests not a nook for me to dwell in every heart, in every brain?*

135

Not every brow that boldly thinks erect with manhood's honest pride?
Does not each bosom shelter me that beats with honor's generous tide?
Not every workshop brooding woe, not every hut that harbors grief?
Ha! Am I not the breath of life that pants and struggles for relief? "

Ah, poor, panting, struggling, misery-laden Ireland! How God laughs with glee to see his shackles weight your misery!

The scene is shifting, the stage is dark'ning—a strange eclipse obscures the shafted light! Darker, darker! Now a low, red fire gleams like a winking eye along the foreground; it runs, it hisses like a snake; there another leaps up, there another; France, Germany, Italy—the continent blazes with the fires of the Commune! That spirit which, drunken with blood, reeled from the guillotine at '93, to be crushed beneath the upbuilding of the Empire, has once more arisen. And out of the hot hells of Fury, and Jealousy, and Hate, out of the pitiless struggle between "vested rights" and wrongs with high ancestral lineage, and the great outcrying of a piteous ignorance against an oppression whose injustice it feels but cannot analyze, grows the sublime idea which priests have anathematized and States have outlawed—"the sacred dogma of EQUALITY."

In so far as that ideal was made possible of conception, in so far as the masses began to understand something of the causes for their ills, in so far the purpose of Liberty was served: no matter that the arms of Oppression were triumphant, the dawn of the thought of equal liberty upon the mass of the unthinking was a far greater victory than any triumph of arms.

So when the fires died down, and the low reflection gleamed for an instant over those quiescent Indian valleys and Altaian ranges, where the main plot of old centuries had been laid, and then paled out before the white flare lighting the tableau of the second act, Liberty stood with chained hands lifted toward her enemy, while a proud look, playing like an iridescent flame in her eyes, said, plain as lips could speak it, "I have unbound their thoughts; they will one day unbind my hands."

Slowly the curtain falls on the fair prisoner and the glowering God.

The solemn ocean interlude rolls in again; again the rising curtain shows the curving slope, the rock-romance of hills, the wide, green valley with its threading silver, the sweeping mountains with the mirage of the blue Pacific lifted high in the sky behind them, the frosted pines, the orange groves. Moving upon the nearer stage

136

two great masses of humanity are seen facing each other; the fires of ambition, of stubborn pride, of determination for the mastery flash like flint-sparks in the eyes of both. Rage is gathering as the stage-light darkens!

Yet these two opposing forces are not all. From under the groves of bridal bloom comes a mournful, chant-like requiem; under the bloom four million voices cry in pain; upon the darkened faces, upturned to that darkening sky, fall the white petals helplessly, as Hope falls on the faces of the dead—to die beside them. In the beautiful land of the sun four million human beings clank the chains of the chattel slave! Ah! what music!

Liberty! Liberty was a wraith, fleeting ghost-like through the lonely rice-swamps, terrible *ignis fatuus* of the quagmire, strange, mystical, vanishing moon-shimmer on the darkly ominous waters lying so silent, so level, beneath the droop of Spanish moss and cypress! There it was they drove thee, *there*—THERE—whère the quaking earth shivered with its branded burden, where the fever and the miasm were thy breathing, and thy sacred eyes were dimmed with winding-sheets of mist that floated, O so dankly, O so coldly, a steam of tears that rose as fast as their dews might fall: there wast thou exiled, Thou, the God-hunted, Thou, the Law-driven, THOU, THE IMMORTAL! Yet, Oh, so dear men love thee, Liberty, that even here in thy last terrible citadel of woe, Humanity linked arms with Death, and wooed thee still! Wooed thee, with the ringing bay of bloodhounds in its ears; wooed thee, with the wolf of hunger gnawing at its throat; wooed thee with the clinging miasm winding its anacondine folds around its fever-thin body; wooed thee with the dark pathos of a dying eye, while the diseased and hungered limbs lay stiffening in their agony. And thou wast true, O Liberty! Out of thy bitter exile thou didst call to them, and point them on to hope; and thou didst call, too, to those strange-eyed dreamers, whose faces shone amidst the rank and file of those dominated by local Hate alone, as shines a clear star among driving clouds. Against them Authority has hurled his curses. Spit upon by the godly, despised by the law-abiding, they yet have dared to say to Church and Law, "Think what you please of me, but free the slave." Aye, the Church persecuted, and the law hunted down, and for the love of God, men set traps to catch their fellow-men: even the "wise men," the wise men at Washington, against whose mandates it is treason to speak, aye, a matter for the scaffold in these days, even the wise men built a trap to uphold the divine institution sent it forth to the people labelled, "The Fugitive Slave Law;¹" and as in other days, human beings died for their opinions—*but the opinions did not die.* Has not one of our latter-day martyrs said, "Men die, but principles live?"

See! The light which has been slowly fading from the right and left shines with a frightful brilliancy upon one point: North and South lie darkened, but Harper's Ferry[2] glows! There is a wild, mad charge, a shifting of the light, a scaffold, a doomed old man bending his grand, white head, to mount the fatal steps with a child-slave's kiss yet warm upon his lips, and then—only a dull, lifeless pendulum in human form, swinging to and fro. And the Church and the Law were satisfied, when those dumb lips were cold, and the dead limbs were stiff, and God and Harper's Ferry had no more to fear from old John Brown[3].

But the Church and the Law have not always been wise; they have not always understood that the martyrs *to* Creed and Code have done as much by their death for the propagation of their principles as the martyrs *of* creed and code; and God and the State sowed a wind whose reaping was a terrible whirlwind, when they hung John Brown.

Across the dim platform the Passions of hate and pride move toward each other; it is the old combat of the forces of Authority, each contending not for the vindication of right, but for the maintenance of power over the other. It is a terrific struggle of brute strength and strategy and cunning and ferocity, and well might those who conceived the ideal beautiful of freedom, shrink horror-struck from the blood-soaked path their feet must tread to reach it. Not strange if some should pause and shudder and cry out, "Is it worth the sacrifice?" But up from the dust where Hope lay trodden, and out of the trenches where the sacrificed lay hid, and over the plains all scarred with bullets and plowed with shells, breathed the whisper, "It is not vain." It was not in vain; for as at Waterloo the struggle of ambition against ambition defeated the first purpose of Authority, the centralization of power, and gave a partial victory to her whom both hated, so Antietam, Fredericksburg, Vicksburg, Gettysburg, while in themselves representing only the brutish struggle of opposition, based on the desire to domineer, really wrought out the victory of that ideal which dwelt in the minds of those anathematized by God and outlawed by the State. For when the hot lips of the iron mouths grew cold, Liberty forsook her lonely fastness, came forth upon the desolated plain, and mounting still to the summits of the blue-hazed hills looked away over the ruined homes, the depopulated cities, the gloom-clouded faces, and though her tears fell fast, an ineffable tenderness shone upon her features as the torrent of pale light flowed round her form, defining its snow-whiteness in relief against the sable of four million freedmen smiling o'er their stricken chains.

Swiftly following the tableau fire comes the eastern scene, where, in the very center of its power the Church is shaken by an invader, and Garibaldi[4] becomes the *personnel*

138

of the event. Then follows the Conclave of the Vatican, where by that singular logic known to the Roman Church the vote of fallible beings renders the pope infallible; upon the heels of this, the breaking of that strong tooth of the Church in the expulsion of the Order of the Society of Jesus by the German Reichstag, and the overthrow of kingscraft in France.

The curtain falls. Behind, the scene is being prepared for the last great act!

And now, in the interval of waiting, let us think. So far we have been surveying the completed. While we can understand something of the passions which animated this past, can feel something of the pulsations which throbbed in its arteries, flowed in its veins, we yet can speak of it without over-riding emotion either upon one side or the other. The river of heart has reached the sea—the troubled waters have spread out deep, and up from their depths shine the still reflections of those great lights which gilt the stages of the past. Calmly now we can look at the reaction from the French Revolution to the Empire, and say, "This was inevitable,"—of Napoleon's fall, "this was necessary;" of the awakening of Science, "this was a natural result;" of the uprising of the '48, "this was the premature birth of an idea forced upon the people by the oppression of Authority:" we can forget the choking agony of John Brown, and declare his death a victory. We can look upon the awful waste of blood in the civil war and say, "it was pitiful, but the goblet of woe must needs have been spilled full of the red life wine, ere the hoarse and hollow throat of tyranny were satisfied." We can see where each of the contending principles have lost and gained, and measuring the sum totals against each other, *must* decide that the old despotism is losing ground; that instead of the supreme authority of God the supreme sovereignty of the Individual is the growing idea.

But now we have come to a stage where we can no longer be cool spectators. In what happens now we too must be part and parcel of the action; we too must hope, and toil, and struggle and suffer. We are no longer looking through the clear still atmosphere of the dead: around our forms the wheeling mists are circled, and before our eyes the haze lies thick——the haze of gold or the haze of gray. The dimness of the "yet to be" befogs our sight, and the rush of hope and fear binds all our faculties. You who stand well upon the heights of love, of comfort, of happiness, heeding not the darkness and the sorrow beneath you, behold, with up-cast eyes, the great figures of God and Freedom wound about, showered with light. To you there is no menace in their darting eyes, there is no purpose in their full-drawn statures, there is no jarring in their clarion voices. No! for your senses are stupid in your luxury, your brains are dulled, too dulled to think, your ears are glutted with the ring of gold. In your vain and foolish hearts you dream that what you see there is a shadowy bridal; that there, at last, Religion and Science, Statecraft and Freedom are meeting to embrace each other.

Ah, go on book-makers, press-writers, doctors and lawyers and preachers and teachers! Go on talking your incompatibilities; go on teaching your absurdities! Dream out your short-lived dream! At your feet, beneath the shadow of your capitols and domes, under the tuition of your few-facted, much-fictioned literature, from out your chaos of truth-flavored lies, from before your pulpits, your rostrums and your seats of learning, something is growing. Something that is looking *you* in the eyes, that is analyzing your statements, that is revolving your institutions in its brain, that is crushing your sophistries in its merciless machinery as fine as grain is ground between the whitened mill-rollers. Freethought is looking at you, gentlemen!—more than that, it questions you, it puts you on the witness-stand, it cross-examines you. It says, "Do you believe in God?" and you answer, "Yes." "Do you believe him to be omnipotent, omniscient and all-just?" "Certainly; less than this would not be God." "Then you believe he has the power to order all things as he wills, and being all-just he wills all things according to justice?" "Yes." "Then you believe him to be the impartially-loving father of all his created children?" "Yes." "And each one of those children has an equal right to life and liberty?" "Yes." Then look upon this earth beneath you, this earth of beings whose lives are of so poor account to you, and tell us, where *is* God, and *what* is he doing?

Everyone has a right to life! What mockery! When the control of the necessaries of life is given to the few by the State, and over above the seal of the law the priest has set the seal the Church! Verily,

> *"You do take my life*
> *When you take that whereby I live."*

Is this your Divine Justice?

What irony to tell me I am free if at the same time you have it in your power to withhold the means of my existence! Free! Will you look down here at these whose sight is shadowed with the ebon shadow of despair, these, the homeless, the disinherited, the product of whose toil you take and leave them barely enough to live upon—live to toil on and keep you in your luxury! You, the monied idlers, you, the book-makers and the journalists, who do more to cry down truth, to laud our social lies, our economic despots and our pious frauds than any other propaganda can! You,

140

the doctors, whose drugs have cursed the world with poison-eaten bodies, corroded the health of unborn generations with your medicated slime, and when the sources of life have yielded to the hungry body so poor a stream that for lack of air, and earth, and sun, and food, and clothing, and recreation, it drooped and sickened, have bottled up some nauseating stuff, and with oracular wisdom have taught them to imagine it could undo what years of misery had done! You, the law-makers, who have twisted Nature's code till to be natural is to be a criminal; you, who have lawed away the earth that was not yours to give; you, who even seek to charter the sea and make the commandment "across the middle of this river thou shalt not go unless thou render tribute unto Caesar!" you, who never inquire "what is *justice*," but "what is law!" And you, the teachers, you who prate of the glory of knowledge as the remedy for the evils of the world, and boast your compulsory law of education, while a stronger law than all the wordy sentences ever graven upon statute books, is driving the children out of the schoolground into the factory, into the saw-mill, into the shaft, into the furrow, into the myriad camps of toil, to the dust of the wheel, to the heat of the furnace, till their pallid cheeks and bloodless lips are bleached like bones beneath the desert sun, and their clogged lungs rattle in their breathing pain! Will you look at these, the under-stratum of your social earth, and tell them they are *free*? Will you tell them ignorance is their greatest curse and education their only remedy? Will you say to these children, "We have provided free schools for you, and now we compel you to attend them whether you have anything to eat and wear or not?" Will you tell these people there is a good, kind, merciful God who loves them, meting out justice to them from the skies?

No, you *will* not, you *cannot*. The words will die upon your lips ere you have uttered them.

Do you know what it is they see up there above you, they whose eyes look through the mist of gray and the shroud of darkness? They see your God of justice a pitiless slave-driver, his Church more brutal than the lash, his State more merciless than the bloodhound; they see themselves a thousand million serfs more hopelessly enthralled, more helplessly chained down than e'en the lashed and tortured body of the chattel slave. For them there is no refuge, no escape; in every land the Master rules; no fugitive slave law need now be passed—there is no place to flee—the whole horizon is iron-bound. White and black alike are yoked together, and the master yields no distinction, shows no mercy. The bare pittance of existence is the meed for him who toils, and for him who *cannot*—starvation! with a preacher to help him die! That is the justice that they see there, in the shadow lines above your golden haze. And they see, too, a conflict preparing between those two antagonistic forces such as never before the world has witnessed. They see your God concentrating his strength to fight so bitter a battle with Liberty as shall crush the spirit of individuality forever from the race. They see him ranging his forces, those forces blood-imbrued through all the anguished past, the blacklist, the club, the sword, the rifle, the prison, aye the scaffold; they see them all, and know that ere your God will yield his vested rights, the noblest of the race will have been stricken, the most unselfish will have been tortured in his dungeons, the white robes of innocence will have been reddened in her own martyr's blood, and Death will have shadowed many and many a home, unless *you* shall harken to the voice of Liberty and save yourselves while there is yet time. They see the wide stage spreading out, they see the passions moving over it; they see there, in the center, beneath the rolling brilliance of the Empire Star, the tragic inauguration of the act! They see a grim and blackened thing, a silent thing, the demoniac effigy of Torquemada's[5] spirit, the frozen laugh of the Dark Ages at our boasted civilization; they see twelve stolid fools before this Nineteenth Century gallows; they see the hiding place of that thing masquerading under the sacred name of Justice, which shrinks even from the gaze of the lauding press and the imbecile jurymen, and does unknown its deed of murder; they see four shrouded forms, they hear four muffled voices, a broken sentence, and—an awful hush! And then, O crowning irony of all, they see advancing to speak to them over the bodies of the murdered (and mouthed back from a hundred pulpits comes the echo), Jehovah masked as Jesus. Ah, the divine cowardice of it! Mild is the light in the Nazarene eyes, tender the tone of the Nazarene voice!

"Ah, people whom I love! For whom my life was given long ago on Calvary! What rashness is it that you meditate? Is it that you are weary of the yoke of love I lay on you? Is this your faith? Have I not promised you a sweet release when your dark pilgrimage on earth is o'er? Exiles ye are upon this world of pain, and if oppression comes to weigh you down, if hunger shows his long fangs at your hearth, if your chilled limbs are cramped with bitter cold the while your neighbor hoards his fuel up, if you are driven out upon the street with crying children clinging piteously and begging you for shelter from the storm, if your hard toil is taken by the law to satisfy a corporation's greed, if Fever and Distress gnaw at your heart and still you tread the weary wine-press out, knowing no rest until the death hour comes; if all these things discourage and perplex, know 'tis for love of you I order it. For thus would I point you to paradise, win you from all the pleasures of the world, and fix your hopes on Heaven's eternity." "Whom the Lord loveth, him he chasteneth;" so then it is for love that these things are. For love of you I press your life-blood out; for love of you I load you down with pain; for love of you I take your rights away; for love of you I institute the law that slaves you to the grasping millionaire; for love of you I pile the glutted hoards of Vanderbilt and Gould and Rothschild and the rest[6]; for love of you I rent the right to breathe in a poor tenement of dingy dirt; for love of you I make machines a curse; for love of you I make you toil long hours, and those who cannot toil, I turn adrift to wander as they may—sons into dens where thievery is learned as a fine art; daughters to barter their virginity till competition forces down the price of lust and death is left them as a last resort. Ah, what a golden crown, and sweet-toned harp, what a resplendent white robe, wait the soul whom so God loves while on the earth it dwells. Aye, for the love of you these men were murdered, and for my glory; and through my holy love they roast in hell: for they would take away the instruments whereby I lure you to my blest abode. They would have taught you what your freedom meant; they would have told you to regain your rights; they would have contradicted my commands and lost you heaven, perchance—and if not heaven, *hell*. Keep to your faith, my people, trust in God! Break not the altars where your fathers knelt; trust to your teachers, keep within the law; bow to the Church and kiss the State's great toe! So shall good order be observed, obeyed, and as "Peace reigned in Warsaw," so anon shall "Peace, good-will to man reign on the earth."

These are the words that fall from the lips of him you call "the merciful," "the just." These are the sounds that sink into the ears of those upon whose toil *you* are dependent for your existence; judge you how they will be received. And now, you, the dwellers on the lifted heights, listen to the voice that follows him, for these are words that concern *you*, and if you listen to their warning you may yet save yourselves the desolation and the ruin that otherwise must come. This deep, bell-pealing voice that echoes through the corridors of thought till almost Death's chill sleepers might arise again, is the voice which called for centuries to the Empire, "Cease your oppressions or the people rise;" and to the Kingdom, "Curse not the new world with your tyrannies, it will rebel;" and to the Master, "Put not the lash upon your bonded slave, for the time will come when every stroke will rise like, a warrior armed, to burn and waste and kill." The Empire laughed, the Kingdom ignored, the Planter sneered; but the time came when laugh and sneer died to white ashes. The time came when "France got drunk with blood, to vomit crime," when England "lost the brightest jewel in her coronal," when the South waded in blood and tears and knelt her pride before a conqueror. And now, she, the liberator, the destined conqueror of God, calls out to you, "Yield up your scepters ere they be torn from you; give back the stolen earth, the mine, the sea! Give back the source of life, give back the light! for a black, bitter hour is waiting you, an awful gulf unfathomed in its depth, if now you do not pause and render *justice*.

Ah, thou, whatever be thy awful name, which like a serpent's trail hath marked the earth, whether Jehovah, Buddha, Joss, or Christ? Thou who hast done for *love* what others do for most envenomed *hate*, how hast thou hated these the happy ones. Is this impartial justice then to these, to pour the golden treasures of the earth into their laps, that these may feast and toast and so forget thee and thy promised heaven? Truly thou hast been most unkind to them, since kindness means with thee a tearing out of e'en the heart and entrails of existence. Bah! how thou liest! To what most pitiable trick of speech hast thou been forced! Think'st thou the dwellers in the darkness longer take thy creed of crystalline deception! No!! They laugh at thee, they spew thee out, they spit at thee.

Love! Say! Look—this long procession coming here! Here are the murderers, with their red-hued eyes; here the adulterers, with their lecherous glance; here are the prostitutes, with their mark of shame; here are the gamblers, with their itching hands; here are the thieves, with furtive lips and eyes; here are the liars with their dastard tongues; here all the train that Crime can muster up reviews before thee! And after them, a ghastly, fearful sight, follow the victims of their blackened hearts, slain, ruined, desolated by thy love! And now, behold, another train comes on—a train whose name is legion! Here the dark, bruted faces from the mines, here the hard, sun-browned cheeks from out the furrow, here the dull visage from the lumber-camp, here the wan eyes from whirling factory, here the gaunt giants from the furnace fire, here the tarred hands from off the stream and sea, here all the aching limbs that stand behind the fashionable counter, here, O pitiful sight of all, those whose home is in the street, whose table is the garbage pile, the vast, helpless body of the unemployed. And, ever as they march, they drop, and drop, into the earth that swallows them, and over their graves to the march goes on. These are thy victims, God! These are the creatures of thy Church and Law! Speak no more of the breaking of altars, thou who hast broken every altar that the human heart holds dear! Take thy position at the head of the murderers' column! And when thou hast marched away into the past, thou and thy preachers and thy praters of justice, then will the world *return* to justice and the great law of Nature reign upon the earth. Then will her broad, green acres yield their wealth to him who toils, and him alone; then will the store-houses of Nature yield her fuel and her light, not to the corporation whose high-priced lobbying can buy it, for in that time no wealth nor intrigue can purchase the heritage of all, but to all the sons and daughters of Labor. And then upon *this* earth there shall be no hungry mouths, no freezing limbs; no children spending the hours of youth in gaining a miserable livelihood, no women crying,

> *"It's Oh, to be a slave*
> *Along with the barbarous Turk,*
> *Where woman has never a soul to save .*
> *If this is* Christian *work!"*

no men wandering aimlessly in search of a master for their slavery.

But O, careless dwellers upon the heights, awaken now!—do not wait till reason, persuasion, judgment, coolness are swept down before the rising whirlwind. Bend your energies *now* to the eradication of the Authority idea, to righting the wrongs of your fellow-men. Do it for your own interest, for if you slumber on—ah me! ye will awaken one day when an ominous rumble prefaces the waking of a terrific underground thunder, when the earth shakes in a frightful ague fit, when from out the parched throats of the people a burning cry will come like lava from a crater, "'Bread, bread, bread!' No more preachers, no more politicians, no more lawyers, no more gods, no more heavens, no more promises! Bread!" And then, when you hear a terrible leaden groan, know that at last, here in your free America, beneath the floating banner of the stars and stripes, more than fifty million human hearts have burst! a dynamite bomb that will shock the continent to its foundations and knock the sea back from its shores!

> *"It is no boast, it is no threat,*
> *Thus History's iron law decrees;*
> *The day grows hot! O Babylon,*
> *'Tis cool beneath thy willow trees!"*[7]

Dyer D. Lum[1]

The brightest scholar, the profoundest thinker of the American Revolutionary movement is dead. On Thursday, April 6th, [1893] they found him sleeping the last sleep, in a hotel near the Bowery in New York. Utterly without pain he must have passed away, as he had always wished he might—into the painless rest.

Dyer D. Lum was born at Geneva, N.Y., fifty-three years ago. He was descended from an old Puritan family hence an American as much as it is possible for any Anglo-Saxon to be an American. In early life he was brought up under strict Presbyterian discipline, but piety never seems to have taken any deep root in his sceptical nature. According to one of his own inimitably told stories, such religious sentiments as he had all departed one bright Sunday, when God failed to send a thunderbolt upon him for having played ball, torn his trousers, and uttered an oath on the Lord's day. And yet in the nobler and better sense of the word Dyer D. Lum was a deeply religious man. He was full of that earnest, self-sacrificing devotion to whatever ideal of the future seemed highest to him at any period of his life, and he never stopped at any command of "the inward *must*," though it cost him friends, worldly success, or the danger of death itself.

He has frequently said and written that the labor movement of America really began with the Pittsburgh riots in 1877[2]; previous to that time, however, he had taken part in the great struggle, now recognized as an economic one, known as the civil war. He fought on the northern side, and so bravely that he jumped from the rank of a volunteer private soldier to that of captain by sheer force of merit. At that time, there is no doubt, he believed himself to be fighting in the good cause. But since he became an economic thinker he has often expressed himself sarcastically as having "gone down there out of *patriotism* (?) to fight the battle of *cheap* labor against *dear*." After the war he resumed his trade as bookbinder, and began his studies in the economic field. In 1876 he was associated with Wendell Phillips[3] as candidate for lieutenant-governor of Massachusetts on the Greenback ticket. Out of the old nursery of Greenbackism[4] came nearly all of our present radical thought, while few of its original exponents are any longer satisfied with the Greenback program: it was simply the beginning of the Socialistic movement. Mr. Lum was not one to remain long satisfied with the "illogic" of Greenbackism. He was too consistent in mind to accept a mixed authoritarianism and liberty. At first he went over to authoritarianism, and was for a time State-socialist. Subsequently, however, he became an Anarchist, a contributor to Parsons'[5] *Alarm*[6], and a most cutting critic of State-socialism.

While living in Washington he was appointed on a committee to investigate the conditions of labor, and in the course of that investigation studied the coöperative system of the Mormons (a much abused people here in America.) The result was a pamphlet in which he set forth the principles of their labor exchange, disabusing the reader of many false notions in regard to Mormon life. This pamphlet had a wide circulation.

In 1886 he was conducting a bookbindery at Port Jervis, N.Y., when the question of who should keep alive the paper of the imprisoned Parsons arose. Although Lum was an individualist and Parsons Communist, no one else could be founded and willing to continue the work of the doomed editor. Lum did not hesitate. He sold out his business, went to Chicago, put about $1500 into the work, no penny of which he ever received or expected to receive back, ran the gauntlet of police, detectives, and the crowd of haters of Anarchy, then very numerous in Chicago, and held the banner aloft as long as he could. During this time he was a constant visitor at the prison, the loved and trusted comrade of those who were about to die, the jealous guardian of their highest honor. Like all who knew those men, he grew to love them all, and never in after years was he able to speak much of them without tears filling his eyes. And yet he counselled them to die. When Parsons asked him his advice as to signing the petition, which he and Lum both *knew* from sure sources of information would have saved his life, he said, "I cannot advise you." But when Parsons pressed him, he said, "Die, Parsons." And the other answered, "I am glad you said it. It is what I wished." For this he was blamed by some, blamed as "wanting their death." Yes, he did want their death, as he loved liberty, and honor, and pride, and the future, and their true glory—more than his own life and more than theirs. For those who knew him best knew there was not one moment when he would not have taken his place by their side and walked proudly to the scaffold had the State decreed it.

After the failure of the "Alarm" in Chicago he was enabled, partly through the courtesy of John Most and others, to re-commence its publication in reduced form in New York. But owing to an accumulation of difficulties he could not continue it long. It was a great sorrow to him, for his last promise to Parsons was to do everything to keep the paper alive. From that time on his life was a bitter struggle with poverty whose miseries he endured with shut lips, only his intimate friends knowing how great they were, and even they hardly daring to offer him any help for the fear of offending his proud, uncomplaining spirit. This poverty chained his hands, tied his aspirations, compelled him to a forced inaction that wore him out more than the severest active strain. Although of a strong constitution he became a victim of insomnia: and burnt up the oil of life without replenishing.—Yet no one would have guessed all this to have met and talked with him, always merry, always full of jokes, always ready to sympathize with the humblest thing that suffered or was glad. At one moment talking Philosophy with the scholars, at the next stroking the sore foot of a dog, or playing hide-and-seek with the children, it was hard to determine what lay deepest beneath those smiling grey eyes that never told aught of the hard personal struggle within.

Of his many pamphlets, articles and poems it may be said *all* evinced profound thought; but unfortunately were too often in a heavy style that rendered them difficult to the ordinary reader. In fact few students went deeper into psychological depths than he, and his habit of reading the masters, living in the company of books, made language which to most of us stilted the ordinary channel of his thought. His early studies in Buddhism left a profound impress upon all his future concepts of life, and to the end his ideal of personal attainment was self-obliteration—Nirvana. He had not the slightest use for the Hedonistic doctrines of most of the individualistic school, and often sent the sharp shafts of his wit into the heart of an argument hinging upon the "pleasure the motive of action" premise.

As to his revolutionary beliefs he always avowed them when there was any reason for so doing. When Berkman shot Frick he was one of those who dared to defend the act. But he did not believe in continually talking about it. He did not believe in telling *other* people to "do" anything. He never said, "arm yourselves and prepare." He had his own plans probably; but if he had he trusted to himself, and neither depended upon nor asked aught from others. For the rest he believed in revolution as he believed in cyclones; when the time comes for the cloud to burst it bursts, and so will burst the pent-up storm in the people when it can no longer be contained. So he believed, and trusted in the future.

And I who trust in his philosophy trust that in that fire-hued day the spirit of my beloved teacher and friend will burn in the hearts of the strugglers for freedom, till it consumes away all fear, all dependence, all the dross of our "American slavery," and leaves them erect, proud, free, dauntless as he who has left to them the rich legacy of a life of thought and work in their behalf.

FREEDOM, *London, June 1893.*

149

Our Martyrs

The chieftain's fame in old and recent days
Time's tablets have illum'ed with bloody deeds
By axe and sword to aid oppression's needs
Or State's distress; but higher meed of bays
Than e'en the poet wrought in classic lays
Is yours, comrades, for he who hears and heeds
The smothered sighs oppression always breeds
Possesses what no victor's sword portrays,
And what surpasses all the sculptor's art.
Heroic souls! Your words our souls imbue
With deeper zeal, and in each lowly heart
Resolves take form to carve for the applause
More dear than man e'er gained in statecraft's cause
And name more grand than hireling swords can hew.

Crime and Punishment

A lecture delivered before the Social Science Club
of Philadelphia, March 15th, 1903.

Men are of three sorts: the turn backs, the rush-aheads, and the indifferents. The first and the second are comparatively few in number. The really conscientious conservative, eternally looking backward for his models and trying hard to preserve that which is, is almost as scarce an article as the genuine radical, who is eternally attacking that which is and looking forward to some indistinct but glowing vision of a purified social life. Between them lies the vast nitrogenous body of the indifferents, who go through life with no large thoughts or intense feelings of any kind, the best that can be said of them being that they serve to dilute the too fierce activities of the other two. Into the callous ears of these indifferents, nevertheless, the opposing voices of conservative and radical are continually shouting; and for years, for centuries, the conservative wins the day, not because he really touches the consciences of the indifferent so much (though in a measure he does that) as because his way causes his hearer the least mental trouble. It is easier to this lazy, inert mentality to nod its head and approve the continuance of things as they are, than to listen to proposals for change, to consider, to question, to make an innovating decision. These require activity, application,—and nothing is so foreign to the hibernating social conscience of your ordinary individual. I say "social" conscience, because I by no means wish to say that these are conscienceless people; they have, for active use, sufficient conscience to go through their daily parts in life, and they think that is all that is required. Of the lives of others, of the effects of their attitude in cursing the existences of thousands whom they do not know, they have no conception; they sleep; and they hear the voices of those who cry aloud about these things, dimly, as in dreams; and they do not wish to awaken.

Nevertheless, at the end of the centuries they always awaken. It is the radical who always wins at last. At the end of the centuries institutions are reviewed by this aroused social conscience, are revised, sometimes are utterly rooted out.

Thus it is with the institutions of Crime and Punishment. The conservative holds that these things have been decided from all time; that crime is a thing-in-itself, with no other cause than the viciousness of man; that punishment was decreed from Mt. Sinai, or whatever holy mountain happens to be believed in his country; that society is best served by strictness and severity of judgment and punishment. And he wishes only to make his indifferent brothers keepers of other men's consciences along these lines. He would have all men be hunters of men, that crime may be tracked down and struck down.

The radical says: All false, all false and wrong. Crime has not been decided from all time: crime, like everything else, has had its evolution according to place, time, and circumstance. "The demons of our sires become the saints that we adore,"—and the saints, the saints and the heroes of our fathers, are criminals according to our codes. Abraham, David, Solomon,—could any respectable member of society admit that he had done the things they did? Crime is not a thing-in-itself, not a plant without roots, not a something proceeding from nothing; and the only true way to deal with it is to seek its causes as earnestly, as painstakingly, as the astronomer seeks the causes of the perturbations in the orbit of the planet he is observing, sure that there must be one, or many, somewhere. And Punishment, too, must be studied? The holy mountain theory is a failure. Punishment is a failure. And it is a failure not because men do not hunt down and strike enough, but because they hunt down and strike at all; because in the chase of those who do ill, they do ill themselves; they brutalize their own characters, and so much the more so because they are convinced that this time the brutal act is done in accord with conscience. The murderous deed of the criminal was *against* conscience, the torture or the murder of the criminal by the official is *with* conscience. Thus the conscience is diseased and perverted, and a new class of imbruted men created. We have punished and punished for untold thousands of years, and we have not gotten rid of crime, we have not diminished it. Let us consider then.

The indifferentist shrugs his shoulders and remarks to the conservative: "What have I to do with it? I will hunt nobody and I will save nobody. Let every one take care of himself. I pay my taxes; let the judges and the lawyers take care of the criminals.

And as for you, Mr. Radical, you weary me. Your talk is too heroic. You want to play Atlas and carry the heavens on your shoulders. Well, do it if you like. But don't imagine I am going to act the stupid Hercules and transfer your burden to my shoulders. Rave away until you are tired, but let me alone."

"I will not let you alone. I am no Atlas. I am no more than a fly; but I will annoy you, I will buzz in your ears; I will not let you sleep. You must think about this."

That is about the height and power of my voice, or of any individual voice, in the present state of the question. I do not deceive myself. I do not imagine that the question of crime and punishment will be settled till long, long after the memory of me shall be as completely swallowed up by time as last year's snow is swallowed by the sea. Two thousand years ago a man whose soul revolted at punishment, cried out: "Judge not, that ye be not judged;" and yet men and women who have taken his name upon their lips as holy, have for all those two thousand years gone on judging as if their belief in what he said was only lip-belief; and they do it to-day. And judges sit upon benches and send men to their death,—even judges who do not themselves believe in capital punishment; and prosecutors exhaust their eloquence and their tricks to get men convicted; and women and men bear witness against sinners; and then they all meet in church and pray, "Forgive us our trespasses *as* we forgive those who trespass against us!"

Do they mean anything at all by it?

And I know that just as the voice of Jesus was not heard, and is not heard, save here and there; just as the voice of Tolstoi is not heard, save here and there; and others great and small are lost in the great echoless desert of indifferentism, having produced little perceptible effect, so my voice also will be lost, and barely a slight ripple of thought be propagated over that dry and fruitless expanse; even that the next wind of trial will straighten and leave as unimprinted sand.

Nevertheless, by the continued and unintermitting action of forces infinitesimal compared with the human voice, the greatest effects are at length accomplished. A wave-length of light is but the fifty-thousandth part of an inch, yet by the continuous action of waves like these have been produced all the creations of light, the entire world of sight, out of masses irresponsive, dark, colorless. And doubt not that in time this cold and irresponsive mass of indifference will feel and stir and realize the force of the great sympathies which will change the attitude of the human mind as a whole towards Crime and Punishment, and erase both from the world.

Not by lawyers and not by judges shall the final cause of the criminal be tried; but lawyer and judge and criminal together shall be told by the Social Conscience, "Depart in peace."

A great ethical teacher once wrote words like unto these: "I have within me the capacity for every crime."

Few, reading them, believe that he meant what he said. Most take it as the sententious utterance of one who, in an abandonment of generosity, wished to say something large and leveling. But I think he meant exactly what he said. I think that with all his purity Emerson[1] had within him the turbid stream of passion and desire; for all his hard-cut granite features he knew the instincts of the weakling and the slave; and for all the sweetness, the tenderness, and the nobility of his nature, he had the tiger and the jackal in his soul. I think that within every bit of human flesh and spirit that has ever crossed the enigma bridge of life, from the prehistoric racial morning until now, all crime and all virtue were germinal. Out of one great soul-stuff are we sprung, you and I and all of us; and if in you the virtue has grown and not the vice, do not therefore conclude that you are essentially different from him whom you have helped to put in stripes and behind bars. Your balance may be more even, you may be mixed in smaller proportions altogether, or the outside temptation has not come upon you.

I am no disciple of that school whose doctrine is summed up in the teaching that Man's Will is nothing, his Material Surroundings all. I do not accept that popular socialism which would make saints out of sinners only by filling their stomachs. I am no apologist for characterlessness, and no petitioner for universal moral weakness. I believe in the individual. I believe that the purpose of life (in so far as we can give it a purpose, and it has none save what we give it) is the assertion and the development of strong, self-centered personality. It is therefore that no religion which offers vicarious atonement for the misdoer, and no philosophy which rests on the cornerstone of irresponsibility, makes any appeal to me. I believe that immeasurable mischief has been wrought by the ceaseless repetition for the last two thousand years of the formula: "Not through any merit of mine shall I enter heaven, but through the sacrifice of Christ."—Not through the sacrifice of Christ, nor any other sacrifice, shall any one attain strength, save in so far as he takes the spirit and the purpose of the sacrifice into his own life and lives it. Nor do I see anything as the result of the teaching that all men are the helpless victims of external circumstance and under the same conditions will act precisely alike, than a lot of spineless, nerveless, bloodless crawlers in the tracks of stronger men,—too desirous of ease to be honest, too weak to be successful rascals.

Let this be put as strongly as it can now, that nothing I shall say hereafter may be interpreted as a gospel of shifting and shirking.

But the difference between us, the Anarchists, who preach self-government and none else, and Moralists who in times past and present have asked for individual responsibility, is this, that while they have always framed creeds and codes for the purpose of *holding others to account,* we draw the line upon ourselves. Set the standard as high as you will; live to it as near as you can; and if you fail, try yourself, judge yourself, condemn yourself, if you choose. Teach and persuade your neighbor if you can; consider and compare his conduct if you please; speak your mind if you desire; but if he fails to reach your standard or his own try him not, judge him not, condemn him not. He lies beyond your sphere; you cannot know the temptation nor the inward battle nor the weight of the circumstances upon him. You do not know how long he fought before he failed. Therefore you cannot be just. Let him alone.

This is the ethical concept at which we have arrived, not by revelation from any superior power, not through the reading of any inspired book, not by special illumination of our inner consciousness; but by the study of the results of social experiment in the past as presented in the works of historians, psychologists, criminologists, sociologists, and legists.

Very likely so many "ists" sound a little oppressive, and there may be those to whom they may even have a savor of pedantry. It sounds much simpler and less ostentatious to say "Thus saith the Lord," or "The Good Book says." But in the meat and marrow these last are the real presumptions, these easy-going claims of familiarity with the will and intent of Omnipotence. It may sound more pedantic to you to say, "I have studied the accumulated wisdom of man, and drawn certain deductions therefrom," than to say "I had a talk with God this morning and he said thus and so;" but to me the first statement is infinitely more modest. Moreover there is some chance of its being true, while the other is highly imaginative fiction.

This is not to impugn the honesty of those who inherit this survival of an earlier mental state of the race, and who accept it as they accept their appetites or anything else they find themselves born with. Nor is it to belittle those past efforts of active and ardent souls who claimed direct divine inspiration as the source of their doctrines. All religions have been, in their great general outlines, the intuitive graspings of the race at truths which it had not yet sufficient knowledge to demonstrate,—rude and imperfect statements of ideas which were yet but germinal, but which, even then, mankind had urgent need to conceive, and upon which it afterwards spends the efforts of generations of lives to correct and perfect. Thus the very ethical concept of which I have been speaking as peculiarly Anarchistic, was preached as a religious doctrine by the fifteenth century Tolstoi, Peter Chilciky; and in the sixteenth century, the fanatical sect of the Anabaptists[2] shook Germany from center to circumference by a doctrine which included the declaration that "pleadings in courts of law, oaths, capital punishment, and all absolute power were incompatible with the Christian faith." It was an imperfect illumination of the intellect, such only as was possible in those less enlightened days, but an illumination that defined certain noble conceptions of justice. They appealed to all they had,—the Bible, the inner light, the best that they knew, to justify their faith. We to whom a wider day is given, who can appeal not to one book but to thousands, who have the light of science which is free to all that can command the leisure and the will to know, shining white and open on these great questions, dim and obscure in the days of Peter Chilciky, we should be the last to cast a sneer at them for their heroic struggle with tyranny and cruelty; though to-day the man who would claim their claims on their grounds would justly be rated atavist or charlatan.

Nothing or next to nothing did the Anabaptists know of history. For genuine history, history which records the growth of a whole people, which traces the evolution of its mind as seen in its works of peace,—its literature, its art, its constructions—is the creation of our own age. Only within the last seventy-five years has the purpose of history come to have so much depth as this. Before that it was a mere register of dramatic situations, with no particular connection, a chronicle of the deeds of prominent persons, a list of intrigues, scandals, murders big and little; and the great people, the actual builders and preservers of the race, the immense patient, silent mass who painfully filled up all the waste places these destroyers made, almost ignored. And no man sought to discover the relations of even the recorded acts to any general causes; no man conceived the notion of discovering what is political and moral growth or political and moral suicide. That they did not do so is because writers of history, who are themselves incarnations of their own time spirit, could not get beyond the unscientific attitude of mind, born of ignorance and fostered by the Christian religion, that man is something entirely different from the rest of organized life; that he is a free moral agent, good if he pleases and bad if he pleases, that is, according as he accepts or rejects the will of God; that every act is isolated, having no antecedent, morally, but the will of its doer. Not until modern science had fought its way past prisons, exilements, stakes, scaffolds, and tortures, to the demonstration that man is no freewill freak thrust by an omnipotent joker upon a world of cause and sequence to play havoc therein, but just a poor differentiated bit of protoplasm as much subject to the general processes of matter and mind as his ancient progenitor in the depths of the Silurian sea, not until then was it possible for any real conception of the scope of history to begin. Not until then was it said: "The actions of men are the effects of large and general causes. Humanity as a whole has a regularity of movement as fixed as the movement of the tides; and given certain physical and social environments, certain developments may be predicted with the certainty of a mathematical calculation." Thus crime, which for so many ages men have gone on punishing more or less light-heartedly, so far from having its final cause in individual depravity, bears a steady and invariable relation to the production and distribution of staple food supplies, a thing over which society itself at times can have no control (as on the occasion of great natural disturbances), and in general does not yet know how to manage wisely: how much less, then, the individual! This regularity of the recurrence of crime was pointed out long before by the greatest statisticians of Europe, who, indeed, did not go so far as to question why it was so, nor to compare these regularities with other regularities, but upon whom the constant repetition of certain figures in the statistics of murder, suicide, assault, etc., made a profound impression. It was left to the new historians, the great pioneer among whom was H.T. Buckle[3] in England, to make the comparisons in the statistics, and show that individual crimes as well as virtues are always calculable from general material conditions.

This is the basis from which we argue, and it is a basis established by the comparative history of civilizations. In no other way could it have been really established. It might have been guessed at, and indeed was. But only when the figures are before us, figures obtained "by millions of observations extending over different grades of civilization, with different laws, different opinions, different habits, different morals" (I am quoting Buckle), only then are we able to say surely that the human mind proceeds with a regularity of operation overweighing all the creeds and codes ever invented, and that if we would begin to understand the problem of the treatment of crime we must go to something far larger than the moral reformation of the criminal. No prayers, no legal enactments, will ever rid society of crime. If they would, there have been prayers enough and preachments enough and laws enough and prisons enough to have done it long ago. But pray that the attraction of gravitation shall cease. Will it cease? Enact that water shall freeze at 100° heat. Will it freeze? And no more will men be sane and honest and just when they are compelled to live in an insane, dishonest, and unjust society, when the natural operation of the very elements of their being is warred upon by statutes and institutions which must produce outbursts destructive both to themselves and to others.

Away back in 1835 Quetelet[4], the French statistician, wrote: "Experience demonstrates, in fact, by every possible evidence, this opinion, which may seem paradoxical at first, that it is society which prepares the crime, and that the guilty one is but the instrument which executes it." Every crime, therefore, is a charge against society which can only be rightly replied to when society consents to look into its own errors and rectify the wrong it has done. This is one of the results which must, in the end, flow from the labors of the real historians; one of the reasons why history was worth writing at all.

Now the next point in the problem is the criminal himself. Admitting what cannot be impeached, that there is cause and sequence in the action of man; admitting the pressure of general causes upon all alike, what is the reason that one man is a criminal and another not?

From the days of the Roman jurisconsults until now the legists themselves have made a distinction between crimes against the law of nature and crimes merely against the law of society. From the modern scientific standpoint no such distinction can be maintained. Nature knows nothing about crime, and nothing ever was a crime until the social Conscience made it so. Neither is it easy when one reads their law books, even accepting their view-point, to understand why certain crimes were catalogued as against the law of nature, and certain others as of the more artificial character. But I presume what were in general classed as crimes against nature were Acts of Violence committed against persons. Aside from these we have a vast, an almost interminable number of offenses big and little, which are in the main attacks upon the institution of property, concerning which some very different things have to be said than concerning the first. As to these first there is no doubt that these are real crimes, by which I mean simply anti-social acts. Any action which violates the life or liberty of any individual is an anti-social act, whether done by one person, by two, or by a whole nation. And the greatest crime that ever was perpetrated, a crime beside which all individual atrocities diminish to nothing, is War; and the greatest, the least excusable of murderers are those who order it and those who execute it. Nevertheless, this chiefest of murderers, the Government, its own hands red with the blood of hundreds of thousands, assumes to correct the individual offender, enacting miles of laws to define the varying degrees of his offense and punishment, and putting beautiful building stone to very hideous purposes for the sake of caging and tormenting him therein.

We do get a fig from a thistle—sometimes! Out of this noisome thing, the prison, has sprung the study of criminology. It is very new, and there is considerable painstaking nonsense about it. But the main results are interesting and should be known by all who wish to form an intelligent conception of what a criminal is and how he should be treated. These men who are cool and quiet and who move among criminals and study them as Darwin did his plants and animals, tell us that these prisoners are reducible to three types: The Born Criminal, the Criminaloid, and the Accidental Criminal. I am inclined to doubt a great deal that is said about the born criminal. Prof. Lombroso[5] gives us very exhaustive reports of the measurements of their skulls and their ears and their noses and their thumbs and their toes, etc. But I suspect that if a good many respectable, decent, never-did-a-wrong-thing-in-their-lives people were to go up for measurement, malformed ears and disproportionately long thumbs would be equally found among them if they took the precaution to represent themselves as criminals first. Still, however few in number (and they are really very few), there are some born criminals,—people who through some malformation or deficiency or excess of certain portions of the brain are constantly impelled to violent deeds. Well, there are some born idiots and some born cripples. Do you punish them for their idiocy or for their unfortunate physical condition? On the contrary, you pity them, you realize that life is a long infliction to them, and your best and tenderest sympathies go out to them. Why not to the other, equally a helpless victim of an evil inheritance? Granting for the moment that you have the right to punish the mentally responsible, surely you will not claim the right to punish the mentally irresponsible! Even the law does not hold the insane man guilty. And the born criminal is irresponsible; he is a sick man, sick with the most pitiable chronic disease; his treatment is for the medical world to decide, and the best of them,—not for the prosecutor, the judge, and the warden.

It is true that many criminologists, including Prof. Lombroso himself, are of opinion that the best thing to do with the born criminal is to kill him at once, since he can be only a curse to himself and others. Very heroic treatment. We may inquire, Is he to be exterminated at birth because of certain physical indications of his criminality? Such neo-Spartanism would scarcely commend itself to any modern society. Moreover the diagnosis might be wrong, even though we had a perpetual and incorruptible commission of the learned to sit in inquiry upon every pink-skinned little suspect three days old! What then? Is he to be let go, as he is now, until he does some violent deed and then be judged more hardly because of his natural defect? Either proposition seems not only heartless and wicked but,—what the respectable world is often more afraid of being than either,—ludicrous. If one is really a born criminal he will manifest criminal tendencies in early life, and being so recognized should be cared for according to the most humane methods of treating the mentally afflicted.

The second, or criminaloid, class is the most numerous of the three. These are criminals, first, because being endowed with strong desires and unequal reasoning powers they cannot maintain the uneven battle against a society wherein the majority of individuals must all the time deny their natural appetites, if they are to remain unstained with crime. They are, in short, the ordinary man (who, it must be admitted, has a great deal of paste in him) plus an excess of wants of one sort and another, but generally phyiscal. Society outside of prisons is full of these criminaloids, who sometimes have in place of the power of genuine moral resistance a sneaking cunning by which they manage to steer a shady course between the crime and the punishment.

It is true these people are not pleasant subjects to contemplate; but then, through that very stage of development the whole human race has had to pass in its progress from the beast to the man,—the stage, I mean, of overplus of appetite opposed by weak moral resistance; and if now some, it is not certain that their number is very great, have reversed the proportion, it is only because they are the fortunate heritors of the results of thousands of years of struggle and failure, struggle and failure, but *struggle* again. It is precisely these criminaloids who are most sinned against by society, for they are the people who need to have the right way of doing things made easy, and who, when they act criminally, need the most encouragement to help the feeble and humiliated moral sense to rise again, to try again.

The third class, the Accidental or Occasional Criminals, are perfectly normal, well-balanced people, who, through tremendous stress of outward circumstance, and possibly some untoward mental disturbance rising from those very notions of the conduct of life which form part of their moral being, suddenly commit an act of violence which is at utter variance with their whole former existence; such as, for instance, the murder of a seducer by the father of the injured girl, or of a wife's paramour by her husband. If I believed in severity at all I should say that these were the criminals upon whom society should look with most severity, because they are the ones who have most mental responsibility. But that also is nonsense; for such an individual has within him a severer judge, a more pitiless jailer than any court or prison,—his conscience and his memory. Leave him to these; or no, in mercy take him away from these whenever you can; he will suffer enough, and there is no fear of his action being repeated.

Now all these people are with us, and it is desirable that something be done to help the case. What does Society do? Or rather what does Government do with them? Remember we are speaking now only of crimes of violence. It hangs, it electrocutes, it exiles, it imprisons. Why? For punishment. And why punishment? "Not," says Blackstone, "by way of atonement or expiation for the crime committed, for that must be left to the just determination of the Supreme Being, but as a precaution against future offenses of the same kind." This is supposed to be effected in three ways: either by reforming him, or getting rid of him altogether, or by deterring others by making an example of him.

Let us see how these precautions work. Exile, which is still practised by some governments, and imprisonment are, according to the theory of law, for the purpose of reforming the criminal that he may no longer be a menace to society. Logic would say that anyone who wished to obliterate cruelty from the character of another must himself show no cruelty; one who would teach regard for the rights of others must himself be regardful. Yet the story of exile and prison is the story of the lash, the iron, the chain and every torture that the fiendish ingenuity of *the non-criminal class can devise by way of teaching criminals to be good!* To teach men to be good, they are kept in airless cells, made to sleep on narrow planks, to look at the sky through iron grates, to eat food that revolts their palates, and destroys their stomachs,—battered and broken down in body and soul; and this is what they call reforming men!

Not very many years ago the Philadelphia dailies told us (and while we cannot believe all of what they say, and are bound to believe that such cases are exceptional, yet the bare facts were true) that Judge Gordon[6] ordered an investigation into the workings of the Eastern Penitentiary officials: and it was found that an insane man had been put into a cell with two sane ones, and when he cried in his insane way and the two asked that he be put elsewhere, the warden gave them a strap to whip him with; and they tied him in some way to the heater, with the strap, so that his legs were burned when he moved; all scarred with the burns he was brought into the court, and the other men frankly told what they had done and why they had done it. This is the way they reform men.

Do you think people come out of a place like that better? with more respect for society? with more regard for the rights of their fellow men? I don't. I think they come out of there with their hearts full of bitterness, much harder than when they went in. That this is often the case is admitted by those who themselves believe in punishment, and practice it. For the fact is that out of the Criminaloid class there develops the Habitual Criminal, the man who is perpetually getting in prison; no sooner is he out than he does something else and gets in again. The brand that at first scorched him has succeeded in searing. He no longer feels the ignominy. He is a "jail-bird," and he gets to have a cynical pride in his own degradation. Every man's hand is against him, and his hand is against every man's. Such are the reforming effects of punishment. Yet there was a time when he, too, might have been touched, had the right word been spoken. It is for society to find and speak that word.

This for prison and exile. Hanging? electrocution? These of course are not for the purpose of reforming the criminal! These are to deter others from doing as he did; and the supposition is that the severer the punishment the greater the deterrent effect. In commenting upon this principle Blackstone[7] says: "We may observe that punishments of unreasonable severity ... have less effect in preventing crimes and amending the manners of a people than such as are more merciful in general..." He further quotes Montesquieu[8]: "For the excessive severity of laws hinders their execution; when the punishment surpasses all measure, the public will frequently, out of humanity, prefer impunity to it." Again Blackstone: "It is a melancholy truth that among the variety of actions which men are daily liable to commit, no less than one hundred and sixty have been declared by act of Parliament to be felonies ... worthy of instant death. So dreadful a list instead of diminishing *increases* the number of offenders."

Robert Ingersoll[9], speaking on "Crimes against Criminals" before the New York State Bar Association, a lawyer addressing lawyers, treating of this same period of which Blackstone writes, says: "There is something in injustice, in cruelty, which tends to defeat itself. There never were so many traitors in England as when the traitor was drawn and quartered, when he was tortured in every possible way,—when his limbs, torn and bleeding, were given to the fury of mobs, or exhibited pierced by pikes or hung in chains. The frightful punishments produced intense hatred of the government, and traitors increased until they became powerful enough to decide what treason was and who the traitors were and to inflict the same torments on others."

The fact that Blackstone was right and Ingersoll was right in saying that severity of punishment increases crime, is silently admitted in the abrogation of those severities by acts of Parliament and acts of Congress. It is also shown by the fact that there are no more murders proportionately in States where the death penalty does not exist than in those where it does. Severity is therefore admitted by the State itself to have no deterrent influence on the intending criminal. And to take the matter out of the province of the State, we have only to instance the horrible atrocities perpetrated by white mobs upon negroes charged with outrage. Nothing more fiendishly cruel can be imagined; yet these outrages multiply. It would seem, then, that the notion of making a terrible example of the misdoer is a complete failure. As a specific example of this, Ingersoll (in this same lecture) instanced that "a few years before a man was hanged in Alexandria, Va. One who witnessed the execution on that very day murdered a pedler in the Smithsonian grounds at Washington. He was tried and executed; and one who witnessed his hanging went home and on the same day murdered his wife." Evidently the brute is rather aroused than terrified by scenes of execution.

What then? If extreme punishments do not deter, and if what are considered mild punishments do not reform, is any measure of punishment conceivable or attainable which will better our case?

Before answering this question let us consider the class of crimes which so far has not been dwelt upon, but which nevertheless comprises probably nine-tenths of all offenses committed. These are all the various forms of stealing,—robbery, burglary, theft, embezzlement, forgery, counterfeiting, and the thousand and one ramifications and offshoots of the act of taking what the law defines as another's. It is impossible to consider crimes of violence apart from these, because the vast percentage of murders and assaults committed by the criminaloid class are simply incidental to the commission of the so-called lesser crime. A man often murders in order to escape with his booty, though murder was no part of his original intention. Why, now, have we such a continually increasing percentage of stealing?

Will you persistently hide your heads in the sand and say it is because men grow worse as they grow wiser? that individual wickedness is the result of all our marvelous labors to compass sea and land, and make the earth yield up her wealth to us? Dare you say that?

It is not so? THE REASON MEN STEAL IS BECAUSE THEIR RIGHTS ARE STOLEN FROM THEM BEFORE THEY ARE BORN.

A human being comes into the world; he wants to eat, he wants to breathe, he wants to sleep; he wants to use his muscles, his brain; he wants to love, to dream, to create. These wants constitute him, the whole man; he can no more help expressing these activities than water can help running down hill. If the freedom to do any of these things is denied him, then by so much he is a crippled creature, and his energy will force itself into some abnormal channel or be killed altogether. Now I do not mean that he has a "natural right" to do these things inscribed on any lawbook of Nature. Nature knows nothing of rights, she knows powers only, and a louse has as much natural right as a man to the extent of its power. What I do mean to say is that man, in common with many other animals, has found that by associative life he conquers the rest of nature, and that this society is slowly being perfected; and that this perfectionment consists in realizing that the solidarity and safety of the whole arises from the freedom of the parts; that such freedom constitutes Man's Social Right; and that any institution which interferes with this right will be destructive of the association, will breed criminals, will work its own ruin. This is the word of the sociologist, of the greatest of them, Herbert Spencer[10].

Now do we see that all men eat,—eat well? You know we do not. Some have so much that they are sickened with the extravagance of dishes, and know not where next to turn for a new palatal sensation. They cannot even waste their wealth. Some, and they are mostly the hardest workers, eat poorly and fast, for their work allows them no time to enjoy even what they have. Some,—I have seen them myself in the streets of New York this winter, and the look of their wolfish eyes was not pleasant to see—stand in long lines waiting for midnight and the plate of soup dealt out by some great newspaper office, stretching out, whole blocks of them, as other men wait on the first night of some famous star at the theater! Some die because they cannot eat at all. Pray tell me what these last have to lose by becoming thieves. And why shall they not become thieves? And is the action of the man who takes the necessities which have been denied to him really criminal? Is he morally worse than the man who crawls in a cellar and dies of starvation? I think not. He is only a little more assertive. Cardinal Manning[11] said: "A starving man has a natural right to his neighbor's bread." The Anarchist says: "A hungry man has a social right to bread." And there have been whole societies and races among whom that right was never questioned. And whatever were the mistakes of those societies, whereby they perished, this was not a mistake, and we shall do well to take so much wisdom from the dead and gone, the simple ethics of the stomach which with all our achievement we cannot despise, or despising, shall perish as our reward.

"But," you will say, and say truly, "to begin by taking loaves means to end by taking everything and murdering, too, very often." And in that you draw the indictment against your own system. If there is no alternative between starving and stealing, (and for thousands there is none) then there is no alternative between society's murdering its members, or the members disintegrating society. Let Society consider its own mistakes, then: let it answer itself for all these people it has robbed and killed: let it cease its own crimes first!

To return to the faculties of Man. All would breathe; and some do breathe. They breathe the air of the mountains, of the seas, of the lakes,—even the atmosphere in the gambling dens of Monte Carlo, for a change! Some, packed thickly together in closed rooms where men must sweat and faint to save tobacco, breathe the noisome reek that rises from the spittle of their consumptive neighbors. Some, mostly babies, lie on the cellar doors along Bainbridge street, on summer nights, and bathe their lungs in that putrid air where a thousand lungs have breathed before, and grow up pale and decayed looking as the rotting vegetables whose exhalations they draw in. Some, far down underground, meet the choke-damp, and—do not breathe at all! Do you expect healthy morals out of all these poisoned bodies?

Some sleep. They have so much time that they take all manner of expensive drugs to try what sleeping it off a different way is like! Some sleep upon none too easy beds a few short hours, too few not to waken more tired than ever, and resume the endless grind of waking life. Some sleep bent over the books they are too tired to study, though the mind clamors for food after the long day's physical toil. Some sleep with hand upon the throttle of the engine, after twenty-six hours of duty, and—crash!—they have sleep enough!

Some use their muscles: they use them to punch bags, and other gentlemen's stomachs when their heads are full of wine. Some use them to club other men and women, at $2.50 a day. Some exhaust them welding them into iron, or weaving them into wool, for ten or eleven hours a day. And some become atrophied sitting at desks till they are mere specters of men and women.

Some love; and there is no end to the sensualities of their love, because all normal expressions have lost their savor through excess. Some love, and see their love tried and worn and threadbare, a skeleton of love, because the practicality of life is always there to repress the purely emotional. Some are so stricken in health, so robbed of power to feel, that they never love at all.

And some dream, think, create; and the world is filled with the glory of their dreams. But who knows the glory of the dream that never was born, lost and dead and buried away somewhere there under the roofs where the exquisite brain was ruined by the heavy labor of life? And what of the dream that turned to madness and destroyed the thing it loved the best?

These are the things that make criminals, the perverted forces of man, turned aside by the institution of property, which is the giant social mistake to-day. It is your law which keeps men from using the sources and the means of wealth production unless they pay tribute to other men, it is this, and nothing else, which is responsible for all the second-class of crimes and all those crimes of violence incidentally committed while carrying out a robbery. Let me quote here a most sensible and appropriate editorial which recently appeared in the Philadelphia *North American*, in comment upon the proposition of some foolish preacher to limit the right of reproduction to rich families:

> *"The earth was constructed, made habitable, and populated without the advice of a commission of superior persons, and until they appeared and began meddling with affairs, making laws and setting themselves up as rulers, poverty and its evil consequences were unknown to humanity. When social science finds a way to remove obstructions to the operation of natural law and to the equitable distribution of the products of labor, poverty will cease to be the condition of the masses of people, and misery, CRIME and problems of population will disappear."*

And they will never disappear until it does. All hunting down of men, all punishments, are but so many ineffective efforts to sweep back the tide with a broom. The tide will fling you, broom and all, against the idle walls that you have built to fence it in. Tear down those walls or the sea will tear them down for you.

Have you ever watched it coming in,—the sea? When the wind comes roaring out of the mist and a great bellowing thunders up from the water? Have you watched the white lions chasing each other towards the walls, and leaping up with foaming anger as they strike, and turn and chase each other along the black bars of their cage in rage to devour each other? And tear back? And leap in again? Have you ever wondered in the midst of it all *which particular drops of water* would strike the wall? If one could know all the factors one might calculate even that. But who can know them all? Of one thing only we are sure: *some must strike it.*

They are the criminals, those drops of water pitching against that silly wall and broken. Just why it was these particular ones we cannot know; but some had to go. Do not curse them; you have cursed them enough. Let the people free.

There is a class of crimes of violence which arises from another set of causes than economic slavery, acts which are the result of an antiquated moral notion of the true relations of men and women. These are the Nemesis of the institution of property in love. If every one would learn that the limit of his right to demand a certain course of conduct in sex relations is himself; that the relation of his beloved ones to others is not a matter for him to regulate, any more than the relations of those whom he does not love; if the freedom of each is unquestioned, and whatever moral rigors are exacted are exacted of oneself only; if this principle is accepted and followed, crimes of jealousy will cease. But religions and governments uphold this institution and constantly tend to create the spirit of ownership with all its horrible consequences.

Ah, you will say, perhaps it is true; perhaps when this better social condition is evolved, and this freer social spirit, we shall be rid of crime,—at least nine-tenths of it. But meanwhile must we not punish to protect ourselves?

The protection does not protect. The violent man does not communicate his intention; when he executes it, or attempts its execution, more often than otherwise it is some unofficial person who catches or stops him. If he is a born criminal, or in other words an insane man, he should, I reiterate, be treated as a sick person,—not punished, not made to suffer. If he is one of the accidental criminals, his act will not be repeated; his punishment will always be with him. If he is of the middle class, your punishment will not reform him, it will only harden him; and it will not deter others.

As for thieves, the great thief is within the law, or he buys it; and as for the small one, see what you do! To protect yourself against him, you create a class of persons who are sworn to the service of the club and the revolver; a set of spies; a set whose business it is to deal constantly with these unhappy beings, who in rare instances are softened thereby but in the majority of cases become hardened to their work as butchers to the use of the knife; a set whose business it is to serve cell and lock and key; and lastly, the lowest infamy of all, the hangman. Does any one want to shake his hand, the hand that kills for pay?

Now against all these persons individually there is nothing to be said: they may probably be very humane, well-intentioned persons when they start in; but the end of all this is imbrutement. One of our dailies recently observed that "the men in charge of prisons have but too often been men who ought themselves to have been prisoners." The Anarchist does not agree with that. He would have no prisons at all. But I am quite sure that if that editor himself were put in the prison-keeper's place, he too would turn hard. And the opportunities of the official criminal are much greater than those of the unofficial one. Lawyer and governmentalist as he was, Ingersoll said: "It is safe to say that governments have committed far more crimes than they have prevented." Then why create a second class of parasites worse than the first? Why not put up with the original one?

Moreover, you have another thing to consider than the simple problem of a wrong inflicted upon a guilty man. How many times has it happened that the innocent man has been convicted! I remember an instance of a man so convicted of murder in Michigan. He had served twenty-seven years in Jackson penitentiary (for Michigan is not a hang-State) when the real murderer, dying, confessed. And the State *pardoned* that innocent man! Because it was the quickest legal way to let him out! I hope he has been able to pardon the State.

Not very long ago a man was hanged here in this city. He had killed his superintendent. Some doctors said he was insane; the government experts said he was not. They said he was faking insanity when he proclaimed himself Jesus Christ. And he was hanged. Afterwards the doctors found two cysts in his brain. The State of Pennsylvania had killed a sick man! And as long as punishments exist these mistakes will occur. If you accept the principle at all, you must accept with it the blood-guilt of innocent men.

Not only this, but you must accept also the responsibility for all the misery which results to others whose lives are bound up with that of the convict, for even he is loved by some one, much loved perhaps. It is a foolish thing to turn adrift a house full of children, to become criminals in turn, perhaps, in order to frighten some indefinite future offender by making an example of their father or mother. Yet how many times has it not happened.

And this is speaking only from the practical, selfish side of the matter. There is another, one from which I would rather appeal to you, and from which I think you would after all prefer to be appealed to. Ask yourselves, each of you, whether you are quite sure that you have feeling enough, understanding enough, and *have you suffered* enough, to be able to weigh and measure out another man's life or liberty, no matter what he has done? And if you have not yourself, are you able to delegate to any judge the power which you have not? The great Russian novelist, Dostoyevsky[12], in his psychological study of this same subject, traces the sufferings of a man who had committed a shocking murder; his whole body and brain are a continual prey to torture. He gives himself up, seeking relief in confession. He goes to prison, for in barbarous Russia they have not the barbarity of capital punishment for murderers, unless political ones. But he finds no relief. He remains for a year, bitter, resentful, a prey to all miserable feelings. But at last he is touched by love, the silent, unobtrusive, all-conquering love of one who knew it all and forgave it all. And the regeneration of his soul began.

"The criminal slew," says Tolstoy: "are you better, then, when you slay? He took another's liberty; and is it the right way, therefore, for you to take his? Violence is no answer to violence."

> "Have good will
> To all that lives, letting unkindness die,
> And greed and wrath; so that your lives be made
> As soft airs passing by."

So said Lord Buddha, the Light of Asia.

And another said: "Ye have heard that it hath been said 'an eye for an eye, and a tooth for a tooth'; but I say unto you, resist not him that is evil."

Yet the vengeance that the great psychologist saw was futile, the violence that the greatest living religious teacher and the greatest dead ones advised no man to wreak, that violence is done daily and hourly by every little-hearted prosecutor who prosecutes at so much a day, by every petty judge who buys his way into office with common politicians' tricks, and deals in men's lives and liberties as a trader deals in pins, by every neat-souled and cheap-souled member of the "unco guid" whose respectable bargain-counter maxims of morality have as much effect to stem the great floods and storms that shake the human will as the waving of a lady's kid glove against the tempest. Those who have not suffered cannot understand how to punish; those who have understanding *will* not.

I said at the beginning and I say again, I believe that in every one of us all things are germinal: in judge and prosecutor and prison-keeper too, and even in those small moral souls who cut out one undeviating pattern for all men to fit, even in them there are the germs of passion and crime and sympathy and forgiveness. And some day things will stir in them and accuse them and awaken them. And that awakening will come when suddenly one day there breaks upon them with realizing force the sense of the unison of life, the irrevocable relationship of the saint to the sinner, the judge to the criminal; that all personalities are intertwined and rushing upon doom together. Once in my life it was given to me to see the outward manifestation of this unison. It was in 1897. We stood upon the base of the Nelson monument in Trafalgar Square. Below were ten thousand people packed together with upturned faces. They had gathered to hear and see men and women whose hands and limbs were scarred all over with the red-hot irons of the tortures in the fortress of Montjuich. For the crime of an unknown person these twenty-eight men and women, together with four hundred others, had been cast into that terrible den and tortured with the infamies of the inquisition to make them reveal that of which they knew nothing. After a year of such suffering as makes the decent human heart sick only to contemplate, with nothing proven against them, some even without trial, they were suddenly released with orders to leave the country within twenty-four hours. They were then in Trafalgar Square, and to the credit of old England be it said, harlot and mother of harlots though she is, for there was not another country among the great nations of the earth to which those twenty-eight innocent people could go. For they were paupers impoverished by that cruel State of Spain in the terrible battle for their freedom; they would not have been admitted to free America. When Francesco Gana, speaking in a language which most of them did not understand, lifted his poor, scarred hands, the faces of those ten thousand people moved together like the leaves of a forest in the wind. They waved to and fro, they rose and fell; the visible moved in the breath of the invisible. It was the revelation of the action of the Unconscious, the fatalistic unity of man.

Sometimes, even now as I look upon you, it is as if the bodies that I see were as transparent bubbles wherethrough the red blood boils and flows, a turbulent stream churning and tossing and leaping, and behind us and our generation, far, far back, endlessly backwards, where all the bubbles are broken and not a ripple remains, the silent pouring of the Great Red River, the unfathomable River,—backwards through the unbroken forest and the untilled plain, backwards through the forgotten world of savagery and animal life, back somewhere to its dark sources in deep Sea and old Night, the rushing River of Blood—no fancy—real, tangible blood, the blood that hurries in your veins while I speak, bearing with it the curses and the blessings of the Past. Through what infinite shadows has that river rolled! Through what desolate wastes has it not spread its ooze! Through what desperate passages has it been forced! What strength, what invincible strength is in that hot stream! You are just the bubble on its crest; where will the current fling you ere you die? At what moment will the fierce impurities borne from its somber and tenebrous past be hurled up in you? Shall you then cry out for punishment if they are hurled up in another? if, flung against the merciless rocks of the channel, while you swim easily in the midstream, they fall back and hurt other bubbles?

Can you not feel that

> "Men are the heart-beats of Man, the plumes that feather his wings,
> Storm-worn since being began with the wind and the thunder of things.
> Things are cruel and blind; their strength detains and deforms,
> And the wearying wings of the mind still beat up the stream of their storms.
> Still, as one swimming up-stream, they strike out blind in the blast,
> In thunder of vision and dream, and lightning of future and past.
> We are baffled and caught in the current and bruised upon edges of shoals:
> As weeds or as reeds in the torrent of things are the wind-shaken souls.
> Spirit by spirit goes under, a foam-bell's bubble of breath,
> That blows and opens asunder and blurs not the mirror of Death."

Is is not enough that "things are cruel and blind?" Must we also be cruel and blind? When the whole thing amounts to so little at the most, shall we embitter it more, and crush and stifle what must so soon be crushed and stifled anyhow? Can we not, knowing what remnants of things dead and drowned are floating through us, haunting our brains with specters of old deeds and scenes of violence, can we not learn to pardon our brother to whom the specters are more real, upon whom greater stress was laid? Can we not, recalling all the evil things that we have done, or left undone only because some scarcely perceptible weight struck down the balance, or because some kindly word came to us in the midst of our bitterness and showed that not all was hateful in the world; can we not understand him for whom the balance was not struck down, the kind word unspoken? Believe me, forgiveness is better than wrath,—better for the wrong-doer, who will be touched and regenerated by it, and better for you. And you are wrong if you think it is hard: it is easy, far easier than to hate. It may sound like a paradox, but the greater the injury the easier the pardon.

Let us have done with this savage idea of punishment, which is without wisdom. Let us work for the freedom of man from the oppressions which make criminals, and for the enlightened treatment of all the sick. And though we may never see the fruit of it, we may rest assured that the great tide of thought is se ng our way, and that

"While the tired wave, vainly breaking,
Seems here no painful inch to gain,
Far back through creeks and inlets making,
Comes silent, flooding in, the main."

McKinley's Assassination from the Anarchist Standpoint

Six years have passed since William McKinley[1] met his doom at Buffalo and the return stroke of justice took the life of his slayer, Leon Czolgosz[2]. The wild rage that stormed through the brains of the people, following that revolver shot, turning them into temporary madmen, incapable of seeing, hearing, or thinking correctly, has spent itself. Figures are beginning to appear in their true relative proportions, and there is some likelihood that sane words will be sanely listened to. Instead of the wild and savage threats, "Brand the Anarchists with hot iron," "Boil in oil," "Hang to the first lamp-post," "Scourge and shackle," "Deport to a desert island," which were the stock phrases during the first few weeks following the tragedy, and were but the froth of the upheaved primitive barbarity of civilized men, torn loose and raging like an unreasoning beast, we now hear an occasional serious inquiry: "But what have the Anarchists to say about it? Was Czolgosz really an Anarchist? Did he say he was? And what has Anarchism to do with assassination altogether?"

To those who wish to know what the Anarchists have to say, these words are addressed. We have to say that *not Anarchism, but the state of society which creates men of power and greed and the victims of power and greed*, is responsible for the death of both McKinley and Czolgosz. Anarchism has this much to do with assassination, that as it teaches the possibility of a society in which the needs of life may be fully supplied for all, and in which the opportunities for complete development of mind and body shall be the heritage of all; as it teaches that the present unjust organization of the production and distribution of wealth must finally be completely destroyed, and replaced by a system which will insure to each the liberty to work, without first seeking a master to whom he must surrender a tithe of his product, which will guarantee his liberty of access to the sources and means of production; as it teaches that all this is possible without the exhaustion of body and mind which is hourly wrecking the brain and brawn of the nations in the present struggle of the workers to achieve a competence, it follows that Anarchism does create rebels. Out of the blindly submissive, it makes the discontented, out of the unconsciously dissatisfied, it makes the consciously dissatisfied. Every movement for the social betterment of the peoples, from time immemorial, has done the same. And since among the ranks of dissatisfied people are to be found all manner of temperaments and degrees of mental development—just as are found among the satisfied also—it follows that there are occasionally those who translate their dissatisfaction into a definite act of reprisal against the society which is crushing them and their fellows. Assassination of persons representing the ruling power is such an act of reprisal. There have been Christian assassins, Republican assassins, Socialist assassins, and Anarchist assassins; in no case was the act of assassination an expression of any of these religious or political creeds, but of temperamental reaction against the injustice created by the prevailing system of the time (excluding, of course, such acts as were merely the result of personal ambition or derangement). Moreover, Anarchism less than any of these can have anything to do in determining a specific action, since, in the nature of its teaching, every Anarchist must act purely on his own initiative and responsibility; there are no secret societies nor executive boards of any description among Anarchists. But that among a mass of people who realize fully what a slaughter-house capitalism has made of the world, how even little children are daily and hourly crippled, starved, doomed to the slow death of poisoned air, to ruined eyesight, wasted limbs, and polluted blood; how through the sapping of the present generation's strength the unborn are condemned to a rotten birthright, all that riches may be heaped where they are not needed; who realize that all this is unnecessary and stupid as it is wicked and revolting; that among these there should be some who rise up and strike back, whether wisely or unwisely, effectively or ineffectively, is no matter for wonder; the wonder is there are not more. *The hells of capitalism create the desperate; the desperate act,—desperately!*

And in so far as Anarchism seeks to arouse the consciousness of oppression, the desire for a better society, and a sense of the necessity for unceasing warfare against capitalism and the State, the authors of all this unrecognized but Nemesis-bearing crime, in so far it is responsible and does not shirk its responsibility: "For it is impossible but that offences come; but woe unto them through whom they come."

Many offences had come through the acts of William McKinley. Upon his hand was the "damned spot" of official murder, the blood of the Filipinos, whom he, in pursuance of the capitalist policy of imperialism, had sentenced to death. Upon his head falls the curse of all the workers against whom, time and time again, he threw the strength of his official power. Without doubt he was in private life a good and kindly man; it is even probable he saw no wrong in the terrible deeds he had commanded done. Perhaps he was able to reconcile his Christian belief, "Do good to them that hate you," with the slaughters he ordered; perhaps he murdered the Filipinos "to do them good"; the capitalist mind is capable of such contortions. But whatever his private life, he was the representative of wealth and greed and power; in accepting the position he accepted the rewards and the dangers, just as a miner, who goes down in the mine for $2.50 a day or less, accepts the danger of the firedamp. McKinley's rewards were greater and his risks less; moreover, he didn't need the job to keep bread in his mouth; but he, too, met an explosive force—the force of a desperate man's will. And he died; *not as a martyr, but as a gambler who had won a high stake and was struck down by the man who had lost the game*: for that is what capitalism has made of human well-being—a gambler's stake, no more.

Who was this man? No one knows. A child of the great darkness, a spectre out of the abyss! Was he an Anarchist? We do not know. None of the Anarchists knew him, save as a man with whom some few of them had exchanged a few minutes' conversation, in which he said that he had been a Socialist, but was then dissatisfied with the Socialist movement. The police said he was an Anarchist; the police said he attributed his act to the influence of a lecture of Emma Goldman[3]. But the police have lied before, and, like the celebrated Orchard[4], they need "corroborative evidence." All that we really know of Czolgosz is his revolver shot and his dying words: "I killed the President because he was the enemy of the people, the good, working people." All between is blank. What he really said, if he said anything, remains in the secret papers of the Buffalo Police Department and the Auburn prison. If we are to judge inferentially, considering his absolutely indifferent behavior at his "trial," he never said anything at all. He was utterly at their mercy, and had they been able to twist or torture any word of his into "conspiracy," they would have done it. Hence it is most probable he said nothing.

Was he a normal or abnormal being? In full possession of his senses, or of a disturbed or weak mentality? Again we do not know. All manner of fables arose immediately after his act as to his boyhood's career; people knew him in his childhood as evil, stupid, cruel; even some knew him who had heard him talk about assassinating the President years before; other legends contradicted these; all were equally unreliable. His indifference at the "trial" may have been that of a strong man enduring a farce, or of a clouded and non-realizing mind. His last words were the words of a naïve and devoted soul, a soul quite young, quite unselfish, and quite forlorn. If martyrdom is insisted upon, which was the martyr, the man who had had the good of life, who was past middle years, who had received reward and distinction to satiety, who had ordered others killed without once jeopardizing his own life, and to whom death came more easily than to millions who die of long want and slow tortures of disease, or this young strong soul which struck its own blow and paid with its own life, so capable of the utterest devotion, so embittered and ruined in its youth, so hopeless, so wasted, so cast out of the heart of pity, so altogether alone in its last agony? This was the greater tragedy—a tragedy bound to be repeated over and over, until "the good working people" (in truth they are not so good) learn that the earth is theirs and the fullness thereof, and that there is no need for any one to enslave himself to another. This Anarchism teaches, and this the future will realize, though many martyrdoms lie between.

The Eleventh of November, 1887

Memorial Oration

Let me begin my address with a confession. I make it sorrowfully and with self-disgust; but in the presence of great sacrifice we learn humility, and if my comrades could give their lives for their belief, why, let me give my pride. Yet I would not give it, for personal utterance is of trifling importance, were it not that I think at this particular season it will encourage those of our sympathizers whom the recent outburst of savagery may have disheartened, and perhaps lead some who are standing where I once stood to do as I did later.

This is my confession: Fifteen years ago last May when the echoes of the Haymarket bomb rolled through the little Michigan village where I then lived, I, like the rest of the credulous and brutal, read one lying newspaper headline, "Anarchists throw a bomb in a crowd in the Haymarket in Chicago," and immediately cried out, "They ought to be hung."—This, though I had never believed in capital punishment for ordinary criminals. For that ignorant, outrageous, blood-thirsty sentence I shall never forgive myself, though I know the dead men would have forgiven me, though I know those who loved them forgive me. But my own voice, as it sounded that night, will sound so in my ears till I die,—a bitter reproach and shame. What had I done? Credited the first wild rumor of an event of which I knew nothing, and, in my mind, sent men to the gallows without asking one word of defense! In one wild, unbalanced moment threw away the sympathies of a lifetime, and became an executioner at heart. And what I did that night millions did, and what I said millions said. I have only one word of extenuation for myself and all those people—ignorance. I did not know what Anarchism was. I had never seen it used save in histories, and there it was always synonymous with social confusion and murder. I believed the newspapers. I thought these men had thrown that bomb, unprovoked, into a mass of men and women, from a wicked delight in killing. And so thought all those millions of others. But out of those millions there were some few thousand—I am glad I was one of them—who did not let the matter rest there.

I know not what resurrection of human decency first stirred within me after that,—whether it was an intellectual suspicion that may be I did not know all the truth of the case and could not believe the newspapers, or whether it was the old strong undercurrent of sympathy which often prompts the heart to go out to the accused, without a reason; but this I do know that though I was no Anarchist at the time of the execution, it was long and long before that, that I came to the conclusion that the accusation was false, the trial a farce, that there was no warrant either in justice or in law for their conviction; and that the hanging, if hanging there should be, would be the act of a society composed of people who had said what I said on the first night, and who had kept their eyes and ears fast shut ever since, determined to see nothing and to know nothing but rage and vengeance. Till the very end I hoped that mercy might intervene, though justice did not; and from the hour I knew neither would nor ever could again, I distrusted law and lawyers, judges and governors alike. And my whole being cried out to know what it was these men had stood for, and why they were hanged, seeing it was not proven they knew anything about the throwing of the bomb.

Little by little, here and there, I came to know that what they had stood for was a very high and noble ideal of human life, and what they were hanged for was preaching it to the common people,—the common people who were as ready to hang them, in their ignorance, as the court and the prosecutor were in their malice! Little by little I came to know that these were men who had a clearer vision of human right than most of their fellows; and who, being moved by deep social sympathies, wished to share their vision with their fellows, and so proclaimed it in the market-place. Little by little I realized that the misery, the pathetic submission, the awful degradation of the workers, which from the time I was old enough to begin to think had borne heavily upon my heart, (as they must bear upon all who have hearts to feel at all), had smitten theirs more deeply still,—so deeply that they knew no rest save in seeking a way out,—and that was more than I had ever had the sense to conceive. For me there had never been a hope there should be no more rich and poor; but a vague idea that there might not be so rich and so poor, if the workingmen by combining could exact a little better wages, and make their hours a little shorter. It was the message of these men, (and their death swept that message far out into ears that would never have heard their living voices), that all such little dreams are folly. That not in demanding little, not in striking for an hour less, not in mountain labor to bring forth mice, can any lasting alleviation come; but in demanding, much,—all,—in a bold self-assertion of the worker to toil any hours he finds sufficient, not that another finds for him,—here is where the way out lies. That message, and the message of others, whose works, associated with theirs, their death drew my notice, took me up, as it were, upon a mighty hill, wherefrom I saw the roofs of the workshops of the little world. I saw the machines, the things that men had made to ease their burden, the wonderful things, the iron genii, I saw them set their iron teeth in the living flesh of the men who made them; I saw the maimed and crippled stumps of men go limping away into the night that engulfs the poor, perhaps to be thrown up in the flotsam and jetsam of beggary for a time, perhaps to suicide in some dim corner where the black surge throws its slime.

I saw the rose fire of the furnace shining on the blanched face of the man who tended it, and knew surely as I knew anything in life, that never would a free man feed his blood to the fire like that.

I saw swart bodies, all mangled and crushed, borne from the mouths of the mines to be stowed away in a grave hardly less narrow and dark than that in which the living form had crouched ten, twelve, fourteen hours a day; and I knew that in order that I might be warm—I, and you, and those others who never do any dirty work—those men had slaved away in those black graves, and been crushed to death at last.

I saw beside city streets great heaps of horrible colored earth, and down at the bottom of the trench from which it was thrown, so far down that nothing else was visible, bright gleaming eyes, like a wild animal's hunted into its hole. And I knew that free men never chose to labor there, with pick and shovel in that foul, sewage-soaked earth in that narrow trench, in that deadly sewer gas ten, eight, even six hours a day. Only slaves would do it.

I saw deep down in the hull of the ocean liner the men who shoveled the coal—burned and seared like paper before the grate; and I knew that "the record" of the beautiful monster, and the pleasure of the ladies who laughed on the deck, were paid for with these withered bodies and souls.

I saw the scavenger carts go up and down, drawn by sad brutes driven by sadder ones; for never a man, a man in full possession of his self-hood, would freely choose to spend all his days in the nauseating stench that forces him to swill alcohol to neutralize it.

And I saw in the lead works how men were poisoned, and in the sugar refineries how they went insane; and in the factories how they lost their decency; and in the

179

stores how they learned to lie; and I knew it was slavery made them do all this. I knew the Anarchists were right,—the whole thing must be changed, the whole thing was wrong,—the whole system of production and distribution, the whole ideal of life.

And I questioned the government then; they had taught me to question it. What have you done—you the keepers of the Declaration and the Constitution—what have you done about all this? What have you done to preserve the conditions of freedom to the people?

Lied, deceived, fooled, tricked, bought and sold and got gain! You have sold away the land, that you had no right to sell. You have murdered the aboriginal people, that you might seize the land in the name of the white race, and then steal it away from them again, to be again sold by a second and a third robber. And that buying and selling of the land has driven the people off the healthy earth and away from the clean air into these rot-heaps of humanity called cities, where every filthy thing is done, and filthy labor breeds filthy bodies and filthy souls. Our boys are decayed with vice before they come to manhood; our girls—ah, well might John Harvey write:

> "Another begetteth a daughter white and gold,
> She looks into the meadow land water, and the world
> Knows her no more; they have sought her field and fold
> But the City, the City hath bought her,
> It hath sold
> Her piecemeal, to students, rats, and reek of the graveyard mould."

You have done this thing, gentlemen who engineer the government; and not only have you caused this ruin to come upon others; you yourselves are rotten with this debauchery. You exist for the purpose of granting privileges to whoever can pay most for you, and so limiting the freedom of men to employ themselves that they must sell themselves into this frightful slavery or become tramps, beggars, thieves, prostitutes, and murderers. And when you have done all this, what then do you do to them, these creatures of your own making? You, who have set them the example in every villainy? Do you then relent, and remembering the words of the great religious teacher to whom most of you offer lip service on the officially religious day, do you go to these poor, broken, wretched creatures and love them? Love them and help them, to teach them to be better? No: you build prisons high and strong, and there you beat, and starve, and hang, finding by the working of your system human beings so unutterably degraded that they are willing to kill whomsoever they are told to kill at so much monthly salary.

This is what the government is, has always been, the creator and defender of privilege; the organization of oppression and revenge. To hope that it can ever become anything else is the vainest of delusions. They tell you that Anarchy, the dream of social order without government, is a wild fancy. The wildest dream that ever entered the heart of man is the dream that mankind can ever help itself through an appeal to law, or to come to any order that will not result in slavery wherein there is any excuse for government.

It was for telling the people this that these five men were killed. For telling the people that the only way to get out of their misery was first to learn what their rights upon the earth were;—freedom to use the land and all within it and all the tools of production—and then to stand all together and take them, themselves, and not to appeal to the jugglers of the law. Abolish the law—that is abolish privilege,—and crime will abolish itself.

They will tell you these men were hanged for advocating force. What! These creatures who drill men in the science of killing, who put guns and clubs in hands they train to shoot and strike, who hail with delight the latest inventions in explosives, who exult in the machine that can kill the most with the least expenditure of energy, who declare a war of extermination upon people who do not want their civilization, who ravish, and burn, and garotte and guillotine, and hang, and electrocute, they have the impertinence to talk about the unrighteousness of force! True, these men did advocate the right to resist invasion by force. You will find scarcely one in a thousand who does not believe in that right. The one will be either a real Christian or a non-resistant Anarchist. It will not be a believer in the State. No, no; it was not for advocating forcible resistance on principle, but for advocating forcible resistance to their tyrannies, and for advocating a society which would forever make an end of riches and poverty, of governors and governed.

The spirit of revenge, which is always stupid, accomplished its brutal act. Had it lifted its eyes from its work, it might have seen in the background of the scaffold that bleak November morning the dawn-light of Anarchy whiten across the world.

So it came first,—a gleam of hope to the proletaire, a summons to rise and shake off his material bondage. But steadily, steadily the light had grown, as year by year the scientist, the literary genius, the artist, and the moral teacher, have brought to it the tribute of their best work, their unpaid work, the work they did for love. To-day it means not only material emancipation, too; it comes as the summing up of all those lines of thought and action which for three hundred years have been making towards freedom; it means fulness of being, the free life.

And I say it boldly, notwithstanding the recent outburst of condemnation, notwithstanding the cry of lynch, burn, shoot, imprison, deport, and the Scarlet Letter A to be branded low down upon the forehead, and the latest excuse for that fond esthetic decoration "the button," that for two thousand years no idea has so stirred the world as this,—none which had such living power to break down barriers of race and degree, to attract prince and proletaire, poet and mechanic, Quaker and Revolutionist. No other ideal but the free life is strong enough to touch the man whose infinite pity and understanding goes alike to the hypocrite priest and the victim of Siberian whips; the loving rebel who stepped from his title and his wealth to labor with all the laboring earth; the sweet strong singer[1] who sang

> *"No Master, high or low";*

the lover who does not measure his love nor reckon on return; the self-centered one who "will not rule, but also will not ruled be"; the philosopher who chanted the Overman; the devoted woman of the people; ay, and these too,—these rebellious flashes from the vast cloud-hung ominous obscurity of the anonymous, these souls whom governmental and capitalistic brutality has whipped and goaded and stung to blind rage and bitterness, these mad young lions of revolt, these Winkelrieds[2] who offer their hearts to the spears.

Collected Poetry

Bastard Born

Why do you clothe me with scarlet of shame?
   Why do you point with your finger of scorn?
What is the crime that you hissingly name
   When you sneer in my ears, "Thou bastard born?"

Am I not as the rest of you,
   With a hope to reach, and a dream to live?
With a soul to suffer, a heart to know
   The pangs that the thrusts of the heartless give?

I am no monster! Look at me—
   Straight in my eyes, that they do not shrink!
Is there aught in them you can see
   To merit this hemlock you make me drink?

This poison that scorches my soul like fire,
   That burns and burns until love is dry,
And I shrivel with hate, as hot as a pyre,
   A corpse, while its smoke curls up to the sky?

Will you touch my hand? It is flesh like yours;
   Perhaps a little more brown and grimed,
For it could not be white while the drawers' and hewers',
   My brothers, were calloused and darkened and slimed.

Yet touch it! It is no criminal's hand!
   No children are toiling to keep it fair!
It is free from the curse of the stolen land,
   It is clean of the theft of the sea and air!

It has set no seals to a murderous law,
   To sign a bitter, black league with death!
No covenants false do these fingers draw
   In the name of "The State" to barter Faith!

It bears no stain of the yellow gold
    That earth's wretches give as the cost of heaven!
No priestly garment of silken fold
    I wear as the price of their "sins forgiven"!

Still do you shrink! Still I hear the hiss
    Between your teeth, and I feel the scorn
That flames in your gaze! Well, what is this,
    This crime I commit, being "bastard born"?

What! You whisper my "eyes are gray,"
    The "color of hers," up there on the hill,
Where the white stone gleams, and the willow spray
    Falls over her grave in the starlight still!

My "hands are shaped like" those quiet hands,
    Folded away from their life, their care;
And the sheen that lies on my short, fair strands
    Gleams darkly down on her buried hair!

My voice is toned like that silent tone
    That might, if it could, break up through the sod
With such rebuke as would shame your stone,
    Stirring the grass-roots in their clod!

And my heart-beats thrill to the same strong chords;
    And the blood that was hers is mine to-day;
And the thoughts she loved, I love; and the words
    That meant most to her, to me most say!

She was my mother—I her child!
    Could ten thousand priests have made us more?
Do you curse the bloom of the heather wild?
    Do you trample the flowers and cry "impure"?

Do you shun the bird-songs' silver shower?
    Does their music arouse your curling scorn
That none but God blessed them? The whitest flower,
    The purest song, were but "bastard born"!

This is my sin,—I was born of her!
    This is my crime,—that I reverence deep!
God, that her pale corpse may not stir,
    Press closer down on her lids—the sleep!

Would you have me hate her? Me, who knew
    That the gentlest soul in the world looked there,
Out of the gray eyes that pitied you
    E'en while you cursed her? The long brown hair

That waived from her forehead, has brushed my cheek,
    When her soft lips have drunk up my salt of grief;
And the voice, whose echo you hate, would speak
    The hush of pity and love's relief!

And those still hands that are folded now
    Have touched my sorrows for years away!
Would you have me question her whence and how
    The love-light streamed from her heart's deep ray?

Do you question the sun that it gives its gold?
    Do you scowl at the cloud when it pours its rain
Till the fields that were withered and burnt and old
    Are fresh and tender and young again?

Do you search the source of the breeze that sweeps
    The rush of the fever from the tortured brain?
Do you ask whence the perfume that round you creeps
    When your soul is wrought to the quick with pain?

She was my Sun, my Dew, my Air,
    The highest, the purest, the holiest;
PEACE—was the shade of her beautiful hair,
    LOVE—was all that I knew on her breast!

Would you have me forget? Or remembering
    Say that her love had bloomed from Hell?
Then BLESSED BE HELL! And let Heaven sing
    "*Te Deum laudamus*," until it swell

And ring and roll to the utterest earth,
    That the damned are free,—since out of sin
Came the whiteness that shamed all ransomed worth
    Till God opened the gates, saying "Enter in!"
        *   *   *   *   *
What! In the face of the witness I bear
    To her measureless love and her purity,
Still of your hate would you make me to share,
    Despising that she gave life to me?

You would have me stand at her helpless grave,
    To dig through its earth with a venomed dart!
This is Honor! and Right! and Brave!
    To fling a stone at her pulseless heart!

This is Virtue! To blast the lips
    Speechless beneath the Silence dread!
To lash with Slander's scorpion whips
    The voiceless, defenseless, helpless dead!
        *   *   *   *   *
God! I turn to an adder now!
    Back upon you I hurl your scorn!
Bind the scarlet upon your brow!
    Ye it is, who are "bastard born"!

Touch me not! These hands of mine
    Despise your fairness—the leper's white!
Tanned and hardened and black with grime,
    They are clean beside your souls to-night!

Basely born! 'Tis ye are base!
    Ye who would guerdon holy trust
With slavish law to a tyrant race,
    To sow the earth with the seed of lust.

Base! By Heaven! Prate of peace,
    When your garments are red with the stain of wars.
Reeling with passion's mad release
    By your sickly gaslight damn the stars!

Blurred with wine ye behold the snow
    Smirched with the foulness that blots within!
What of purity can ye know,
    Ye ten-fold children of Hell and Sin?

Ye to judge her! Ye to cast
    The stone of wrath from your house of glass!
Know ye the Law, that ye dare to blast
    The bell of gold with your clanging brass?

Know ye the harvest the reapers reap
    Who drop in the furrow the seed of scorn?
Out of this anguish ye harrow deep,
    Ripens the sentence: "*Ye*, bastard born!"

Ay, sin-begotten, hear the curse;
    Not mine—not hers—but the fatal Law!
"Who bids one suffer, shall suffer worse;
    Who scourges, himself shall be scourged raw!

"For the thoughts ye think, and the deeds ye do,
    Move on, and on, till the flood is high,
And the dread dam bursts, and the waves roar through,
    Hurling a cataract dirge to the sky!

"To-night ye are deaf to the beggar's prayer;
    To-morrow the thieves shall batter your wall!
Ye shall feel the weight of a starved child's care
    When your warders under the Mob's feet fall!

"'Tis the roar of the whirlwind ye invoke
    When ye scatter the wind of your brother's moans;
'Tis the red of your hate on your own head broke,
    When the blood of the murdered spatters the stones!

"Hark ye! Out of the reeking slums,
    Thick with the fetid stench of crime,
Boiling up through their sickening scums,
    Bubbles that burst through the crimson wine,

"Voices burst—with terrible sound,
   Crying the truth your dull souls ne'er saw!
We are *your* sentence! The wheel turns round!
   The bastard spawn of your bastard law!"

This is bastard: That Man should say
   How Love shall love, and how Life shall live!
Setting a tablet to groove God's way,
   Measuring how the divine shall give!

O, Evil Hearts! Ye have maddened me,
   That I should interpret the voice of God!
Quiet! Quiet! O angered Sea!
   Quiet! I go to her blessed sod!

    *   *   *   *   *

Mother, Mother, I come to you!
   Down in your grasses I press my face!
Under the kiss of their cold, pure dew,
   I may dream that I lie in the dear old place!

Mother, sweet Mother, take me back,
   Into the bosom from whence I came!
Take me away from the cruel rack,
   Take me out of the parching flame!

Fold me again with your beautiful hair,
   Speak to this terrible heaving Sea!
Over me pour the soothing of prayer,
   The words of the Love-child of Galilee:

"Peace—be still!" Still,—could I but hear!
   Softly,—I listen.—O fierce heart, cease!
Softly,—I breathe not,—low,—in my ear,—
   Mother, Mother—I heard you!—Peace!

Enterprise, Kansas, January, 1891.

The Gods and the People

What have you done, O skies,
That the millions should kneel to you?
Why should they lift wet eyes,
Grateful with human dew?

Why should they clasp their hands,
And bow at thy shrines, O heaven,
Thanking thy high commands
For the mercies that thou hast given?

What have those mercies been,
O thou, who art called the Good,
Who trod through a world of sin,
And stood where the felon stood?

What is that wondrous peace
Vouchsafed to the child of dust,
For whom all doubt shall cease
In the light of thy perfect trust?

How hast Thou heard their prayers
Smoking up from the bleeding sod,
Who, crushed by their weight of cares,
Cried up to Thee, Most High God?

    *   *   *   *   *

Where the swamps of Humanity sicken,
Read the answer, in dumb, white scars!
You, Skies, gave the sore and the stricken
The light of your far-off stars!

The children who plead are driven,
Shelterless, through the street,
Receiving the mercy of Heaven
Hard-frozen in glittering sleet!

The women who prayed for pity,
Who called on the saving Name,
Through the walks of your merciless city
Are crying the rent of shame.

The starving, who gazed on the plenty
In which they might not share,
Have died in their hunger, rent by
The anguish of unheard prayer!

The weary who plead for remission,
For a moment, only, release,
Have sunk, with unheeded petition:
This the Christ-pledged Peace.

These are the mercies of Heaven,
These are the answers of God
To the prayers of the agony-shriven,
From the paths where the millions plod!

The silent scorn of the sightless!
The callous ear of the deaf!
The wrath of might to the mightless!
The shroud, and the mourning sheaf!

Light—to behold their squalor!
Breath—to draw in life's pain!
Voices to plead and call for ·
Heaven's help—hearts to bleed—in vain!

    *   *   *   *   *

What have you done, O Church,
That the weary should bless your name?
Should come with faith's holy torch
To light up your alter'd fane?

Why should they kiss the folds
Of the garment of your High Priest?
Or bow to the chalice that holds
The wine of your Sacred Feast?

Have you blown out the breath of their sighs?
Have you strengthened the weak, the ill?
Have you wiped the dark tears from their eyes,
And bade their sobbing be still?

Have you touched, have you known, have you felt,
Have you bent and softly smiled
In the face of the woman, who dwelt
In lewdness—to feed her child?

Have you heard the cry in the night
Going up from the outraged heart,
Masked from the social sight
By the cloak that but angered the smart?

Have you heard the children's moan,
By the light of the skies denied?
Answer, O Walls of Stone,
In the name of your Crucified!

   * * * * *

Out of the clay of their heart-break,
From the red dew of its sod,
You have mortar'd your brick, for Christ's sake,
And reared a palace to God!

Your painters have dipped their brushes
In the tears and the blood of the race,
Whom, LIVING, your dark frown crushes—
And limned—a DEAD Savior's face!

You have seized, in the name of God, the
Child's crust from famine's dole;
You have taken the price of its body
And sung a mass for its soul!

You have smiled on the man, who, deceiving,
Paid exemption to ease your wrath!
You have cursed the poor fool who believed him,
Though her body lay prone in your path!

You have laid the seal on the lip!
You have bid us to be content!
To bow 'neath our master's whip,
And give thanks for the scourge—"heav'n sent."

These, O Church, are your thanks;
These are the fruits without flaw,
That flow from the chosen ranks
Who keep in your perfect law:

Doors hard-locked on the homeless!
Stained glass windows for bread!
On the living, the law of dumbness,
And the law of need, for—the *dead!*

Better the dead, who, not needing,
Go down to the vaults of the Earth,
Than the living whose hearts lie bleeding,
Crushed by you at their very birth.
      *   *   *   *   *
What have you done, O State,
That the toilers should shout your ways;
Should light up the fires of their hate
If a "traitor" should dare dispraise?

How do you guard the trust
That the people repose in you?
Do you keep to the law of the just,
And hold to the changeless true?

What do you mean when you say
"The home of the free and brave"?
How free are your people, pray?
Have you no such thing as a slave?

What are the lauded "rights,"
Broad-sealed by your Sovereign Grace?
What are the love-feeding sights
You yield to your subject race?

*   *   *   *   *

The rights!—Ah! the right to toil,
That another, idle, may reap;
The right to make fruitful the soil
And a meagre pittance to keep!

The right of a woman to own
Her body, spotlessly pure,
And starve in the street—alone!
The right of the wronged—to endure!

The right of the slave—to its yoke!
The right of the hungry—to pray!
The right of the toiler—to vote
For the master who buys his day!

You have sold the sun and the air!
You have dealt in the price of blood!
You have taken the lion's share
While the lion is fierce for food!

You have laid the load of the strong
On the helpless, the young, the weak!
You have trod out the purple of wrong;—
Beware where its wrath shall wreak!

"Let the Voice of the People be heard!
O—"You strangled it with your rope!
Denied the last dying word,
While your Trap and your Gallows spoke!

But a thousand voices rise
Where the words of the martyr fell;
The seed springs fast to the Skies
Watered deep from that bloody well!

*   *   *   *   *

Hark! Low down you will hear
The storm in the underground!
Listen, Tyrants, and fear!
Quake at that muffled sound!

"Heavens that mocked our dust,
Smile on, in your pitiless blue!
Silent as you are to us,
So silent are we to you!

"Churches that scourged our brains!
Priests that locked fast our hands!
We planted the torch in your chains
Now gather the burning brands!

"States, that have given us LAW,
When we asked for THE RIGHT TO EARN BREAD!
The Sword that Damocles¹ saw
By a hair swings over your head!

What ye have sown ye shall reap:
Teardrops, and Blood, and Hate,
Gaunt gather before your Seat,
And knock at your palace gate!

"There are murderers on your Thrones!
There are thieves in your Justice-halls!
White Leprosy cancers their stones,
And gnaws at their worm-eaten walls!

"And the Hand of Belshazzar's Feast²
Writes over, in flaming light:
THOUGHT'S KINGDOM NO MORE TO THE PRIEST;
NOR THE LAW OF RIGHT UNTO MIGHT."

And Thou Too

The moonlight rolls down like a river,
The silence streams out like a sea;
And far where the eastern winds quiver,
My farewell goes floating to thee.

Like night, when the sunset is fading
And starbeams troop up in the skies,
Through a cold, dark and lonely forever
Gleams the light of the poet eyes.

And sometimes when I am weary,
When the path is thorny and wild,
I'll look back to the Eyes in the twilight,
Back to the eyes that smiled.

And pray that a wreath like a rainbow
May slip from the beautiful past,
And crown me again with the sweet, strong love
And keep me, and hold me fast.

For the way is not strown with petal soft,
It is covered with hearts that weep,
And the wounds I tread touch a deeper source
Than you think it mine to keep.

Down the years I shall move without you,
Yet ever must feel the blow
That caused me a deeper pain to give
Than you will ever know.

For the tears that dropped on my hands that night
'Neath the mystical shining moon,
Were a sacred dew, consecrated there,
On the rose-altered heart of June.

And the heart that beat against mine like a bird
That is fluttering, wounded sore,
With its nest all broken, deserted, torn,
Will beat there forevermore.

But the world moves on, and the piteous Earth
Still groans in the monster pain;
And the star that leads me points onward yet,
Though the red drops fall like rain!

Ah, not to a blaze of light I go,
Nor shouts of a triumph train;
I go down to kiss the dregs of woe,
And drink up the Cup of Pain.

And whether a scaffold or crucifix waits
'Neath the light of my silver star,
I know and I care not: I only know
I shall pause not though it be far.

Though a crucified life or an agonized death,
Though long, or quick and sharp,
I am firmly wrought in the endless thread
Of Destiny's woof and warp.

And I do not shrink, though a wave of pain
Sobs over me now and then,
As I think of those "saddest of all sad words,"
The pitiful "might have been."

"It might have been"—it is not to be;
And the tones of your "swan's farewell"
Ring sadly, solemnly deep to me
Like the voice of a sobbing bell.

Ay, gather your petals and take them back
To the dead heart under the dew;
And crown it again with the red love bloom,
For the dead are always true.

But go not "back to the sediment"
In the slime of the moaning sea,
For a better world belongs to you,
And a better friend to me.

St. Johns, Michigan, 1888.

The Dirge of the Sea

Come! Come! I have waited long!
   My love is old,
      My arms are strong;
         I would woo thee, now,
            With the wave-kiss cold
               On they pallid brow;
Thou art mine, thou art mine! My very own!
   Thine ears shall hear
      My eternal moan;
         Always near
            Thou'lt feel my lips,
               And the bathing tear
                  Where my sorrow drips.
Thou, my king forever, behold thy throne!
   Reign in thy majesty, all alone.

      None! None wept for thee,
         Nearing the verge
            Of eternity!
               I, thy solemn dirge
                  Will chant for aye
                     Wide as the wave-merge
                        Into sky.
I love thee! Thou art my chosen own!
   Thy heart, like mine,
      Was cold as stone,

Thine eyes could shine
Like my blue waves fair;
Thy lips, like wine,
Curved to kisses rare!
Hard as my waves were the eyes that shone,
And the wine as deadly! Come, love, alone!
Float! Float, on the swelling wave!
Long is the hearse,
Wide the grave;
Thy pall is a curse
From the fading shore
A broken verse
From a heart wrung sore!
"Life's stream's wreck-strown!" Ah, like my own!
The words are low
As a dying groan;
The voice thrills so,
It might rouse thy breast
With pity's glow,
Wert thou like the rest!
But thou, my hero, wert never known
To feel as a human; thou stoodst, alone.

Down! Down! Behold the wrecks!
I strew the deep
With these human specks!
No faith I keep
With their moral trust;
See how I heap
Their crumbling dust!
I sneered in their faces, my own, my own,
As they knelt to pray
When the ships went down;
I flung my spray
In their dying eyes,
And laughed at the way
It drowned their cries!

On the shore they heard the exultant tone,
   And said: "The Sea laughs." Ah, I laughed alone.

     Now! Now, we twain shall go,
       Love-locked,
         Laughing so!
           The fools ye mocked
             With your tender eyes,
               The trusts ye rocked
                 With your cradling lies,
E'en like these wretches, my own, my own,
   Shall rot in clay
     Or crumbled bone,
       Thou shalt hold thy way,
         Day-kissed and fair,
           Where the wild waves play
             In the sun-thick air!
My arms, my kiss, my tears, my moan,
   Ye shall know for aye, where we wander lone.
     Love! Love! Thou wert like to me!
       Thy luring gaze
         Rolled relentlessly!
           The marsh-light blaze
             To some human soul,
               Down the darkn'ing maze
               To Ruin's goal.
Ah, how ye crushed them, my beautiful own!
  Like whistled leaves
    Around thee stown,
      Whirled the dead beliefs
        Of each long-mourned life!
         Here, no one grieves:
           Neither tears nor strife
Appeal to the Sea, where its wrecks are thrown!
   Thou shalt stand in their midst, and smile, alone!

Laugh! Laugh! O form of light!
Death hides
Thy faithless sight!
The flowing tides
Of thy heart are still;
Yet are wrecks thy brides,
For it is my will
That that which on earth made thy heaven,
my own,
May strew around
Thy eternal throne!
The gurgling sound
Of the dying cry,
The gushing wound
Of heart-agony,
Were thy joy in life! Now the Sea makes known
Thy realm in death! Thy heaven, alone!

Years! Years, ye shall mix with me!
Ye shall grow a part
Of the laughing Sea;
Of the moaning heart
Of the glittered wave
Of the sun-gleam's dart
In the ocean-grave.
Fair, cold, and faithless wert thou, my own!
For that I love
Thy heart of stone!
From the heights above
To the depths below,
Where dread things move,
There is naught can show
A life so trustless! Proud be thy crown!
Ruthless, like none, save the Sea, alone!

April, 1891.

I Am

I am! The ages on the ages roll:
    And what I am, I was, and I shall be:
    By slow growth filling higher Destiny,
And widening, ever, to the widening Goal.
I am the Stone that slept; down deep in me
    That old, old sleep has left its centurine trace;
I am the plant that dreamed; and lo! still see
    That dream-life dwelling on the Human Face.
I slept, I dreamed, I wakened: I am Man!
    The hut grows Palaces; the depths breed light;
    Still *on! Forms* pass; but *Form* yields kinglier Might!
The singer, dying where his song began,
    In Me yet lives; and yet again shall he
    Unseal the lips of greater songs To Be;
    For mine the thousand tongues of *Immortality*.

January, 1892.

Love's Ghost

Among the leaves and the rolls of moonlight,
The moon, which weaves lace on the road-white
Among the winds, and among the flowers,
Our blithe feet wander—life is ours!

Life is ours, and life is loving;
All our powers are locked in loving;
Hearts, and eyes, and lips are moving
With the ecstasy of loving.

Ah! the roses! they are blooming;
And the June air, throbbing, tuning,
Sings of Love's eternal summer—
Chants of Joy, life's only Comer;
And we clasp our hands together,
Singing in the war, sweet weather;
Kissing, thrilling with caressing,
All the sweet from Love's rose pressing.

Ah, so easy!—Earth is Heaven,—
    Darkness, shadows, do not live;
Like the rose our hearts are given,
Like the rose whose bloom is given,
To the sun-gold, and the heaven.
Not because it wills or wishes,
    But because 'tis life to give.
    *   *   *   *   *
Dreary, dreary, snow-filled darkness!
Heavy, weary, voiceless darkness!

We have drifted, drifted, drifted, you and I,
Far apart as snows and roses, sea and sky.
We have drifted, drifted, drifted, far asunder,
And my lonely voice uplifted in sad wonder,
Wakes no echo—only falls,
Heavy with its own sad calls.

All your love was of the summer;
    Born to die among the roses,
    Wither, scatter, like the roses,
Leaving me the gray-browed Comer,
With the ashes on his forehead,
    And the winter in his hair,
With the footsteps slow and solemn
    Going down the endless stair,
Joy is gone and you, my Lover,
Gone in other ways to hover;
Gone among the summer places,
Gone to seek for summer faces.

Bright-faced Joy was not for me;
    Born among the snows and pines,
Gray-faced Sorrow was to be
    Imaged in my mournful lines.

Love, not born for cold and sorrow,
    Only for the sweet sunshine,
I shall keep your face forever
    Hidden in this heart of mine.
In its light, one spot will brighten,
    Keeping fair the sacred tomb;
Like old moonlight it will whiten
    The inviolable room;
Like the moonlight it will whiten,

Softly, all the darkened room;
And the broken stalk may put forth
    Memory's ghost of Love's old bloom.

March, 1892.

Life or Death

A Soul, half through the Gate, said unto Life:
"What does thou offer me?" And Life replied:
"Sorrow, unceasing struggle, disappointment; after these
Darkness and silence." The Soul said unto Death:
"What dos *thou* offer me?" And Death replied:
"In the beginning what Life gives at last."
Turning to Life: "And if I live and struggle?"
"Others shall live and struggle after thee
Counting it easier where thou hast passed."
"And by their struggles?" "Easier place shall be
For others, still to rise to keener pain
Of conquering Agony!" "And what have I
To do with all these others? Who are they?"
"Yourself!" "And all who went before?" "Yourself."
"The darkness and the silence, too, have end?"
"They end in light and sound; peace ends in pain,
Death ends in Me, and thou must glide from Self
To Self, as light to shade and shade to light again.
Choose!" The Soul, sighing, answered: "I will live."

Philadelphia, May, 1892.

The Toast of Despair

We have cried,—and the Gods are silent;
　　We have trusted,—and been betrayed;
We have loved,—and the fruit was ashes;
　　We have given,—the gift was weighed.

We know that the heavens are empty,
　　That friendship and love are names;
That truth is an ashen cinder,
　　The end of life's burnt-out flames.

Vainly and long we have waited,
　　Through the night of the human roar,
For a single song on the harp of Hope,
　　Or a ray from a day-lit shore.

Songs aye come floating, marvelous sweet,
　　And bow-dyed flashes gleam;
But the sweets are Lies, and the weary feet
　　Run after a marsh-light beam.

In the hour of our need the song departs,
　　And the sea-moans of sorrow swell;
The siren mocks with a gurgling laugh
　　That is drowned in the deep death-knell.

The light we chased with our stumbling feet
　　As the goal of happier years,
Swings high and low and vanishes,—
　　The bow-dyes were of our tears.

God is a lie, and Faith is a lie,
　　And a tenfold lie is Love;
Life is a problem without a why,
　　And never a thing to prove.

It adds, and subtracts, and multiplies,
    And divides without aim or end;
Its answers all false, though false-named true,—
    Wife, husband, lover, friend.

We know it now, and we care no more;
    What matters life or death?
We tiny insects emerge from earth,
    Suffer, and yield our breath.

Like ants we crawl on our brief sand-hill,
    Dreaming of "mighty things,"—
Lo, they crunch, like shells in the ocean's wrath,
    In the rush of Time's awful wings.

The sun smiles gold, and the plants white,
    And a billion stars smile, still;
Yet, fierce as we, each wheels toward death,
    And cannot stay his will.

The build, ye fools, your mighty things,
    That Time shall set at naught;
Grow warm with the song the sweet Lie sings,
    And the false bow your tears have wrought.

For us, a truce to Gods, loves, and hopes,
    And a pledge to fire and wave;
A swifter whirl to the dance of death,
    And a loud huzza for the Grave!

Philadelphia, 1892.

Mary Wollstonecraft[1]

The dust of a hundred years
   Is on thy breast,
And thy day and thy night of tears
   Are centurine rest.
Thou to whom joy was dumb,
   Life a broken rhyme,
Lo, thy smiling time is come,
   And our weeping time.
Thou who hadst sponge and myrrh
   And a bitter cross,
Smile, for the day is here
   That we know our loss;—
Loss of thine undone deed,
   Thy unfinished song,
Th' unspoken word for our need,
   Th' unrighted wrong;
Smile, for we weep, we weep,
   For the unsoothed pain,
The unbound wound burned deep,
   That we might gain.
Mother of sorrowful eyes
   In the dead old days,
Mother of many sighs,
   Of pain-shod ways;
Mother of resolute feet
   Through all the thorns,
Mother soul-strong, soul-sweet,—
   Lo, after storms
Have broken and beat thy dust
   For a hundred years,
Thy memory is made just,
   And the just man hears.

Thy children kneel and repeat:
   "Though dust be dust,
Though sod and coffin and sheet
   And moth and rust
Have folded and molded and pressed,
   Yet they cannot kill;
In the heart of the world at rest
   She liveth still."

Philadelphia, April 27, 1893.

The Suicide's Defense[1]

(Of all the stupidities wherewith the law-making power has signaled its own incapacity for dealing with the disorders of society, none appears so utterly stupid as the law which punishes an attempted suicide. To the question "What have you to say in your defense?" I conceive the poor wretch might reply as follows.)

To say in my defense? Defense of what?
Defense to whom? And why defense at all?
Have I wronged any? Let that one accuse!
Some priest there mutters I "have outraged God"!
Let God then try me, and let none dare judge
Himself as fit to put Heaven's ermine on!
Again I say, let the wronged one accuse.
Aye, silence! There is none to answer me.
And whom could I, a homeless, friendless tramp,
To whom all doors are shut, all hearts are locked,
All hands withheld—whom could I wrong, indeed
By taking that which benefited none
And menaced all?
Aye, since ye will it so,
Know then your risk. But mark, 'tis not defense,
'Tis accusation that I hurl at you.

See to't that ye prepare your own defense.
My life, I say, is an eternal threat
To you and yours; and therefore it were well
To have foreborne your unasked services.
And why? Because I hate you! Every drop
Of blood that circles in your plethoric veins
Was wrung from out the gaunt and sapless trunks
Of men like me, who in your cursed mills
Were crushed like grapes within the wine-press ground.
To us ye leave the empty skin of life;
The heart of it, the sweet of it, ye pour
To fete your dogs and mistresses withal!
Your mistresses! Our daughters! Bought, for bread,
To grace the flesh that once was father's arms!

Yes, I accuse you that ye murdered me!
Ye killed the Man—and this that speaks to you
Is but the beast that ye have made of me!
What! Is it life to creep and crawl and beg,
And slink for shelter where rats congregate?
And for one's ideal dream of a fat meal?
Is it, then, life, to group like pigs in sties,
And bury decency in common filth,
Because, forsooth, your income must be made,
Though human flesh rot in your plague-rid dens?
Is it, then, life, to wait another's nod,
For leave to turn yourself to gold for him?
Would it me life to you? And was I less
Than you? Was I not born with hopes and dreams
And pains and passions even as were you?

But these ye have denied. Ye seized the earth,
Though it was none of yours, and said: "Hereon
Shall none rest, walk or work, till first to me
Ye render tribute!" Every art of man,
Born to make light of the burdens of the world,
Ye also seized, and made a tenfold curse

To crush the man beneath the thing he made.
Houses, machines, and lands—all, all are yours;
And us you do not need. When we ask work
Ye shake your heads. Homes?—Ye evict us. Bread?—
"Here, officer, this fellow's begging. Jail's
the place for him!" After the stripes, what next?—
Poison!—I took it!—Now you say 'twas sin
To take this life which troubled you so much.
Sin to escape insult, starvation, brands
Of felony, inflicted for the crime
Of asking food! Ye hypocrites! Within
Your secret hearts the sin is that I *failed!*
Because I failed ye judge me to the stripes,
And the hard toil denied when I was free.
So be it. But beware!—a prison cell's
An evil bed to grow morality!
Black swamps breed black miasms; sickly soils
Yield poison fruit; snakes warmed to life will sting.
This time I was content to go alone;
Perchance the next I shall not be so kind.

Philadelphia, September, 1894.

The Road Builders

("Who built the beautiful roads?" queried a friend of the present order, as we walked one day along the macadamized driveway of Fairmount Park[1].)

I saw them toiling in the blistering sun,
Their dull, dark faces leaning toward the stone,
Their knotted fingers grasping the rude tools,
Their rounded shoulders narrowing in their chest,
The sweat drops dripping in great painful beads.
I saw one fall, his forehead on the rock,

The helpless hand still clutching at the spade,
The slack mouth full of earth.

And he was dead.
His comrades gently turned his face, until
The fierce sun glittered hard upon his eyes,
Wide open, staring at the cruel sky.
The blood yet ran upon the jagged stone;
But it was ended. He was quite, quite dead:
Driven to death beneath the burning sun,
Driven to death upon the road he built.

He was no "hero", he; a poor, black man,
Taking "the will of God" and asking naught;
Think of him thus, when next your horse's feet
Strike out the flint spark from the gleaming road;
Think that for this, this common thing, The Road,
A human creature died; 'tis a blood gift,
To an o'erreaching world that does not thank.
Ignorant, mean and soulless was he? Well,—
Still human; and you drive upon his corpse.

Philadelphia, July 24, 1900.

Ave et Vale[1]

Comrades, what matter the watch-night tells
    That a New Year comes or goes?
What to us are the crashing bells
    That clang out the Century's close?

What to us is the gala dress?
    The whirl of the dancing feet?
The glitter and blare in the laughing press,
    And din of the merry street?

Do we not know that our brothers die
    In the cold and the dark to-night?
Shelterless faces turned toward the sky
    Will not see the New Year's light!

Wandering children, lonely, lost,
    Drift away on the human sea,
While the price of their lives in a glass is tossed
    And drunk in a revelry!

Ah, know we not in their feasting halls
    Where the loud laugh echoes again,
That brick and stone in the mortared walls
    Are the bones of murdered men?

Slowly murdered! By day and day,
    The beauty and strength are reft,
Till the Man is sapped and sucked away,
    And a Human Rind is left!

A Human Rind, with old, thin hair,
    And old, thin voice to pray
For alms in the bitter winter air,—
    A knife at his heart always.

And the pure in heart are impure in flesh
    For the cost of a little food:
Lo, when the Gleaner of Time shall thresh,
    Let these be accounted good.

For these are they who in bitter blame
    Eat the bread whose salt is sin;
Whose bosoms are burned with the scarlet shame,
    Till their hearts are seared within.

The cowardly jests of a hundred years
    Will be thrown where they pass to-night,
Too callous for hate, and too dry for tears,
    The saddest of human blight.

Do we forget them, these broken ones,
 That our watch to-night is set?
Nay, we smile in the face of the year that comes
 Because we do not forget.

We do not forget the tramp on the track,
 Thrust out in the wind-swept waste,
The curses of Man upon his back,
 And the curse of God in his face.

The stare in the eyes of the buried man
 Face down in the fallen mine;
The despair of the child whose bare feet ran
 To tread out the rich man's wine;

The solemn light in the dying gaze
 Of the babe at the empty breast,
The wax accusation, the sombre glaze
 Of its frozen and rigid rest;

They are all in the smile that we turn to the east
 To welcome the Century's dawn;
They are all in our greeting to Night's high priest,
 As we bid the Old Year begone.

Begone and have done, and go down and be dead
 Deep drowned in your sea of tears!
We smile as you die, for we wait the red
 Morn-gleam of a hundred-years

That shall see the end of the age-old wrong,—
 The reapers that have not sown,—
The reapers of men with their sickles strong
 Who gather, but have not strown.

For the earth shall be his and the fruits thereof
 And to him the corn and wine,
Who labors the hills with an even love
 And knows not "thine and mine."

And the silk shall be to the hand that weaves,
    The pearl to him who dives,
The home to the builder; and all life's sheaves
    To the builder of human lives.

And none go blind that another see,
    Or die that another live;
And none insult with a charity
    That is not theirs to give.

For each of his plenty shall freely share
    And take at another's hand:
Equals breathing the Common Air
    And toiling the Common Land.

A dream? A vision? Aye, what you will;
    Let it be to you as it seems:
Of this Nightmare Real we have our fill;
    To-night is for "pleasant dreams."

Dreams that shall waken the hope that sleeps
    And knock at each torpid Heart
Till it beat drum taps, and the blood that creeps
    With a lion's spring upstart!

For who are we to be bound and drowned
    In this river of human blood?
Who are we to lie in a swound,
    Half sunk in the river mud?

Are we not they who delve and blast
    And hammer and build and burn?
Without us not a nail made fast!
    Not a wheel in the world should turn!

Must we, the Giant, await the grace
    That is dealt by the puny hand
Of him who sits in the feasting place,
    While we, his Blind Jest, stand

Between the pillars? Nay, not so:
    Aye, if such things were true,
Better were Gaza again, to show
    What the giant's rage may do!

But yet not this: it were wiser far
    To enter the feasting hall
And say to the Masters, "These things are
    Not for you alone, but all."

And this shall be in the Century
    That opes on our eyes to-night;
So here's to the struggle, if it must be,
    And to him who fights the fight.

And here's to the dauntless, jubilant throat
    That loud to its Comrade sings,
Till over the earth shrills the mustering note,
    And the World Strike's signal rings.

Philadelphia, January 1, 1901.

Marsh-Bloom

(To Gaetano Bresci[1])

Requiem, requiem, requiem,
Blood-red blossom of poison stem
    Broken for Man,
Swamp-sunk leafage and dungeon-bloom,
Seeded bearer of royal doom,
    What now is the ban?

What to thee is the island grave?
With desert wind and desolate wave
    Will they silence Death?

Can they weight thee now with the heaviest stone?
Can they lay aught on thee with "Be alone,"
   That hast conquered breath?

Lo, "it is finished"—a man for a king!
Mark you well who have done this thing:
   The flower has roots;
Bitter and rank grow the things of the sea;
Ye shall know what sap ran thick in the tree
   When ye pluck its fruits.

Requiem, requiem, requiem,
Sleep on, sleep on, accused of them
   Who work our pain;
A wild Marsh-blossom shall blow again
From a buried root in the slime of men,
   On the day of the Great Red Rain.

Philadelphia, July, 1901.

Written–in–Red

(To Our Living Dead in Mexico's Struggle.)

Written in red their protest stands,
For the Gods of the World to see;
On the dooming wall their bodiless hands
Have blazoned "Upharsin," and flaring brands
Illumine the message: "Seize the lands!
Open the prisons and make men free!"
Flame out the living words of the dead
   Written—in—red.

Gods of the World! Their mouths are dumb!
Your guns have spoken and they are dust.
But the shrouded Living, whose hearts were numb,
Have felt the beat of a wakening drum
Within them sounding—the Dead Men's tongue—
Calling: "Smite off the ancient rust!"
Have beheld "Resurrexit," the word of the Dead,
      Written—in—red.

Bear it aloft, O roaring flame!
Skyward aloft, where all may see.
Slaves of the World! Our cause is the same;
One is the immemorial shame;
One is the struggle, and in One name—
MANHOOD—we battle to set men free.
"Uncurse us the Land!" burn the words of the Dead,
      Written—in—red.

The Worm Turns

Germinal[1]

(The last word of Angiolillo.[2])

Germinal!—The Field of Mars is plowing,
And hard the steel that cuts, and hot the breath
Of the great Oxen, straining flanks and bowing
Beneath his goad, who guides the share of Death.

Germinal!—The Dragon's teeth are sowing,
And stern and white the sower flings the seed
He shall not gather, though full swift the growing;
Straight down Death's furrow treads, and does not heed.

Germinal!—The Helmet Heads are springing
Far up the Field of Mars in gleaming files;
With wild war notes the bursting earth is ringing.
*   *   *   *   *
Within his grave the sower sleeps, and smiles.

London, October, 1897.

Ut Sementem Feceris, Ita Metes[1]

(To the Czar, on a woman, a political prisoner, being flogged to death in Siberia.)

How many drops must gather to the skies
Before the cloud-burst comes, we may not know;
How hot the fires in under hells must glow
Ere the volcano's scalding lavas rise,
Can none say; but all wot the hour is sure!
Who dreams of vengeance has but to endure!
He may not say how many blows must fall,
How many lives be broken on the wheel,
How many corpses stiffen 'neath the pall,
How many martyrs fix the blood-red seal;
But certain is the harvest time of Hate!
And when weak moans, by an indignant world
Re-echoed, to a throne are backward hurled,
Who listens, hears the mutterings of Fate!

Philadelphia, February, 1890.

Santa Agueda[1]

(Where the torturer Canovas breathed his last.)

Santa Agueda, thou that wast accursed
With presence of a demon dressed in Man,
Blessed art thou, for on thy stones there ran
The vampire blood from bitter torture nursed;
Along thy streets there flashed the lightning-burst,
"Delivered!" flaming on from eye to eye,
Though lips said "killed," and all thy gateways hearsed
In lying black, made mourning mockery.
Blessed art thou! From thee went forth the cry,
"Vengeance yet loves, Renunciation hates,
And justice smites: *the torturer shall die;*"
Across his path the steel-nerved slayer waits
"And both shall burn together,"—one in light
Of unconsuming hell and reddened night;
And one with feet on hell and brow dawn-rayed, *pure white.*
Philadelphia, August, 1898.

The Feast of Vultures

(As the three Anarchists, Vaillant, Henry and Caserio, were led to their several executions, a voice from the prison cried loudly, "Vive l'anarchie!" Through watch and ward the cry escaped, and no man owned the voice; but the cry is still resounding through the world.)

A moan in the gloam in the air-peaks heard—
The Bird of Omen—the wild, fierce Bird,
   Aflight
     In the night,
       Like a whiz of light,
Arrowy winging before the storm,
   Far away flinging,
   The whistling, singing,
White-curdled drops, wind-blown and warm,
   From its beating, flapping,
     Thunderous wings;
   Crashing and clapping ·
     The split night swings,
   And rocks and totters,
     Bled of its levin,
   And reels and mutters
     A curse to Heaven!
Reels and mutters and rolls and dies,
With a wild light streaking its black, blind eyes.
   Far, far, far,
     Through the red, mad morn,
   Like a hurtling star,
     Through the air upborne,
   The Herald-Singer,
   The Terror-Bringer,
Speeds—and behind, through the cloud-rags torn,
   Gather and wheel a million wings,
   Clanging as iron where the hammer rings;
     The whipped sky shivers,

The White Gate shakes,
The ripped throne quivers,
The dumb God wakes,
And feels in his heart the talon-stings—
The dead bodies hurled from beaks for slings.
"Ruin! Ruin!" the Whirlwind cries,
And it leaps at his throat and tears his eyes;
"Death for death, as ye long have dealt;
The heads of your victims your head shall pelt;
The blood ye wrung to get drunk upon,
Drink, and be poisoned! On, Herald, on!"
Behold, behold,
How a moan is grown!
A cry hurled high 'gainst a scaffold's joist!
The Voice of Defiance—the loud, wild Voice!
Whirled
Through the world,
A smoke-wreath curled
(Breath 'round hot kisses) around a fire!
See! the ground hisses
With curses, and glisses
With red-streaming blood-clots of long-frozen ire,
Waked by the flying
Wild voice as it passes;
Groaning and crying,
The surge of the masses
Rolls and flashes
With thunderous roar—
Seams and lashes
The livid shore—
Seams and lashes and crunches and beats,
And drags a ragged wall to its howling retreats!
Swift, swift, swift,
'Thwart the blood-rain's fall,
Through the fire-shot rift
Of the broken wall,
The prophet-crying

The storm-strong sighing,
Flies—and from under Night's lifted pall,
   Swarming, menace ten million darts,
   Uplifting fragments of human shards!
      Ah, white teeth chatter,
         And dumb jaws fall,
      While winged fires scatter
         Till gloom gulfs all
Save the boom of the cannon that storm the forts
That the people bombard with their comrades' hearts;
   "Vengeance! Vengeance!" the voices scream,
   And the vulture pinions whirl and stream!
"Knife for knife, as ye long have dealt;
The edge ye whetted for us be felt,
   Ye chopper of necks, on your own! your own!
   Bare it, Coward! On, Prophet, on!"

   Behold how high
   Rolls a prison cry!

Philadelphia, August, 1894.

Night at the Grave in Waldheim[1]

Quiet they lie in their shrouds of rest,
    Their lids kissed close 'neath the lips of peace;
Over each pulseless and painless breast
The hands lie folded and softly pressed,
As a dead dove presses a broken nest;
    Ah, broken hearts were the price of these!

The lips of their anguish are cold and still,
    For them are the clouds and the gloom all past;
No longer the woe of the world can thrill
The chords of those tender hearts, or fill
The silent dead-house! The "people's will"
    Has snapped asunder the strings at last.

"The people's will!" All, in years to come,
    Dearly ye'll weep that ye did not save!
Do ye not hear now the muffled drum,
The trampling foot and the ceaseless hum,
Of the million marchers,—trembling, dumb,
    In their tread to a yawning, giant grave?

And yet, ah! yet there's a rift of white!
    'Tis breaking over the martyrs' shrine!
Halt there, ye doomed ones,—it scathes the night,
As lightning darts from its scabbard bright
And sweeps the face of the sky with light!
    "No more shall be spilled out the blood-red wine!"

These are the words it has written there,
    Keen as the lance of the northern morn;
The sword of Justice gleams in its glare,
And the arm of Justice, upraised and bare,

Is true to strike, aye, 'tis strong to dare;
    It will fall where the curse of our land is born.

No more shall the necks of the nations be crushed,
    No more to dark Tyranny's throne bend the knee;
No more in abjection be ground to the dust!
By their widows, their orphans, our dead comrades' trust,
By the brave heart-beats stilled, by the brave voices hushed,
    We swear that humanity yet shall be free!

Pittsburgh, 1889.

The Hurricane

("We are the birds of the coming storm."–August Spies[1].)

The tide is out, the wind blows off the shore;
Bare burn the white sands in the scorching sun;
The sea complains, but its great voice is low.

    Bitter thy woes, O People,
      And the burden
    Hardly to be borne!
    Wearily grows, O People,
      All the aching
    Of thy pierced heart, bruised and torn!
    But yet thy time is not,
      And low thy moaning.
    Desert thy sands!
    Not yet is thy breath hot,
      Vengefully blowing;
    It wafts o'er lifted hands.

The tide has turned; the vane veers slowly round;
Slow clouds are sweeping o'er the blinding light;
White crests curl on the sea,—its voice grows deep.

224

Angry thy heart, O People,
　　And its bleeding
Fire-tipped with rising hate!
Thy clasped hands part, O People,
　　For thy praying
Warmed not the desolate!
God did not hear thy moan:
　　Now it is swelling
To a great drowning cry;
A dark wind-cloud, a groan,
　　Now backward veering
From that deaf sky!

The tide flows in, the wind roars from the depths,
The whirled-white sand heaps with the foam-white waves;
Thundering the sea rolls o'er its shell-crunched wall!

Strong is thy rage, O People,
　　In its fury
　　Hurling thy tyrants down!
Thou metest wage, O People.
　　Very swiftly,
Now that thy hate is grown:
Thy time at last is come;
　　Thou heapest anguish,
Where thou thyself wert bare!
No longer to thy dumb
　　God clasped and kneeling,
Thou answerest thine own prayer.

Sea Isle City, N. J., August, 1889.

In Memoriam

*To General M. M. Trumbull[1] (No man better than General Trumbull
defended my martyred comrades in Chicago.)*

Back to thy breast, O Mother, turns thy child,
   He whom thou garmentedst in steel of truth,
   And sent forth, strong in the glad heart of youth,
To sing the wakening song in ears beguiled
By tyrants' promises and flatterers' smiles;
These searched his eyes, and knew nor threats nor wiles
   Might shake the steady stars within their blue,
Nor win one truckling word from off those lips,—
   No—not for gold nor praise, nor aught men do
To dash the Sun of Honor with eclipse,
O, Mother Liberty, those eyes are dark,
   And the brave lips are white and cold and dumb;
   But fair in other souls, through time to come,
Fanned by thy breath glows the Immortal Spark.

Philadelphia, May, 1894.

John P. Altgeld[1]

*(After an incarceration of six long years in Joliet state prison for an act
of which they were entirely innocent, namely, the throwing of the
Haymarket bomb[2], in Chicago, May 4, 1886, Oscar Neebe, Michael
Schwab, and Samuel Fielden, were liberated by Governor Altgeld, who
thus sacrificed his political career to an act of justice.)*

There was a tableau! Liberty's clear light
   Shone never on a braver scene than that.
   Here was a prison, there a Man who sat
High in the Halls of state! Beyond, the might

Of ignorance and Mobs, whose hireling press
Yells at their bidding like the slaver's hounds,
  Ready with coarse caprice to curse or bless,
To make or unmake rulers!—Lo, there sounds
  A grating of the doors! And three poor men,
Helpless and hated, having naught to give,
Come from their long-sealed tomb, look up, and live,
  And thank this Man that they are free again.
And He—to all the world this Man dares say,
  "Curse as you will! I have been just this day."

Philadelphia, June, 1893.

"Light Upon Waldheim"

(The figure on the monument over the grave of the Chicago martyrs[1] in Waldheim Cemetery is a warrior woman, dropping with her left hand a crown upon the forehead of a fallen man just past his agony, and with her right drawing a dagger from her bosom.)

Light upon Waldheim! And the earth is gray;
  A bitter wind is driving from the north;
The stone is cold, and strange cold whispers say:
  "What do ye here with Death? Go forth! Go forth!"

Is this thy word, O Mother, with stern eyes,
  Crowning thy dead with stone-caressing touch?
May we not weep o'er him that martyred lies,
  Slain in our name, for that he loved us much?

May we not linger till the day is broad?
  Nay, none are stirring in this stinging dawn—
None but poor wretches that make moan to God:
  What use are these, O thou with dagger drawn?

"Go forth, go forth! Stand not to weep for these,
　Till, weakened with your weeping, like the snow
Ye melt, dissolving in a coward peace!"
　Light upon Waldheim! Brother, let us go!

London, October, 1897.

Notes

Introduction

1 Avrich, Paul. *An American Anarchist: The Life of Voltairine de Cleyre*. Princeton: Princeton University Press 1978.

2 Goldman, Emma. *Voltairine de Cleyre*. Berkeley Heights, NJ: Oriole Press, 1932.

3 Avrich, Paul. *An American Anarchist: The Life of Voltairine de Cleyre*. Princeton: Princeton University Press 1978.

4 *ibid.*

In Defense of Emma Goldman and the Right of Expropriation

Philadelphia: The Author, 1894. From a lecture delivered in New York on December 16, 1893.

London: Liberty Press, 1894.

London: Serialized in *Liberty* 11/1894–1/1895.

The Herald of Revolt, (reprint) 1913.

Note that there are errors in the original text, including the misspelling of Goldman throughout.

1 Cardinal Manning—Cardinal priest of Sts. Andrew and Gregory on the Coelian Hill and second archbishop of Westminster. In response to the deaths in London's Trafalgar Square on November 13, 1887, Manning wrote "Necessity has no law and a starving man has a natural right to his neighbour's bread." "Distress in London: A Note on Outdoor Relief" *Fortnightly Review*, 40, January–June 1888.

2 Paine's *Rights of Man*—First published in 1790. An exposition on the rights of man, and a plan to apply those rights in a reform of the English Government. Written partially as a response to Edmond Burke's *Reflections on the Revolution in France,* and dedicated to General Washington and The Marquis de Lafayette.

3 Emma Goldman (1869–1940)—Born in 1869 in a Jewish ghetto in Russia where her family ran a small inn. Dedicated her life to political radicalism after four anarchists were hung in Chicago who were accused of murdering policemen during the Haymarket meeting on May 3, 1886. From 1906 to 1917 she edited the anarchist magazine *Mother Earth*. Died May 14, 1940. At the time of this talk by de Cleyre, Goldman was serving a twelve month prison sentence for incitement to riot after urging a rally of the unemployed in New York to take their own bread if necessary.

4 Pilate—Pontius Pilate, was the Roman governor of Judaea from 26 CE to 36 CE. The Bible claims that Pilate initially refused to condemn Jesus of Nazareth but under pressure washed his hands of the whole affair.

5 *Fortnightly Review*—Published between 1865 and 1934, the *Fortnightly Review* was a respected and influential literary journal. Published writers such as George Eliot, Ezra Pound, James Joyce, and H.G. Wells.

6 Botany Bay, inlet, New South Wales, SE Australia, just south of Sydney. Visited in 1770, by James Cook, who proclaimed British sovereignty over the east coast of Australia. Named by Sir Joseph Banks. In 1788, the first shipload of British prisoners arrived, establishing it as one of England's most important penal colonies in the nineteenth century.

7 Thomas Earle White—Member of Philadelphia anarchist study group along with de Cleyre in the early 1890s. As a lawyer he represented the anarchist Charles Mowbray after his arrest in Philadelphia in 1894. He also represented Emma Goldman in the Philadelphia Free Speech Fight of 1909.

8 Coeur d'Alenes—A reference to the 1892 strike of silver miners and the mass round-up and ill treatment of union men that followed.

9 Studebaker Wagon Works' strikers—A reference to the Chicago carriage and wagon makers' strike of 1893.

10 Henry Clay Frick (1949–1919)—American industrialist that started Frick and Co. In 1889 Andrew Carnegie made him chairman of the Carnegie Steel Co. His lockout of the workers and use of Pinkerton detectives resulted in the 1892 Homestead Strike and Alexander Berkman's unsuccessful attempt on his life in July 1892.

11 Pinkertons—A reference to the Pinkerton Detective Agency, founded in 1850 by Scottish immigrant Allan Pinkerton. Pinkerton was hired by both Carnegie and Frick to put down strikes, and the agency worked for management during the Homestead Strike and lock out. Between 1866 and 1892 they participated in over seventy labor disputes on the side of the employers.

12 Delmonico's—A reference to an upscale New York restaurant, Delmonico's (1824–1923), that was patronized by people such as Queen Victoria, Charles Dickens, and Oscar Wilde.

13 Samuel Ward McAllister (1827–1895)—New York Society leader who wrote *Society as I have found it* (1890).

14 Marc Antony—Great Roman Emperor 61–30 B.C.

15 Claus Timmerman—German anarchist communist. Editor of *Der Anarchist* (1889–1895), *Brandfackel* [the Torch of War] (1893–94) and *Sturmvogel* [Storm Bird] (1897–99). He had been arrested along with Goldman and sentenced to six months imprisonment.

16 Anarchist communism is based on the central thesis of mutual aid, arguing that goods should be distributed by need and not necessarily productivity. Hence the maxim "From each according to their ability; to each acording to their need". Anarchist individualism can encompass a wide range of ideas— mutualism, Stirner's egoism, etc—but in economic and personal dealings it argues for the primacy of the individual rather than class or community.

17 Algernon Charles Swinburne (1837–1909)—English poet and writer. Most of his political work appears in *Songs before Sunrise* (1871), and *Songs of Two Nations* (1875).

18 Anaxagoras (c500–c428)—Greek philosopher seen by de Cleyre and other freethinkers as an early atheist.

19 Hypatia of Alexandria (c370–c415)—Mathematician and thinker who was attacked by a Christian mob and stabbed to death with broken pottery shards.

20 John Huss (1369–1415)—Bohemian Roman Catholic priest burnt at the stake as a heretic.

21 Giordano Bruno (1548–1600)—Dominican monk and victim of the Spanish Inquisition. Venerated by the American anarchist movement as a martyr to freedom of thought.

22 Robert Emmet (1778–1803)—Irish nationalist and organizer of a failed rebellion against English rule. Executed.

23 Sophia Perovskaya (1853–1881)—Russian revolutionary and populist. Hung for with other members of Narodnaya Volya for assassinating Alexander II, Czar of Russia, in March 1881. She was the first woman political prisoner in Russia to be executed.

24 Parsons, Fischer, Engel, Spies, Lingg—A reference to the Haymarket martyrs.

25 A reference to Alexander Berkman who was currently serving a 22-year prison sentence for the attempted assassination of Henry Clay Frick.

26 Paulino Pallas (1862–1893)—Spanish anarchist who threw two bombs at the captain general of Catalonia in September 1893 in revenge for the Spanish officer's role in the violent repression of the Jerez uprising in January 1892. Executed by firing squad.

They Who Marry Do Ill

Mother Earth, January, 1908.

1 Henrietta P. Westbrook—Delivered the lecture "They who marry do well" before the Liberal League.

2 Thomas Henry Huxley (1825–1895)—Prominent scientist and scholar who was a chief supporter of Darwin immediately after the publication of *The Origin of the Species.*

3 Eduard Von Hartman (1842–1906)—German Philosopher, author of *Philosophy of the Unconscious.*

4 Dyer D. Lum (1840–1893)—Anarchist militant. He was a teacher and mentor to de Cleyre as well as a lover. The two met in 1888 and had a five-year relationship, although there are few details as to the extent and frequency of their intimacy. Lum committed suicide in 1893. In her eulogy to Lum, de Cleyre calls him "the brightest scholar, the profoundest thinker of the American Revolutionary movement."

5 Alice Roosevelt, daughter of Theodore Roosevelt, married Nicholas Longworth in a highly publicized marriage on February 17, 1906.

6 Ernest Crosby (1856–1907)—Ex-lawyer and anti-imperialist writer who co-founded the anti-imperialist organization American League of New York and served in various leadership roles with the American Anti-Imperialist League of Chicago and the Anti-Imperialist League of New York. Prominent Tolstoyan.

7 Leonard Abbott (1878–1953)—American socialist, then anarchist. Abbott met Ernest Crosby at a meeting called to exert public pressure for a reduction in Alexander Berkman's prison sentence. He would go on to become a close friend of Emma Goldman and a major force in the Modern School movement. De Cleyre paraphrases parts of Abbott's obituary of Crosby (*Some Reminiscences of Ernest Crosby*) published in the February 1907 *Mother Earth*.

8 Hugh O. Pentecost (1848–1906)—A speaker and lawyer, editor of the publication *The Twentieth Century*. While running for District Attorney of New York City, he reneged on his former support for the Haymarket men. He was strongly criticized for this act in the obituary de Cleyre wrote for him that appeared in the March 1907 issue of *Mother Earth*.

9 Chicago Anarchists—A reference to the Haymarket martyrs: August Spies, Michael Schwab, Samuel Fielden, Albert R. Parsons, Adolph Fischer, George Engel, Louis Lingg, and Oscar Neebe.

Anarchism and American Traditions

New York: Mother Earth Publishing Association, 1909.

Also published in *Mother Earth* in December 1908. Subsequent reprintings:

Milan: (Italian translation by Maria Rovetti) 1909.

Chicago: Free Society Group of Chicago, 1932.

1 William Penn (1644–1718)—English Quaker who founded the U.S. state of Pennsylvania. He was the son of British Admiral Sir William Penn.

2 General John Burgoyne, aka "General Johnnie"—Born in 1722 in Sutton, Bedfordshire, England. General for the British during the U.S. war for independence. He was defeated by U.S. forces in the Saratoga Campaign of 1777.

3 "Remember Paoli"— A reference to the "Paoli Massacre" of September 21, 1777 in Paoli, Pennsylvania where hundreds of U.S. soldiers were killed and wounded in a night bayonet attack by the British. "Remember Paoli" became the battle cry for the U.S. forces throughout the rest of the war.

4 On August 16, 1777, Elizabeth Page Stark, known as "Molly" gained infamy when her husband, Brigadier General John Stark, led his militia against the forces of General John Burgoyne engaging them with the war cry, "There they are boys. We beat them today or Molly Stark's a widow."

5 General Wayne "Mad Anthony Wayne" was born in Philadelphia in 1745. He is credited with preventing the first mutiny in the U.S. forces in 1781. The nickname "Mad Anthony Wayne" was given to him by his soldiers as a reflection of both his fierce temper and his reckless courage.

6 Boston Tea Party Indians were patriots who dresses as Native Americans when they raided British ships and dumped 342 crates of tea in the Boston Harbor.

7 Kentucky Resolutions—A reference to a series of resolutions passed by the legislature of the state protesting the Alien and Sedition Acts. The most radical of which was the Kentucky Resolution of 1799, which asserted that states had the power to nullify the laws of the Federal Government.

8 Alien Laws—Four laws passed in 1798 by the federalist controlled congress to curb domestic dissent known collectively as the Alien and Sedition Laws.

9 Shays' Rebellion led by Daniel Shays, a former revolutionary army captain, was aimed against politicians and laws that were felt to be unfair to farmers and laborers.

10 Robert Hunter (1874–1942)—American Socialist and author of *Poverty* (1904), *Socialists at Work* (1908), and *Violence in the Labor Movement* (1914) among others. He left the Socialist party in 1914.

The Dominant Idea

New York: Mother Earth Publishing Association, 1910.

1 Determinism—Philosophical theory which opposes the doctrine of free will in that it suggests all man's volitions are invariably determined by pre-existing circumstances.

2 Kaffirs and Boers—Kaffirs is often used in South Africa to generally describe any black native who is not the descendant of an imported slave, but on the eastern frontier of the Cape Colony of Africa the term is usually restricted to a member of the Amaxosa tribe. The Boers—a group of Dutch farmers from the Netherlands who, in 1652, settled in South Africa.

3 Saint Teresa of Avila (1515–1582)—Catholic writer of mystical theology and author of "*Life Written by Herself.*"

4 Terence Powderly (1849–1924)—Son of Irish immigrants residing in Pennsylvania. Powderly worked as a machinist and joined the Knights of Labor in 1874 and after five years was appointed as grand master workman, the union's highest post.

5 John Burns (1858–1943)—English labor leader and trade unionist. Influential in the huge London Dock Strike of 1889. Became a socialist member of Parliament in 1892.

Direct Action

New York: Mother Earth Publishing Association, 1912.

A lecture delivered in Chicago January, 1912.

1 A reference to John and James McNamara, both active in the International Bridge and Structural Iron Workers and opposed to the closed shop. Both were tried and eventually pled guilty for the bombing of the anti-union *LA Times* building in October 1910.

2 Brook of Siloa—Presumably a biblical reference (Shiloh).

3 Bacon's Rebellion took place 1675–1676. The Rebels were attempting to destroy as many Native Americans as possible and won considerable support amongst poor whites and blacks. It fizzled out after Bacon's death in October 1676.

4 James Greenleaf Whittier (1807–1892)—Abolitionist Quaker poet and founder of the Liberty Party—an offshoot of the Abolitionist Party.

5 A reference to Shadrach Minkins, the first runaway to be arrested under the 1850 Fugitive Slave Law. Immediately after his arrest, however, he was taken away from officials and taken to Canada.

6 A reference to William "Jerry" Henry who was arrested under the Fugitive Slave Law of 1850 on October 1, 1851; rescued by local abolitionists and eventually spirited to Canada.

7 Gerrit Smith (1797–1874)—Abolitionist who served one term in the House of Representatives and was a Presidential candidate in 1848, 1856, and 1860. A financial supporter of John Brown.

8 William D. (Big Bill) Haywood (1869–1928)—A union organizer in the West for the Western Federation of Miners who was tried for conspiracy to murder former Idaho Governor Frank Steunenberg but not convicted. Prominent IWW organizer who at the time of writing was faced with expulsion from the Socialist Party of America for his support of direct cction.

9 Frank Bohn (1866–1944)—As a member of the Socialist Labor Party, Bohn was one of the attendees of the planning meeting to form the IWW. Later joining the Socialist Party, he (like Haywood) was threatened with expulsion for supporting the tactic of direct action in industrial disputes.

10 John Brown (1800–1859)—Abolitionist who led a raid on Harper's Ferry on October 16, 1859.

11 Frederick Douglass—An escaped slave who became famed for his abilities as a writer and orator. He is perhaps most famous for his first autobiography, *Narrative of the Life of Frederick Douglass*.

12 Lucy Colman (1817–1906)—Abolitionist and women's rights activist.

13 Free Soilers, Free-Soil Party—A Third Party in the 1800's whose main platform was the prevention of the spread of slavery into new states.

14 Grange—Otherwise known as the National Grange of the Patrons of Husbandry, founded in 1867 as a social/fraternal association and was concerned with farmers' issues.

15 Farmer's Alliance—Originated in Texas in 1877, it presented farmers' grievances against railroads and other businesses. In 1889, it went national and became the National Farmer's Alliance and Industrial Union.

16 Knights of Labor—Founded in 1869 as a secret organization called the Noble Order of the Knights of Labor by Uriah S. Stephens. "Noble Order" was dropped from the name in 1879. Membership reached its peak at 700,000 members in 1886.

17 Industrial Workers of the World—Formed in Chicago in 1905 as a response to the skill based practices of the American Federation of Labor by representatives of 43 other groups, including the Western Federation of Miners, the Socialist Labor Party, some branches of the Socialist Party, and some sections of the AFL. Numerous anarchists, such as Jay Fox, Lucy Parsons and Josef Peukert, were also in attendance at the founding Convention.

18 Oscar Ameringer (1870–1914)—Socialist politician, columnist, writer, labor organizer and member of the Knights of Labor. In an article entitled "The Bad News From Chicago" immediately after the Haymarket massacre, he discusses the effects of the incident on the Knights' organization.

19 Francisco I. Madero (1873–1913)—A Mexican revolutionary who led the fight to overthrow the dictator Porfirior Diaz and served as its President from 1911 until his overthrow and death in 1913.

20 Illinois Central—A rail line chartered in 1851 that began in Cairo, Illinois at the meeting of the Ohio and Mississippi rivers and ended at Galena, in the northwest part of Illinois.

21 Swinburne's "Hymn of Man"—A poem by Algernon Charles Swinburne (1837–1909). Most of Swinburne's political work appears in *Songs Before Sunrise* (1871) and *Songs of Two Nations* (1871).

Economic Tendency of Freethought

Reprinted from Benjamin Tucker's periodical *Liberty*.

A lecture given before the Boston Secular Society, 1887.

1 Giordano Bruno (1548–1600)—Born Filippo Bruno; he changed his name to Giordano after entering the Dominican order. However, he was eventually excommunicated for his heliocentric view of the universe. For these and other beliefs he was tried and imprisoned in 1592 and burned at the stake in 1600. Venerated by many as a martyr to freedom of thought.

2 Martin Luther (1483–1546)—Augustinian friar and preacher at Wittenburg whose writings and teaching are considered to have sparked the Protestant Reformation.

3 Cardinal Manning—Henry Edward Manning (1807–1892): Catholic theologian and minister who became Cardinal in 1875. See also note 1 of *In Defense of Emma Goldman*, above.

4 Deism—The belief that God exists but the rejection of organized religion.

5 Albert R. Parsons (1848–1887)—An ex-Confederate soldier who moved to Chicago in 1873 and became a prominent anarchist speaker and writer. He spoke at the Haymarket meeting, and, though he was not present when the explosion happened, became one of whom would be called the Haymarket martyrs.

6 Jay Gould (1836–1892)—Began as a speculator on small railroads, and eventually ended up owning various railroad lines across the country.

7 As railroad tycoons and owners of the New York Central line, the Vanderbilt family was one of the wealthiest and most prominent families in America during the mid to late 1800's.

8 A quote from Proudhon that was on the masthead of Benjamin Tucker's paper *Liberty.*

Francisco Ferrer

New York: Mother Earth Publishing Association, 1911.

1 Francisco Ferrer Y Guardia (1859–1909)—Anarchist teacher who founded the Modern School in Barcelona on September 8th, 1901. He was opposed to Church and State schooling as well as to the use of rewards and punishments in education. He was arrested, first for an associate's assassination attempt on King Alfonse XIII in 1906 and a second time after Barcelona's "Tragic Week" in July 1909 for which he was tried as the leader of the workers' insurrection and executed by firing squad.

2 "White Terror"—Defined partially by de Cleyre in the first paragraph, but this particular reference is to is the Barcelona government's response to the "Tragic Week" in which 500 militants, including Ferrer, were arrested.

3 The Castle of Montjuich is situated on the dominating hill of that name near Barcelona. The castle was used as a prison notorious for its cruelty to inmates.

4 Alella—Located on the outskirts of Barcelona to the northeast.

5 Catalonia—A region in the northeast corner of Spain in which Barcelona lies.

6 Toledo—A city 71 km (44 miles) from Madrid, Spain.

7 Mother of Sorrows—Another name for Mary, the mother of Jesus.

8 Ruiz Zorilla (1834–1895)—A participant in the Spanish revolution of 1868, and of the first members of the post-revolutionary cabinet. After the restoration of Alphonso XII, he moved to France and spent the rest of his life trying to stir up revolution in Spain.

9 Alfred Joseph Naquet (1834–1916)—A French politician and chemist who held two professorships until he was arrested in 1867 for participation in a secret society. He participated in the revolution of September 4, 1870 and held several positions in the French government. He is most famous for sponsoring a measure re-establishing divorce that passed in 1884.

10 Mlle. Meunier—A wealthy friend/acquaintance of Ferrer's and the major financial supporter of his work.

11 Dr. Oden de Buen—A professor at Barcelona University who occasionally lectured on geography and natural science in public lectures held by the Modern School.

12 Albert Bloch and Paraf Javal—*La Substancia Universal. Libro Primero: Primeros Principios. Libro Segundo:El Universo*. 4°. 174pp. Barcelona: Casa Editorial Maucci, 1918.

13 Mateo Morral (1880–1906)—A young anarchist who, on May 31, 1906, threw a bomb at King Alphonse XIII's wedding party and killed himself two days later when he was recognized as the bomber. Ferrer was blamed for being part of the bomb plot and arrested. Morral worked in the publishing house of the Escuela Moderna.

Sex Slavery

New York: Mother Earth Publishing Association, 1914.

A lecture delivered to the Ladies Liberal League in 1895.

1 Moses Harman (1830–1911)—Founder and publisher of *Lucifer, the Light-Bearer*, which became the *American Journal of Eugenics*. He was a proponent of women's rights and the eugenics movement during the late 1800s and early 1900s. Harmon, an anarchist, adopted a position of no censorship in his papers, and at the time of writing he was serving a sentence in Leavenworth prison for publishing articles in *Lucifer* the previous year that were deemed obscene.

2 See note 13 of *In Defense of Emma Goldman*, above.

3 Mrs. Grundy—A fictitious character in Thomas Merton's 1798 play *Speed the Plough* who personifies prudishness and strict propriety.

4 In June 1886, Moses Harman's *Lucifer, the Light-Bearer* published "The Markland Letter" which described a brutal instance of forced sex within marriage and called it rape. Markland, sympathetic to anarchism, claimed the letter was from a "friend." For publishing this letter Harman was initially sentenced to five years imprisonment, finally being re-sentenced to one year's hard labor.

5 August Bebel (1840–1913)— Marxist writer and revolutionary.His work *Women and Socialism* (1879) was highly influential among radicals of many persuasions.

6 Anthony Comstock (1844–1916)—In 1873, he succeeded in getting the U.S. Congress to pass the "Act of the Suppression of Trade in, and Circulation of, Obscene Literature and Articles of Immoral Use." The Act, or "Comstock Law," was popularly named after him. For the next 42 years, until his death in 1915, Comstock held remarkable power as a special, unpaid postal inspector. He was a particular enemy of many anarchists including de Cleyre, Ezra Heywood, Moses Harman, and Emma Goldman.

The Making of an Anarchist

New York: Mother Earth Publishing Association, 1914.

1 Peter Alekseevich Kropotkin (1842–1921)—Russian revolutionary, geologist, and principal theorist of anarchist communism. His works include: *In Russian and French Prisons* (1887), *The Conquest of Bread* (1892, first English translation 1906), *Memoirs of a Revolutionist* (1899), *Fields, Factories and Workshops* (1899), *Mutual Aid* (1902) and *The Great French Revolution* (1909). *Ethics, Origin and Development* (1922), his final work, was published posthumously.

2 Petro-Paulovsky fortress—Where Kropotkin, along with countless other radicals, was held prisoner in Russia.

3 Count Leo Tolstoy (1828–1910)—His unorthodox Christian philosophy espoused non-resistance to evil as the proper response to aggression. His philosophy also expressed concern for the fair treatment of the poor and working class. Tolstoy believed that Christians should reject the State when seeking answers to questions of morality and instead to look within themselves and to God for answers.

Besides those cited by de Cleyre, Tolstoy's works include: *Confession* (1884), *What Then Must We Do?* (1886), and *The Kingdom of God is Within You* (1894).

4 William Wess—Anarchist member of the Hackney Branch of the Socialist League and also a member of what was known as the Freedom group based around the anarchist communist newspaper of the same name.

5 Mrs. Turner and Lizzie—Lizzie is English anarchist John Turner's sister who was married to Scottish anarchist Thomas Bell, who later moved to America. She was extremely close to Voltairine. Mrs. Turner is Mary Turner, John Turner's wife.

6 Convent of Our Lady of Lake Huron, at Sarnis, Ontario—Where de Cleyre received her primary schooling.

7 A reference to the Haymarket martyrs.

8 Thomas Paine (1737–1809)—Born in England, but later emigrated to the Colonies when he realized that the Colonists were within their rights to revolt against a government that imposed taxes on them but which did not give them the right of representation in the Parliament. He suggested there was no reason for the Colonies to stay dependent on England and formulated his philosophy for American independence in his pamphlet *Common Sense*.

9 Clarence Seward Darrow (1857–1938)—When Darrow was a young lawyer, he was impressed by the book *Our Penal Machinery and Its Victims* by John Peter Altgeld. Concurrent with Altgeld's philosophy Darrow believed that the United States criminal system favored the rich over the poor. As an attorney, he defended various labor leaders. Darrow's works include: *Crime, its Cause and Treatment* (1925), *The Prohibition Mania* (1927) and *The Story of My Life* (1932) as well as several novels.

10 Benjamin Tucker's *Liberty*—An anarchist individualist journal published between 1881–1908 by Tucker (1854–1939), a noted radical publisher.

11 Socialist Sections, The Liberal Leagues, The Single Tax Clubs—Liberal Leagues adhered to freethought principles and argued against linking church and state. In 1884 the national Liberal League split into two factions. De Cleyre helped form the Ladies' Liberal League in Philadelphia which contained numerous anarchist members. Single Tax clubs were formed by supporters of the single tax. They often provided a venue where anarchists could speak.

12 Jewish Vorwaerts (Vorwarts)—A reference to the socialist Jewish *Daily Forward* begun in 1897 with Abraham Cahan as editor.

13 John Most (1846–1906)—Highly influential German anarchist who moved to America in 1882 and was editor of the militant, German-language anarchist paper *Freiheit.*

14 Louise Michel (1830–1905)—French anarchist who was a passionate orator and a prolific writer. Active in the Paris Commune. She also was shot by a disturbed man and, like de Cleyre, refused to press charges. In 1891 she organized an International school in London.

15 New Caledonia—A French penal colony in the South pacific where Louise Michel and other Communards were exiled after the defeat of the Paris Commune.

16 Dyer D. Lum—See note 4 of *They Who Marry Do Ill,* above.

17 Theresa Clairmunt (Teresa Claramunt)(1862–1931)—Deported from Spain in 1896 for anarchist activities she returned in 1898 and played a crucial role in the launching of the anarchist paper *El Productor* in 1901.She was one of the organisers of the large Barcelona strike in 1902.

18 Jean Grave (1854–1939)—Activist in the French anarchist movement. Author of *La société mourante et l'anarchie* which de Cleyre translated into English. In 1895 he began publishing "Les temps nouveaux," which was influential also in literary and artistic circles. In 1914, Grave joined Kropotkin in England in signing the "Proclamation of the 16," which supported the Allies during the First World War, thus, subjecting himself to the criticism of anti-war anarchists such as Errico Malatesta and Emma Goldman.

19 Montjuich—After the bombing of a Corpus Christi parade in Barcelona on June 7, 1896, many anarchists were rounded up and tortured in Montjuich prison. De Cleyre later met some of the tortured men in London where their scars caused some public outcry.

The Heart of Angiolillo

New York: Mother Earth Publishing Association, 1912.

Edition printed with permission from the Labadie Collection, University of Michigan.

1 Michele Angiolillo (1861–1897)—Italian anarchist who assassinated the Prime Minister of Spain, Antonio Canovas de Castillo, in August 1897 in revenge for the torture of anarchists in Montjuich prison.

2 Nick Bottom's ears—A character turned into a donkey in William Shakespeare's *A Midsummer Nights Dream*.

3 Montjuich—See note 3 of *Francisco Ferrer*, above.

4 Antonio Noguès, Tomas Ascheri, Jose Molas, Sebastian Sunyer— Were all inmates who were tortured in the prison at Montjuich. Specific accounts of their experiences survive in the form of letters.

5 A reference to the novel *Germinal* by Emile Zola (1885) which served as an important influence on nineteenth century anarchists. The character Souvarine epitomizes the nihilist and attentater. *Germinal* became a popular title for anarchist newspapers and the name of children born to anarchists.

The Mexican Revolt

New York: Mother Earth Publishing Association, 1911.

Edition printed with permission from the Labadie Collection, University of Michigan.

1 Dyer D. Lum—See note 4 of *They Who Marry Do Ill*, above.

2 Ricardo Flores Magon (1874–1922)—Anarchist, Mexican revolutionary writer and activist. Magon was founder of the Mexican Liberal Party (PLM). He lived much of his life in exile in America where he was imprisoned on numerous occasions. During his exile he corresponded and met with Emma Goldman and the anarchist W. C. Owen. He was, for a time, editor of the English language section of the PLM newspaper *Regeneración*.

3 Single Tax—See note 12 of *The Making of an Anarchist*, above.

4 Francisco I. Madero—See note 20 of *Direct Action*, above.

5 Victor Luitpold Berger (1860–1929)—Austria-Hungary born socialist congressman of Wisconsin affiliated with the Socialist Labor Party and the Socialist Democratic Party.

6 Henry George (1839–1897)—Author of, among others, *Our Land and Land Policy* and *Progress and Poverty*, which advocated the theory of the single tax.

The Drama of the Nineteenth Century

Pittsburgh: R. Staley and Co., 1888.

A lecture to the Pittsburgh Secular Society, December 1888.

Edition printed with permission from the Labadie Collection, University of Michigan.

1 Fugitive Slave Law (1850)—With this law, suspected runaway slaves could be arrested without warrant and turned over to a claimant on nothing more than his sworn testimony of ownership.

2 Harper's Ferry—Location across the river from where Brown, the abolitionist, wished to set up his operation to free slaves.

3 John Brown—See note 11 of *Direct Action,* above.

4 Giuseppe Garibaldi (1807–1882)—Initially influenced by Mazzini and the ideas of "Young Italy," Garibaldi fought against the Austrians in Milan and against forces supporting Rome and the Papal States in an effort for Italian independence.

5 Tomas de Torquemada (1420–1498)—In 1483, the pope appointed Torquemada, who had been an assistant inquisitor since 1482, Grand Inquisitor of Castile, and on October 17 extended his jurisdiction over Aragon. Instrumental in having Jews expelled from Spain in 1492, his name, for some, was synonomous with cruelty.

6 Vanderbilt, Gould, Rothchild—A reference to prominent families of wealth and entrepreneurship in the industrial revolution of America at the turn of the nineteenth century.

7 An extract from Ferdinand Freiligrath's poem "Revolution," a staple of the revolutionary movement and quoted by one of the Haymarket anarchists, Samuel Fielden, at his trial.

Dyer D. Lum

In *In Memoriam*. London: Freedom, 1893.

Edition printed with permission from the Labadie Collection, University of Michigan.

1 Dyer D. Lum—See note 4 in *They Who Marry Do Ill*, above.

2 Pittsburgh riots in 1877—A reference to the destruction of property belonging to the Pennsylvania Railroad Company and the Baltimore and Ohio Railroad Companyby striking railroad workers and their supporters. The companies had announced cost cutting plans.

3 Wendell Phillips (1811–1884)—Left the legal profession to dedicate his life to the anti-slavery cause and became a leader of the radical abolitionists who also supported temperance, women's rights, and labor reforms. He was seen by many American anarchists as representing the lost libertarian heritage of America.

4 Greenbackism—The idea that maintaining a flexible supply of paper money served the interests of working people, whereas paper money backed by hard money (such as gold or silver) benefited only the rich. Printing more money was seen as a solution to the country's economic crisis. The Greenback Party, based on this strategy, was formed by Edward Kellogg in 1841.

5 Albert Parsons—See note 5 of *The Economic Tendency of Free Thought*, above.

6 *The Alarm* (1884–1889)—Anarchist newspaper edited by Albert Parsons until his arrest.

Crime and Punishment

Philadelphia: Social Science Club, 1903.

Edition printed with permission from the Labadie Collection, University of Michigan.

Also published in *Selected Works of Voltairine de Cleyre*, edited by Alexander Berkman, Mother Earth Publishing Association, New York, 1914.

1 Ralph Waldo Emerson (1803–1882)—Prominent nineteenth century author, lecturer and transcendentalist.

2 Anabaptists—A violent and extremely radical body of ecclesiastico-civil reformers which first appeared in 1521 at Zwickau, in the present kingdom of Saxony. They were against involvement in political affairs, arguing that they only served god and stressing the separation of church and state. Such thoughts led to them being outlawed in many European countries.

3 Henry Thomas Buckle (1821–1862)—One of the most celebrated English historians of the Victorian Era. Author of *Introduction to the History of Civilization in England* (originally published in two volumes, 1857 and 1861). This was as much a sociological as historical work and appealed to anarchists with such lines as "Governments do no intrinsic good, at best they only correct evils previously imposed by Governments."

4 Adolphe Quetelet (1796–1874)—An influential social statisticians of the nineteenth century influenced by Charles Fourier. His studies of the numerical consistency of crimes prompted much discussion on free will and social determinism. He also collected and analyzed statistics on crime and mortality.

5 Cesare Lombroso (1835–1909)—Italian university professor and criminologist who became known for his studies in the relation between mental and physical characteristics. Lombroso's theories relate certain physical characteristics, such as jaw size, to criminal psychopathology, sociopathy and criminal behavior. He argued that anarchists were criminal types distinguished by physical characteristics such as cranial defomities.

6 Isaac G. Gordon (1819–1893)—Prison reformer who ordered an investigation into the Eastern State Penitentiary which was in the Cherry Hill section of Philadelphia.

7 Sir William Blackstone (1723–1780)—English jurist; professor of common law at Oxford; author of *Commentaries on the Laws of England*, which had considerable influence on the importation and adaptation of English common law in America.

8 Charles de Secondat, Baron de la Brède et de Montesquieu (1689–1755)—Author of *On the Spirit of Laws*, published in 1748. He believed the existence of underlying rules or laws that never change and argued for the creation of separate branches of government so as to prevent the taking of power by one section.

9 Robert Green Ingersoll (1833–1899)—Prominent American freethinker, orator, and writer. Influenced by Voltaire and Tom Paine, his writings were regularly attacked by supporters of the church and religion for their agnosticism.

10 Herbert Spencer (1820–1903)—His system of synthetic philosophy (i.e. the idea of a univeral principle that underlies all phenomena and encompasses all human knowledge) had a large influence on many anarchists, especially with its stress on the primacy of the individual.

11 Cardinal Manning (1808–1892)—See note 1 of *In Defense of Emma Goldman*, above.

12 Fyodor Mikhailovich Dostoevsky (1821–1881)—Russian writer. Author of *The House of the Dead* (1862), *Notes From The Underground* (1864), *Crime and Punishment* (1866), *The Idiot* (1868), and *The Devils* (1871).

McKinley's Assassination from the Anarchist Standpoint

New York: Mother Earth Publishing Association, 1907.

1 William McKinley (1843–1901)—Twenty-fifth president of the United States. With victory in the war with Spain, McKinley took control of the Philippines in 1898 with the idea of maintaining it as a strategic Pacific stronghold. The Filipino people; however, naturally desired their independence, and subsequent incidents of violence ensued as a result of U.S. occupation.

2 Leon Czolgosz (1873–1901)—A worker in a wire mill in Cleveland, Ohio. He moved to Buffalo, New York in 1901, where at the Pan-American Exhibition he assassinated President William McKinley, shooting him twice as he waited in a receiving line. Regarding the assassination Czolgosz stated, "I didn't believe one man should have so much service, and another man have none." Czolgosz was executed on October 29, 1901.

3 Emma Goldman—See note 3 *In Defense of Emma Goldman*, above.

4 Harry Orchard (1867–1954)—Worked as a miner in Idaho during a time of labor disputes. A member of the Western Federation of Miners who was accused of several acts of violence, including the murder of former Idaho Governor Frank Steunenberg in 1905. He confessed and became a prosecution witness implicating Bill Haywood, Charles Moyer, and George Pettibone in the plot to kill Steunenberg. Orchard was seen as a traitor in labor circles with his attempt to implicate the three men who were part of the leadership of the Western Federation of Miners. Ultimately the three men, defended by Clarence Darrow, were acquitted.

The Eleventh of November, 1887

A Memorial Oration Delivered on November 11, 1901, in Chicago.

1 From William Morris' *Chants for Socialists* (1885).

2 A reference to Swiss hero Arnold van Winkelried. According to legend van Winkelried was responsible for the defeat of the Austrian army at the battle of Sempach on July 9, 1386. He allowed the Swiss army to break through the Austrian lines by throwing himself onto the Austrian spears.

Bastard Born

Enterprise, Kansas 1891.

The Gods and the People

London: James Tochattl, 1897.

1 Damocles—Mythological figure who switches places with tyrant king Dionysius to see how the rich and powerful live. Upon dining in a great hall, Damocles discovers the sharp point of a sword dangling above his head. Dionysius suggests that the rich and powerful must always be in fear of imminent death. With this Damocles desires to return to his humble state.

2 *Belshazzar's Feast*—The painting by Rembrandt is derived from the Old Testament Book of Daniel (5: 1-6, 25-8) which tells of a banquet Belshazzar, King of Babylon, gave for his nobles. At this banquet Belshazzar blasphemously served wine in the sacred vessels his father Nebuchadnezzar had looted from the Temple in Jerusalem.This act led to the fall of his kingdom.

And Thou Too

St. Johns, Michigan, 1888.

The Dirge of the Sea

1891.

I Am & Love's Ghost

1892.

Life or Death

Philadelphia, 1892.

The Toast of Despair

Philadelphia, 1892.

Mary Wollstonecraft

Philadelphia, 1893.

1 Influential radical author who advocated for women's rights in *Thoughts on the Education of Daughters* (1787), *A Vindication for the Rights of Men* (1790), a reply to Edmund Burke, and *A Vindication for the Rights of Women* (1792). In 1797, she wed anarchist William Godwin and died bearing their child, who would grow up to become author Mary Shelley.

The Suicide's Defense

Philadelphia, 1894.

1 Commentary suggesting that laws against suicide are absurd and only serve to show how inadequately government regards issues of mental health. Perhaps a personal response given that de Cleyre herself attempted suicide on several occasions and her mentor, Dyer Lum, committed suicide in 1893.

The Road Builders

Philadelphia, 1900.

1 A 4,400-acre ribbon of green bordering the Schuylkill River and Wissahickon Creek in Philadelphia, Pennsylvania.

Ave et Vale

Philadelphia, 1901.

  1 (Latin)—Hail and farewell.

Marsh-Bloom

Philadelphia, 1901.

  1 An Italian anarchist who assassinated King Umberto in 1900. He had allegedly killed himself in his prison cell in May 1901.

Written—In—Red

Voltairine de Cleyre's last poem.

The Worm Turns

Philadelphia: Innes and Sons, 1900.

Germinal

London, 1897.

  1 Germinal—See note 5 of *The Heart of Angiolillo*, above.

  2 Michele Angiolillo (1861–1897)—Italian anarchist who assassinated the Prime Minister of Spain, Antonio Canovas de Castillo, in August 1897 in revenge for the torture of anarchists in Montjuich prison.

Ut Sementem Feceris, Ita Metes

Philadelphia, 1890.

  1 (Latin)—As you sow, so will you reap.

Santa Agueda

Philadelphia, 1898.

  1 Site of the execution of Spanish Prime Minister Antonio Canocas del Castillo by Italian anarchist Michele Angiolillo in August 1897.

The Feast of Vultures

Philadelphia, 1894.

Night at the Grave in Waldheim

Pittsburgh, 1889.

1 Site in Chicago where the Haymarket martyrs are buried. Later, de Cleyre would be buried along side these men.

The Hurricane

Sea Isle City, New Jersey, 1889.

1 Haymarket anarchist executed in November 1887. The quote is from a speech Spies made in 1885, "We are the birds of a coming storm—the prophets of the revolution."

In Memoriam

Philadelphia, 1893.

1 General M. M. Trumbull 9th Iowa Cavalry—Commanding Officers of Fort Smith Sept. 1865 to Feb. 1866 who was influential in the defense of the Haymarket men, writing two pamphlets on the case: *Was it a Fair Trial?* and *The Trial of the Judgement: A Review of the Anarchist Case.*

John P. Altgeld

Philadelphia, 1893.

1 John Peter Altgeld (1847–1902)—Governor of Illinois from 1893–1897. Early in his term as governor, he reviewed the sentences of the surviving prisoners convicted after the Haymarket affair. He saw that a great injustice had been done and issued a pardon for the survivors.

2 A reference to the bomb in Haymarket Square, Chicago thrown at the police on the evening of May 3, 1886.

"Light Upon Waldheim"

London, 1897.

1 A reference to the four protesters who were later arrested and hung as a result of the bomb explosion in Haymarket Square, Chicago.

Other Titles from AK Press

Books

MARTHA ACKELSBERG—*Free Women of Spain*

KATHY ACKER—*Pussycat Fever*

MICHAEL ALBERT—*Moving Forward: Program for a Participatory Economy*

JOEL ANDREAS—*Addicted to War: Why the U.S. Can't Kick Militarism*

ALEXANDER BERKMAN—*What is Anarchism?*

HAKIM BEY—*Immediatism*

JANET BIEHL & PETER STAUDENMAIER—*Ecofascism: Lessons From The German Experience*

BIOTIC BAKING BRIGADE—*Pie Any Means Necessary: The Biotic Baking Brigade Cookbook*

JACK BLACK—*You Can't Win*

MURRAY BOOKCHIN—*Anarchism, Marxism, and the Future of the Left*

MURRAY BOOKCHIN—*Social Anarchism or Lifestyle Anarchism: An Unbridgeable Chasm*

MURRAY BOOKCHIN—*Spanish Anarchists: The Heroic Years 1868–1936, The*

MURRAY BOOKCHIN—*To Remember Spain: The Anarchist and Syndicalist Revolution of 1936*

MURRAY BOOKCHIN—*Which Way for the Ecology Movement?*

DANNY BURNS—*Poll Tax Rebellion*

CHRIS CARLSSON—*Critical Mass: Bicycling's Defiant Celebration*

JAMES CARR–*Bad*

NOAM CHOMSKY—*At War With Asia*

NOAM CHOMSKY—*Language and Politics*

NOAM CHOMSKY—*Radical Priorities*

WARD CHURCHILL—*On the Justice of Roosting Chickens: Reflections on the Consequences of U.S. Imperial Arrogance and Criminality*

WARD CHURCHILL—*Speaking Truth in the Teeth of Power: Lectures on Globalization, Colonialism, and Native North America*

HARRY CLEAVER—*Reading Capital Politically*

ALEXANDER COCKBURN & JEFFREY ST. CLAIR (ed.)—*Dime's Worth of Difference*

ALEXANDER COCKBURN & JEFFREY ST. CLAIR (ed.)—*The Politics of Anti-Semitism*

ALEXANDER COCKBURN & JEFFREY ST. CLAIR (ed.)—*Serpents in the Garden*

DANIEL & GABRIEL COHN-BENDIT—*Obsolete Communism: The Left-Wing Alternative*

EG SMITH COLLECTIVE—*Animal Ingredients A–Z (3rd edition)*

HOWARD EHRLICH—*Reinventing Anarchy, Again*

SIMON FORD—*The Realization and Suppression of the Situationist International: An Annotated Bibliography 1972–1992*

YVES FREMION & VOLNY—*Orgasms of History: 3000 Years of Spontaneous Revolt*

DANIEL GUERIN—*No Gods No Masters*

AGUSTIN GUILLAMON—*The Friends Of Durruti Group, 1937–1939*

ANN HANSEN—*Direct Action: Memoirs Of An Urban Guerilla*

WILLIAM HERRICK—*Jumping the Line: The Adventures and Misadventures of an American Radical*

FRED HO—*Legacy to Liberation: Politics & Culture of Revolutionary Asian/Pacific America*

STEWART HOME—*Assault on Culture*

STEWART HOME—*Neoism, Plagiarism & Praxis*

STEWART HOME—*Neoist Manifestos / The Art Strike Papers*

STEWART HOME—*No Pity*

STEWART HOME—*Red London*

STEWART HOME—*What Is Situationism? A Reader*

JAMES KELMAN—*Some Recent Attacks: Essays Cultural And Political*

KEN KNABB—*Complete Cinematic Works of Guy Debord*

KATYA KOMISARUK—*Beat the Heat: How to Handle Encounters With Law Enforcement*

NESTOR MAKHNO—*The Struggle Against The State & Other Essays*

SUBCOMANDANTE MARCOS—*¡Ya Basta!: Ten Years of the Zapatista Uprising*

G.A. MATIASZ—*End Time*

CHERIE MATRIX—*Tales From the Clit*

ALBERT MELTZER—*Anarchism: Arguments For & Against*

ALBERT MELTZER—*I Couldn't Paint Golden Angels*

RAY MURPHY—*Siege Of Gresham*

NORMAN NAWROCKI—*Rebel Moon*

HENRY NORMAL—*A Map of Heaven*

HENRY NORMAL—*Dream Ticket*

HENRY NORMAL—*Fifteenth of February*

HENRY NORMAL—*Third Person*

FIONBARRA O'DOCHARTAIGH—*Ulster's White Negroes: From Civil Rights To Insurrection*

DAN O'MAHONY—*Four Letter World*

CRAIG O'HARA—*The Philosophy Of Punk*

ANTON PANNEKOEK—*Workers' Councils*

BEN REITMAN—*Sister of the Road: the Autobiography of Boxcar Bertha*

PENNY RIMBAUD—*The Diamond Signature*

PENNY RIMBAUD—*Shibboleth: My Revolting Life*

RUDOLF ROCKER—*Anarcho-Syndicalism*

RON SAKOLSKY & STEPHEN DUNIFER—*Seizing the Airwaves: A Free Radio Handbook*

ROY **SAN FILIPPO**—*A New World In Our Hearts: 8 Years of Writings from the Love and Rage Revolutionary Anarchist Federation*

ALEXANDRE **SKIRDA**—*Facing the Enemy: A History Of Anarchist Organisation From Proudhon To May 1968*

ALEXANDRE **SKIRDA**—*Nestor Mahkno—Anarchy's Cossack*

VALERIE **SOLANAS**—*Scum Manifesto*

CJ **STONE**—*Housing Benefit Hill & Other Places*

ANTONIO **TELLEZ**—*Sabate: Guerilla Extraordinary*

MICHAEL **TOBIAS**—*Rage and Reason*

JIM **TULLY**—*Beggars of Life: A Hobo Autobiography*

TOM **VAGUE**—*Anarchy in the UK: The Angry Brigade*

TOM **VAGUE**—*The Great British Mistake*

TOM **VAGUE**—*Televisionaries*

JAN **VALTIN**—*Out of the Night*

RAOUL **VANEIGEM**—*A Cavalier History Of Surrealism*

FRANCOIS EUGENE **VIDOCQ**—*Memoirs of Vidocq: Master of Crime*

GEE **VOUCHER**—*Crass Art And Other Pre-Postmodern Monsters*

MARK J **WHITE**—*An Idol Killing*

JOHN **YATES**—*Controlled Flight Into Terrain*

JOHN **YATES**—*September Commando*

BENJAMIN **ZEPHANIAH**—*Little Book of Vegan Poems*

BENJAMIN **ZEPHANIAH**—*School's Out*

HELLO—*2/15: The Day The World Said NO To War*

DARK STAR COLLECTIVE —*Beneath the Paving Stones: Situationists and the Beach, May 68*

DARK STAR COLLECTIVE —*Quiet Rumours: An Anarcha-Feminist Reader*

ANONYMOUS —*Test Card F*

CLASS WAR FEDERATION —*Unfinished Business: The Politics of Class War*

CDs

THE **EX**—*1936: The Spanish Revolution*

MUMIA **ABU JAMAL**—*175 Progress Drive*

MUMIA **ABU JAMAL**—*All Things Censored Vol.1*

MUMIA **ABU JAMAL**—*Spoken Word*

FREEDOM ARCHIVES—*Chile: Promise of Freedom*

FREEDOM ARCHIVES—*Prisons on Fire: George Jackson, Attica & Black Liberation*

JUDI **BARI**—*Who Bombed Judi Bari?*

JELLO **BIAFRA**—*Become the Media*

JELLO **BIAFRA**—*Beyond The Valley of the Gift Police*

JELLO **BIAFRA**—*High Priest of Harmful*

JELLO **BIAFRA**—*I Blow Minds For A Living*

JELLO **BIAFRA**—*If Evolution Is Outlawed*

JELLO **BIAFRA**—*Machine Gun In The Clown's Hand*

JELLO **BIAFRA**—*No More Cocoons*

NOAM **CHOMSKY**—*An American Addiction*

NOAM **CHOMSKY**—*Case Studies in Hypocrisy*

NOAM **CHOMSKY**—*Emerging Framework of World Power*

NOAM **CHOMSKY**—*Free Market Fantasies*

NOAM **CHOMSKY**—*New War On Terrorism: Fact And Fiction*

NOAM **CHOMSKY**—*Propaganda and Control of the Public Mind*

NOAM **CHOMSKY**—*Prospects for Democracy*

NOAM **CHOMSKY/CHUMBAWAMBA**—*For A Free Humanity: For Anarchy*

WARD **CHURCHILL**—*Doing Time: The Politics of Imprisonment*

WARD **CHURCHILL**—*In A Pig's Eye: Reflections on the Police State, Repression, and Native America*

WARD **CHURCHILL**—*Life in Occupied America*

WARD **CHURCHILL**—*Pacifism and Pathology in the American Left*

ALEXANDER **COCKBURN**—*Beating the Devil: The Incendiary Rants of Alexander Cockburn*

ANGELA **DAVIS**—*The Prison Industrial Complex*

JAMES **KELMAN**—*Seven Stories*

TOM **LEONARD**—*Nora's Place and Other Poems 1965–99*

CHRISTIAN **PARENTI**—*Taking Liberties: Policing, Prisons and Surveillance in an Age of Crisis*

UTAH **PHILLIPS**—*I've Got To Know*

DAVID **ROVICS**—*Behind the Barricades: Best of David Rovics*

ARUNDHATI **ROY**—*Come September*

VARIOUS—*Better Read Than Dead*

VARIOUS—*Less Rock, More Talk*

VARIOUS—*Mob Action Against the State: Collected Speeches from the Bay Area Anarchist Bookfair*

VARIOUS—*Monkeywrenching the New World Order*

VARIOUS—*Return of the Read Menace*

HOWARD **ZINN**—*Artists In A Time of War*

HOWARD **ZINN**—*Heroes and Martyrs: Emma Goldman, Sacco & Vanzetti, and the Revolutionary Struggle*

HOWARD **ZINN**—*A People's History of the United States: A Lecture at Reed College*

HOWARD **ZINN**—*People's History Project*

HOWARD **ZINN**–*Stories Hollywood Never Tells*

DVDs

NOAM **CHOMSKY**—*Distorted Morality*

ARUNDHATI **ROY**—*Instant-Mix Imperial Democracy*

Ordering Information

AK Press

674-A 23rd Street,
Oakland, CA 94612-1163,
USA

Phone: (510) 208-1700
E-mail: akpress@akpress.org
URL: www.akpress.org
Please send all payments (checks, money orders, or cash at your own risk) in U.S. dollars. Alternatively, we take VISA and MC.

AK Press

PO Box 12766,
Edinburgh, EH8 9YE,
Scotland

Phone: (0131) 555-5165
E-mail: ak@akedin.demon.co.uk
URL: www.akuk.com
Please send all payments (cheques, money orders, or cash at your own risk) in U.K. pounds. Alternatively, we take credit cards.

For a dollar, a pound or a few IRC's, the same addresses would be delighted to provide you with the latest complete AK catalog, featuring several thousand books, pamphlets, zines, audio products and stylish apparel published & distributed by AK Press. Alternatively, check out our websites for the complete catalog, latest news and updates, events, and secure ordering.